TAKE BACK MANUFACTURING

An Imperative for Western Economies

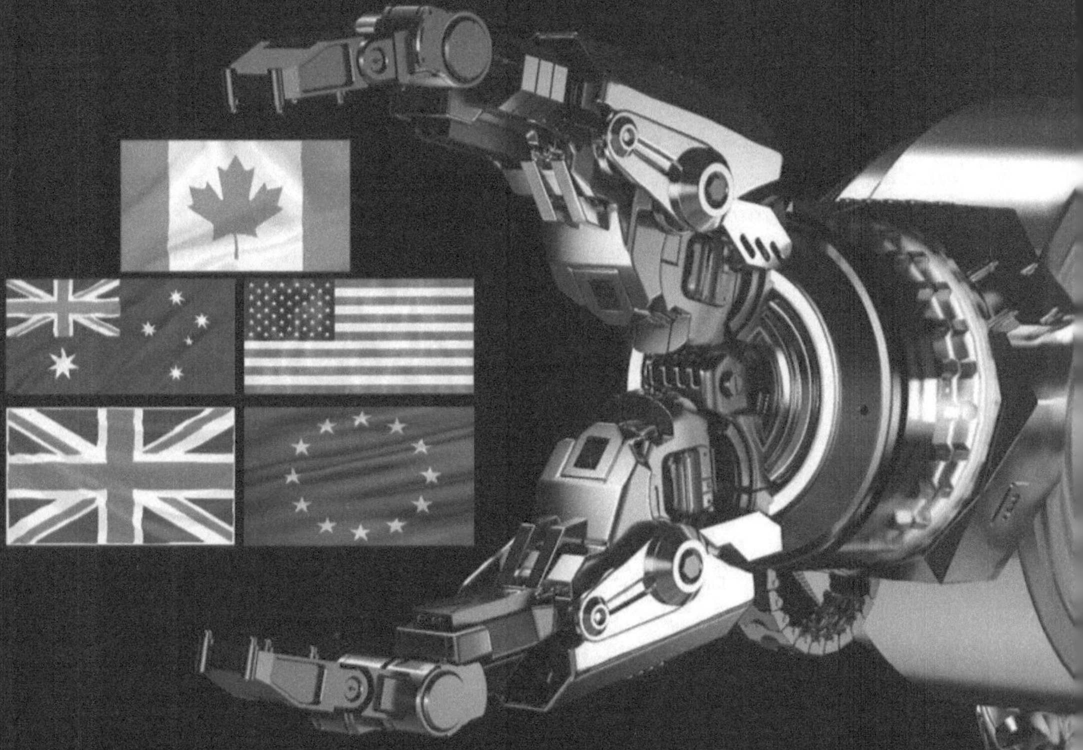

This Book is about the destruction of the manufacturaing sector in our western Societies, with significant loss of national prosperity, and why the imperative for western economies must be to... Take Back Manufacturing!

NIGEL SOUTHWAY

TAKE BACK MANUFACTURING
An Imperative for Western Economies

Copyright © 2024 **Nigel Southway**

ISBN (Paperback): 978-1-964494-63-0
ISBN (Ebook): 978-1-964494-64-7

Printed in the United States of America.

PROMINENT
BOOKS
EDGE

5830 E 2nd St, Ste 7000 #9983
Casper, WY 82609
USA

CONTENTS

INTRODUCTION

WHY TAKE BACK MANUFACTURING?

This book is about how in less than a lifetime we have experienced the destruction of the manufacturing sectors in most Western societies, along with significant loss of national prosperity, and why the imperative must be to Take Back Manufacturing.

The focus will be on Canadian manufacturing and the North American economic situation, but many of the issues are applicable to many Western economies.

This book will explain how, with the correct political will and focus, Canada and North America can recover its manufacturing industries and achieve future prosperity.

The globalized manufacturing approach, with its efficient supply chains supported by liberalized free-trade agreements, has been the business norm through the last four decades, and the prime reason for the hollowing out of the Western industrial base.

Since 1980, the Canadian manufacturing trade deficit has increased ten times, to more than $100 billion. This significant imbalance in trade has eradicated many jobs and small enterprises, with most of the production-capacity investment and technological development being relocated offshore to foreign factories.

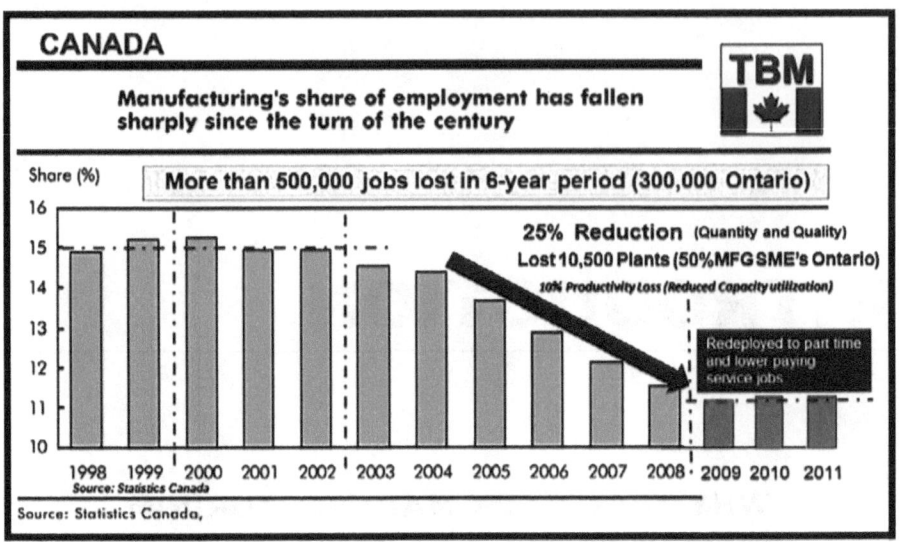

CANADA

Manufacturing's share of employment has fallen sharply since the turn of the century

TBM

Share (%)

More than 500,000 jobs lost in 6-year period (300,000 Ontario)

25% Reduction (Quantity and Quality)
Lost 10,500 Plants (50% MFG SME's Ontario)
10% Productivity Loss (Reduced Capacity utilization)

Redeployed to part time and lower paying service jobs

1998 1999 2000 2001 2002 2003 2004 2005 2006 2007 2008 2009 2010 2011
Source: Statistics Canada

Source: Statistics Canada,

Since 2000, more than 25 percent of the manufacturing workforce (about 500,000 Canadian citizens) has been displaced into lower-paying or more precarious employment due to globalized manufacturing. Those who have remained in manufacturing have seen wage values decline, with many jobs now at almost minimum wage. A high percentage are temporary positions, even though they demand significant knowledge, skill, and experience.

A generation of youth has become disillusioned by the inability to develop a meaningful and sustainable career and have been forced to operate in the so-called "gig economy," where the delicate balance between capital and labor in all forms has been lost, and this has generated significant inequality across the population.

The rhetoric from politicians such as Bill Clinton and his economic advisors in the early stages of modern globalization suggested that we should embrace the inevitable move of the Western economies toward a post-industrialized society.

But now we are predicting yet another significant sea change regarding national economic policies that will, for reasons that we will explain, move our Western economies toward localized trade blocs, and the return of our manufacturing base from the other countries from which we currently import manufactured product. We will explain why many products have been, or soon will be, returning to local manufacturing supply chains to support the consumer base within the new United States-Mexico-Canada Agreement (USMCA) trade pact.

But many trade experts do not consider Canada a logical and typical return destination within this updated trade bloc. The reasons for "why not Canada?" are many. We are a high-cost destination, with a questionable political will to set a consistent national industrial policy that convinces business leaders to invest. Canada presents a small consumer base with flat growth, an unpredictable resource-driven exchange rate, high overall energy costs, non-competitive transportation, and border transactions, as well as high labor expenses and punitive safety and environmental legislations.

The Canadian federal government has done little to assure business leaders that the Canadian dollar will never again get over-inflated by oil and gas resource growth, as we experienced in the last few decades. The adoption of a carbon tax supporting the climate change agenda will make this competitive footprint even worse. Our advantage of a lower corporate tax rate is now diminished due to the US lowering theirs. Although strong in the past, our skilled workforce is diminishing and not being maintained.

My prediction is that the decline in the Canadian manufacturing sector will continue due to the absence of government focus on effective industrial policies and legislation, and its ineffectiveness in addressing national competitive factors such as tariffs, exchange, taxation, and industrial investment.

Our governments, manufacturing sectors and educational support organizations must immediately respond to these challenges and work cohesively to reverse this dismal outlook. We will explain what action they must take in this book.

We will brief you on how nationalistic policies, sustainable supply chain concepts, LEAN business practices and INDUSTRY 4.0 technologies can combine to create future economic and business changes that will provide opportunities to revitalize our manufacturing sectors.

We will also explain how these changes can not only take back manufacturing, but will assist in the reduction of global pollution.

I have written this book to communicate and update the TBM message we have been delivering to many associations, societies, media, and government bodies over the last ten years since we started the TBM advocacy group. Most of us in the TBM Forum hold a common view that, over the last three decades, we have undertaken economic policies and doctrine that have taken us in the wrong direction, both economically and socially. But now, recent facts and logic support a fast-growing expert and public consensus that is at last shifting toward our view.

For many years, all the experts who had the ear of government sanctioned over-liberalized global trade and would not listen to alternatives of more controlled global trade. But now, via the new awakening created by the Trump presidency, the deteriorating relationship with China, the COVID virus, the Russian aggression with Ukraine, and the precarious state of our economies, many in the Western world are now forming opinions in line with our thinking. Although it is great that our message and those of many others has finally gotten through, we fervently hope that any action taken will not be too little, too late.

In the early part of the book, I have used my own journey and experiences in manufacturing to augment the message by contrasting how much has changed over those years in manufacturing. I tell how a few of the changes have been for the better, but that most are certainly for the worse!

Although I have authored this book, many inputs are from others who participated in the TBM Forum (the mission and history of this advocacy group will be explained later in this book). Much of this material has been collected over many years, and although I have tried to give credit to all sources, please forgive me if we did not always record the source fully.

I hope you will forgive my frank openness and strong opinions. As an advocate for something as important as our manufacturing base and future prosperity I did not want to hold back or worry about political correctness. My focus was to ensure the whole message got through. I admit I have been very critical of those responsible, as any improvement must include a process of open and honest critique.

I include topics related to the issues surrounding our ability to take back manufacturing, such as climate change mitigation, immigration, and the need for a rethink of our learning systems, etc.

Also, I may mention economic and political solutions you may not agree with, or have not considered before, and I implore you to keep an open mind.

Unfortunately, we live in a world full of dissention, fake news, political correctness, and cancel culture that can suppress free speech. This is now even apparent with so-called trusted mainstream media sources, who often appear subject to dangerous and unbalanced consensus thinking, even on scientific topics, rather than objective, fact-based questioning and reporting. So, we caution the reader to continuously review facts, rather than the current media rhetoric and worldview.

Although as a Canadian I have focused on the specific Canadian situation, I also comment in general terms about the North American environment that effects all of us who live in North America. Also, it's clear that the issues and solutions are common across most western nations.

I suggest you do not put this book down until you completely understand, and hopefully identify with, the thread and message of the book, so we can take back manufacturing!

THE MAKER CULTURE

I am going to use my own journey in manufacturing to explain just how much our Western culture has changed, and, sadly, not for the better.

I have been lucky on many fronts, including good health and a prosperous career that was initiated by being part of an impactful maker culture that I will explain in this chapter. This positioned me for a full British engineering apprenticeship back when it was a class act. The British engineering apprenticeship system provided, from school-leaving age, an integrated, fully paid on-the-job training and valuable experience in industry, while also studying at a leading British college or university. Then, based on performance and aptitude, you would qualify with a trade or as a technician or professional engineer. I graduated from this system as an engineer. I went on to enjoy a challenging technical and management career with some of the best corporations in the world, including immigrating to Canada in the late 1970s to work in the Canadian aerospace industry and the high-tech electronics industry. I eventually joined a leading-edge consulting team, wrote and published a business textbook, and consulted internationally for many years. I also had the opportunity to give something back by lecturing at Canadian colleges on advanced manufacturing and business practices. I have served as chair of my engineering society and been an active advocate for manufacturing for many years. This has driven me to write this, my second book. I have also been fortunate to have made many fun and interesting business relationships, and many lifelong friends in many different countries and cultures, along the way.

I was born in the southwest of England in the late 1940s, in the county of Somerset in the Mendip Hills, close to the town of Cheddar of cheese fame. I am a post-World War II baby boomer. My family moved to the local city when I was about three years old, so I spent most of my young life until my early twenties as an inner-city kid in the regional seaport city of Bristol, England.

When I was a young boy, the manufacturing culture was all around us. Factories were on every street. I remember going to sleep most nights to the hum and throb of the local cardboard box factory two doors down churning out boxes and containers on three shifts. We had a milk-processing plant and a sugar refinery in our block, as well as some light machining, a pork-butchering plant, and a rubber and leather treatment facility. It was a real collaboration of smells, sounds, smoke, and waste materials. Bristol was famous for many industries: aerospace, tobacco, chemicals, and machine tools, and, to lesser extent, shipbuilding. We had a mixture of food, wine, and spirit production, and furniture manufacturing. We had one of the largest seaports in Britain at the mouth of the Avon, the river that runs through Bristol into the Bristol Channel. So, I lived in a seaport environment with plenty of industry opportunities to develop a good career with. Even with the pressure of large classes due to the baby boomer bulge, and many school buildings being destroyed in the Second World War, our schooling was basic but adequate. The educational system was far more practical than today, with woodworking, metalworking, and technical drawing being standard subjects to prepare students for technical trades. I quickly started to excel at these subjects.

We were far more nationalistic, socialized, and structured than children are today, with after-school activities such as youth clubs and uniformed organizations there for us to join. I had a great career in the Scout movement as a Cub Scout, moving up to Scout and Senior Scout, and ending up with the zenith of the Queen's Scout Award at sixteen. This forced us to learn how to operate in structured organizations, and yet be free to become competitive in personal proficiency. We developed a solid work ethic that propelled us to become useful and self-actualizing citizens.

Due to economic reasons, many families in the '50s and '60s focused on making and repairing things around the home. This included garden structures, fitted closets, kitchen cabinets, and, of course, the maintenance and repair of bicycles, motor scooters, and motor cars. We all participated in this strong maker culture. Later in my teens, I purchased my first car from a wrecker after the insurance had written it off. With some work, I prepared and resubmitted it for a road-worthiness test at a local garage. My friends and I all got our first cars this way. We got used to lifting engines in and out, doing brake jobs, and rebuilding using a welding torch. I spent some of my best times with my father and my friends getting these projects completed. Money was tight, but we were happy and resourceful at making and repairing things. When I parked my repainted and fixed-up car in the high street, some old guy would typically walk by and ask, "Did you do it yourself?" I would say yes with pride, and an admiring discussion would ensue. If you were a young man in the street and could fix things, natural respect would develop for you. That was our maker culture.

Even from those beginnings, I have been a manufacturing engineer in mind and spirit, and it has become my psychological makeup. Although I have gone on to do many other things and have many other interests, I most easily fit the maker idiom. I have always liked to be able to say, "We make those things here!" Being able to turn an idea or need into a product that is valued by others has always provided me great satisfaction. I was fortunate to grow up in a maker society, where making and repairing things was a way of life. This has sadly all but evaporated, much to the detriment of our next generation in the Western world.

In my early teens onward, I found myself, without trying all that hard, at the top of the class in metalwork shop and technical drawing, and close to top in math and physics. I was able to complete six school-leaving certificates at sixteen years old—I had that maker culture well inside me. There was never any doubt I would pursue an industrial apprenticeship. It was the obvious outcome and I had always considered it my destiny.

In our baby boomer youth, everything seemed possible if we wanted it bad enough and worked at it. Contrast our adolescent can-do optimism and our active career journeys with the job-starved, over-educated and under-trained, snowflake, safe-spaced, sexually neurotic, drugged-up, suicide-prone youth of today. Many baby-boomers wonder, and are critical of, why a high percentage of our current youth is in so much despondency and personal strife. But to be fair, I firmly believe they have been true victims of something, and I want to talk about that now.

In just one lifetime, many things have changed in our lives, and not all for the better. Technology has moved us from the slide rule to handheld computers more powerful than most mainframe computers that existed when I started university. We have moved from aging information in hardcopy public libraries and limited radio and television programming to the tremendous power of the internet, which can provide vast amounts of real-time information on all subjects, and the ability to share and communicate globally down to the individual level. This has changed the way we communicate and operate our lives, but it has made us less interested in interacting on a personal level, and certainly prone to mass-media manipulation in terms of our views and how our beliefs are shaped. Through push marketing, it has created an increase in our wants versus our needs for products and services. We have increased our expectations for travel, from taking holidays within our own country to affordable global destinations. Medical science has vastly improved, supporting a better quality of health. It supports the suppression of most disease and illnesses, but we have traded tuberculous, malaria, alcoholism, and cancer from tobacco for HIV/AIDS, obesity, mental illness, and the abuse of recreational drugs. Plus, we are currently facing down a deadly virus, and although the professionals will say we have prevented significant deaths, we do have disputes over questionable policies about solving its long-term effects on our societies. Overall life expectancy has improved around the globe, although in most Western countries this is now flatlining due to mental health and a multitude of sociopathic issues associated with drug use and pace of life.

But the profound differences between the early life of the baby boomers and our current youth is as follows. For baby boomers (born 1945 to about 1964) it was easy to imagine how life would unfold.

It would include an easy job market with good wages, benefits, and a pension plan. A job that typically offered on-the-job training or assisted learning at night school and didn't always depend on having a post-graduate degree. Most of us who graduated from university or college in the 1970s and 1980s were not burdened with extraordinary student debt, as post-secondary education was ridiculously cheap. We imagined getting married in our twenties and starting a family while taking an early plunge into the housing market. This involved scraping together a relatively small down payment and taking on an affordable mortgage. It would have been a house, not a cramped 500-square-foot condominium. Childcare cost wasn't nearly the concern it is today, as it was possible for a middle-class family to survive on one income if that was the choice.

For our young people today, everything has changed. The cost of a post-secondary education is grossly prohibitive. Unless helped by their parents, young students can expect to leave university or college tens of thousands of dollars in debt, especially if they stuck around to get a master's degree to chase that elusive job market. Yes, there are jobs out there, but they don't come with magnificent pay grades and benefits to match the cost of living, and due to a gig economy (casual labor contracts) many jobs stopped coming with pension plans long ago.

Worse, employers have been forced, due to several reasons, to prune their labor costs and offer little if any on-the-job training, and most are not supportive of developing employee skills or offering ground-up apprenticeships.

People in their thirties today have already had to navigate two brutal recessions, and most employment still looks precarious.

Worst of all is housing. Never in the history of Canada has the cost of housing been so disassociated from a person's income. If you live in Toronto or Vancouver, it's obscene. According to an April 2022 column in the Toronto *Globe & Mail* newspaper, a National Bank of Canada report states that mortgage payments as a percentage of household income in Vancouver stands at 89 percent. In Toronto it's 68 percent. It is better in smaller markets, but for many a family home will be a small condominium or townhome, unless they want to move to a rural area and commute.

The thought of raising a family in these conditions—with the added high cost of living forcing both partners to work and pay childcare—has deterred many from starting a family. For many of our young people, a life of travel and exploration is much more appealing than barely making ends meet with kids in the picture. The outcome is that birth rates in the Western world have been trending downward since 2008, with immigration being used to stabilize the level of population. This comes with its own set of issues, which we shall explain.

There are existential reasons for not wanting children, such as the perceived state of the world and the fear of climate change, but by far the main issue is economics.

The current generation has had to face these significant challenges. Unless they are naturally high achievers or are part of the social elite that can afford to ride above these problems, they are badly positioned to cope, and, as we have witnessed, will develop despondency and complacency, and a loss of self-worth. With no dream of a good life ahead, they will struggle to be motivated future citizens, and this puts them at social risk with the poor learning performances and social issues we are now witnessing. It's not their fault, and it should come as no surprise.

The other major difference between the young baby boomers and the current youth is that we have moved toward a so-called "post-industrialized society" and away from making things. The changes mentioned already have bred a population of super-consumers that are far more aligned with the concepts of buying products than making them. Today, any product-purchasing research can be done on the internet. Ordering a product is a mere click away on a website, and delivery via a global supply chain from anywhere in the world is at the door in the next courier run. The only challenge the current generation faces is how to get it out of the over-designed packaging. Assembly, if there is any, is goof-proofed down to the cretin level. The thought of where or how it is manufactured, or what contribution it may have to the local economy, is not given any thought.

Today, many people in professions outside of manufacturing—especially economists, bankers, teachers, journalists, public servants, and politicians—have developed career experience without involvement, feel, understanding, or—and I must say this—respect for the manufacturing process. They have demonstrated that they consider it dark, dirty, dangerous, deafening, smelly, and difficult work. Worse, they have stated that it is not that important, and not a strong part of our economic prosperity in the Western world.

As manufacturing declined, it lost respect from the bulk of the population. It became risky, unreliable, and unrewarding as a provider of jobs and careers, which further diminished its image. Many of the fraternity of manufacturing practitioners have had to relocate to other careers, some of them less exciting or financially rewarding, and even less sustainable, such as low-paying part-time service jobs.

Our youth now finds it difficult, and in many cases impossible to find a worthwhile career, especially in a technical field associated with manufacturing or engineering. We have lost the maker culture in the West, with many of our young people believing we don't make things here anymore. Who can blame them, when every time they look at a product's "made in" marking, it says it was manufactured somewhere else?

It's clear for many reasons, that we will explain in later chapters, why our Western society

has currently lost most of the motivation and commitment toward maintaining a manufacturing base.

Sadly, we have lost four important things in our society in just one lifetime:

A strong and productive spirit of nationalism,

The energy of youth that can visualize a successful future,

A maker culture,

And our respect for all of them.

All of these are essential for a balanced economy and a prosperous society.

In the rest of this book, we will explain how we may be able to get them back.

LIFE IN THE MANUFACTURING FAST LANE

Unlike today's sparse role models for youth, with questionable levels of reality and usefulness, my motivational role models for a career as an industrial apprentice were all around me at age fourteen. I looked enviously at boys only a few years older than me who had full-time jobs as technical apprentices. Well, heck, they must be successful: they had enough money to buy the latest Beatles records, wear top-fashion clothes, get a motor scooter, or even a Mini car on hire purchase, or at the max drive a Mini Cooper that absolutely guaranteed a girlfriend! What more would a fourteen-year-old male expect or want in life? Hail to these older faces—they had it all, and I wanted it too.

In 1966, many important things were happening. England won the World Cup—I doubt I will see that again! The original Star Trek TV series first aired and fueled our vision of personal communicators, hand-held information touch tablets and the transporter beam. I guess two out of three ain't bad. (As a global traveler, I am still waiting for that transporter beam.) The British rock bands that shaped the music of our generation were all in the charts, and, most importantly, I started my engineering apprenticeship at sixteen.

Luckily, the British apprenticeship system under the British Labor government of the time was at its zenith. Most industry sectors were using it to develop the next generation of tradesmen, engineers, and managers, much like the German industrial system today. This was before the later disaster in the 1970s of Maggie Thatcher's Conservatives reset, and the slide of the British industrial machine and prosperity for the average citizen into economic hell and prosperity oblivion.

One of my main interests at the time was aero modeling, so it was not a total surprise that I applied with many other kids to an engineering apprenticeship selection committee at the British Aerospace Corporation (BAC), which, combined with the Rolls-Royce aero engine corporation, had openings for up to 200 apprentices a year, and was the best place for an aircraft-crazy youth to start a career.

BAC was a large national aerospace corporation, a consolidation of many of the big WWII British aerospace names in aircraft design and manufacturing, such as Supermarine, Hawker, Avro, and Bristol. The division I applied to had formerly been the Bristol Aeroplane Company that had produced WWI and WWII aircraft like the Bristol Beaufighter bomber and torpedo aircraft. The Bristol division post-WWII had produced the Bristol Britannia airliner and were at the time developing components for the Harrier Jump Jet and guided weapons systems, as well as communication satellites, and, of course, the Concorde super-sonic airliner, then in early development. Both BAC and the Rolls-Royce engines corporation were located about five miles from my home in North Bristol at Filton, on a large aerodrome campus. This was one of the key centers of the advanced aerospace industry in the UK at that time.

The apprenticeship selection process involved tests that included reading a drawing, explaining some aerospace terms, and writing about a hobby, then an interview. I was told to my surprise that I was a "perfect fit," due to my moral and social commitment with Scouting, being air-craft savvy with my significant aircraft modeling hobby, all the correct school-leaving credentials with a lot of hands-on skills, and a top score in their drawing tests. I was in!

In 1966, we did not have the problems with the maker culture or the motivation and commitment to training our young people described in the previous chapter. When I joined the workforce, the intake of apprentices was huge within the aerospace industry. They were inducting about two hundred young people a year into the local industrial com-plex. Some of us would make it as full engineers in one of the many disciplines, others would become technologists, and some would grade as technicians and skilled tradespeople. Some would fail and exit the industrial learning system due to lack of interest, or they would not be a fit with the environment, but most would find their correct level. The message was "you will go as far as you want if you apply yourself."

This was the power of the British industrial apprentice system. It was a powerful and structured learning system that provided a balance of education, training, and experience. As British engineering apprentices (especially in large organizations), we were extremely lucky to have a complete learning system provided for us. Our academic education integrated with our industrial training and on-the-job experience.

It started with a basic training period—a four-month induction program in an industrial trade school on the business campus—to learn the various key processes, tools, and equipment, and the operating and safety procedures that we would experience when in the factory environment.

One of the best early learning experiences was the "cube test." Trade schools still practice a version of it today. The test was undertaken by all apprentices, no matter what grade or educational program we were destined to follow. We were given the basics of all metalwork processes with a series of projects to make test samples. The most difficult was the cube test, which consisted of a rough cut of mild steel about 1.5 inches cubed. We were to use only hand tools to accurately cut and file the cube to 1-inch square to within three-thousands of an inch in all three planes. The surface finish had to be a certain grade.

This was no mean feat. It was a lesson in patience and perseverance as much as skill and accuracy, and the only assurance we were given was, "Don't worry if you make it undersize. We have plenty of rough cuts for you to restart the process with." I got it completed to specification on the third restart, but some guys never completed the project and ran out of time. We were told if we completed the project, we would get a prize. It was the 1-inch cube I had completed, with my name and the date stamped into it. It still sits on my desk as a reminder of the effort and final moment of pride. What I try to forget is the process of shame that took place on the first two attempts, as I had to walk to the scrap bin in the middle of the shop in full view of the group and drop my bad piece into the bin. The teaching assistants called out my name and rang a bell. Add "character-building" to the list of life lessons. To this day I cringe when I see a scrap bin in the manufacturing process, and I have an aversion to seeing anything scrapped.

Although it appeared so at the time, it was not a career-defining project. When I first talked with the well-respected BAC chief engineer toward the end of my apprenticeship, he asked how many tries it had taken me to complete the cube exercise. I said three and, being a pushy guy, I asked his number of tries. He just laughed and said, "I ran out of time, never finished. It's been twenty years and I still regret it." I didn't laugh, I just felt lucky.

In our first year, we were assigned to a scheduled rotation to gain experience by working in different departments, from fabrication to assembly to quality and testing to the maintenance and support functions. We were assigned to tradesmen or technicians to be their "mates," which translated into: *Do and get anything they wanted and take the abuse and blame for everything.* We got all the jobs the trades guys hated doing, such as steam cleaning and greasing the equipment, sweeping up the job site, fetching and counting parts, preparing tools and materials, holding the part while a trade or tech did his work, etc. I was considered "useful" with manual tasks, and I could hold my own with a tool kit to assist trades guys with their daily tasks. We gained valuable practice and insight, as we were exposed to the challenges and issues the various trades faced in their jobs. At sixteen I was ready to learn and put up with anything, and most of the skilled trades and technicians had been apprentices, so they took us under their wings and treated us like younger brothers or, if they were older, like adopted sons. Our advantage was that we were following a natural career pathway that built on itself. The expression "he's an apprentice, make him work" was code for "look after him, he will become one of us." I can't say it was always easy, but I was young enough to be smart and dumb at the same time. It took a while to realize that these skilled tradesmen had also been apprentices and had already tried all the tricks we were pulling, so they were way ahead of us.

To most of us, the apprenticeship program was more of a challenge to be enjoyed than potential failure to be feared. We were excited about the journey we had been selected to undertake and were glad to be learning with some wages in the pocket, which were spent on cars, clothes, and parties.

Our ongoing education was a paid "day release program" to attend one day and up to two-night classes a week at a local college program to gain a recognized industrial qualification for trade or technician certificates. The technologist and engineering course was structured as a "sandwich program" of six months training in industry and six months formal post-graduate education at a college or university for a three- or four-year period.

The British apprenticeship system in the 1960s was an exceptional learning system, and it built a strong next-generation technical workforce. The key point is that at this time the British apprenticeship system used a continuous grading system to seamlessly stream the aptitude, skills, and academic capability of each apprentice through the engineering, technologist technician, and trade structure. The result was a solidly educated, trained, and experienced workforce with little waste or loss of opportunity for the futures of those involved. Many of us who experienced this agree that this system was effective and fair, and, years later, when asked about our engineering qualifications, we would say with pride that we completed a British engineering apprenticeship—that's how good it was. Local universities or technical schools provided the classroom courses that were fully government sponsored, and they were nationally recognized programs. The industrial training and experience were provided by the organization that employed the apprentice and was sponsored, part funded, and certified by a government body. Canada and the USA have never installed such a powerful industrial learning system, but they did benefit from it, as a considerable number of us who were products of this

British apprenticeship system eventually immigrated to Canada and the USA to support the aerospace and electronic industrial environment in the 1960s and the 1970s.

The crying shame is that this UK apprenticeship system was dismantled by the British Conservative government in the 1970s as they de-focused the economy away from manufacturing, which resulted in the erosion of the manufacturing base. As a point of interest, the apprenticeship system is now being planned for reinstallation in the UK to support their new thrust to get back manufacturing. Also, the reinstalled apprenticeship system will still follow the original structure that I experienced, and which I am explaining here. Here is the link to the new British system:

BIS-15-604-english-apprenticeships-our-2020-vision.pdf (publishing.service.gov.uk)

The only fully functional apprenticeship system in the Western nations is in Germany, which may correlate with their continued success at keeping their own manufacturing base, even with the pressure of globalization.

Such an integrated industrial learning system is a critical success factor in enabling the recovery of manufacturing, and we will explain this in detail in a later chapter.

As we progressed from age sixteen through the apprenticeship, we had the opportunity, if our performance was high enough, to grade up from the technician program of day release to join the technologist or engineering sandwich program. I started as a technician apprentice and graded up to the sandwich program and ended as a graduate apprentice with a degree in electronic engineering. The lesson was: you want it, and work hard, you get it.

In the last years of our apprenticeship, we would join departments for longer experience periods and start to develop individual career paths. Many of us would focus our time on the product design, development, or engineering departments, which resulted in a career within those departments. I chose to focus on manufacturing departments such as production-process planning, production-project management, and manufacturing-technology development. This career path was driven by both aptitude and interest, and to some extent the encouragement from the department managers, who would start to procure the apprentice talent they wanted.

Through this later period of my apprenticeship, I worked in the manufacturing departments as a trainee manufacturing engineer and was assigned to coordinating the manufacture of prototype electronic assemblies. This involved reviewing the early drawings in the design office, which were hand-drawn on drafting boards. All our machine processes were manually operated, so it was handle-turning by skilled operators, not program-driven button-pushing. Some Numerically Controlled (NC) milling and turning machines programed with paper tape were in use, but we would not see computers in manufacturing for at least another ten years. I developed an understanding of manufacturing and fabricating metal components on machine tools by talking with the process planners and machine operators. I also had to become an expert on the design rules for printed-circuit-board technology for electronic assembly, and the testing capability for these circuits. The design engineers respected my knowledge, and I learned how to process these rush low-volume orders through the production departments. I assisted with the development of some new electronic-assembly processes, such as micro-welding of integrated electronic circuits and conformal coating of printed circuit boards for airborne applications. I worked with a machine provider to develop an integrated assembly machine for solar panels for spacecraft applications. These were all exciting learning experiences.

By the time I fully qualified as a manufacturing engineer at twenty-two with a degree-level qualification, I had six years of valuable industrial education, training, and experience, all of it relevant to the continuing success of my career, and I had been paid to undertake it. This prepared me for what was to come next: the director of manufacturing engineering procured me by giving me an offer I could not refuse.

I was offered a position as a power-systems manufacturing engineer working on the project team for the Intelsat 4A communication satellite. This involved going to California to work with Hughes Aircraft (the consortium leader) and planning and building solar panels and battery systems for the satellite. I worked on this program and managed many others, including some European scientific-payload satellites over the next six years. I was involved in the launch of twenty-two satellites.

In 1978, I immigrated to Canada as a senior manufacturing engineer to work in aerospace, and I managed a subsystem build of the Canadian Anik C and D communication satellites that supported TV and telephonics. I also assisted the manufacturing planning for the electronic control units for the Canadarm, the space shuttle robotic manipular arm. I went on to operate in a variety of manufacturing engineering and management roles.

In 1983, I moved from aerospace to the electronics industry as an engineering manager at Motorola, the telecommunications company, and developed the Evolution plan for my division that was focused on improving all facets of the manufacturing process, and new-product-introduction procedures. This was an exciting time to be in electronics manufacturing, as we successfully competed with the leading international companies, and learned how to evolve our operating practices, using what became LEAN and Six Sigma practices to reduce waste and variability within the manufacturing process. We reduced our inventory and "Cost Of Poor Quality," and I developed my version of a change-management process within the organization.

In 1989, I moved on as an industry consultant and joined two kindred spirits from Hewlett-Packard, the computer-hardware company. We formed a consulting practice to educate and consult industry on what was then a new concept called LEAN manufacturing. It was an exciting opportunity, and we quickly developed our education and facilitation product set. Within a year we had documented our technology, and I co-authored the LEAN concept and methodology into the textbook *Cycle Time Management* that was published in 1992 by Productivity Press in the USA.

The CTM book was well received, and it was the only how-to book on the subject at the time. Also, it was a great tool to illustrate and market our services, and I have continued to consult corporations across many manufacturing sectors in different countries on LEAN manufacturing and continuous improvement. My career has been... life in the manufacturing fast lane.

Manufacturing has been exceptionally good to me, and in the next chapter I will explain how my business experiences from 2000 onward drove me toward writing this book.

THE OFFSHORE EXPERIENCE: TBM GENESIS

By the late 1990s, my consulting efforts became focused on assisting clients to reposition their supply chains. Some had operations in Mexico, and in the last years of the 1990s I was asked to assist and eventually general-manage an electronic assembly operation in a Mexican *maquiladora* in Nogales on the US/Mexican border. *Maquiladoras* were manufacturing operations in Mexico close to the US/Mexico border that involved bringing most of the electronic components and associated raw materials into Mexico, utilizing the low-cost labor to assemble the product and then returning the finished or semi-finished product back into the US or Canada with few taxes or tariffs.

My main goal was to stabilize the quality and output of the factory. Although the Mexican management was eager, they were far from experienced or disciplined enough to run a manufacturing environment. The workforce was transient and seasonal and came up from the southern farms on a temporary basis, so turnover was in double digits each week. Monday attendance was a nightmare. In general, Mexicans rate work about fifth on the list after religion, holidays, parties, and festivals. I have many horror stories I could share about the labor and management challenges in running a *maquiladora*. But for all their shortfalls, the people were friendly and, except for their work ethic, wonderful to know.

The challenge was managing the trade-off of inferior quality due to the high labor turnover, added inventory, and transportation costs with the opportunity of much lower labor costs. This business model worked well in some cases, but the transient nature of the labor pool was a huge challenge that many found to be problematic and unsustainable. Eventually, however, Mexican quality control improved and stabilized, and many corporations now have successful manufacturing operations there, although many have moved away from the border towns to stable cities within Mexico.

By the early 2000s, China had been fully opened for trade and many North American corporations were firmly requesting—and in some cases forcing—their suppliers to move manufacturing to this low-cost country. This was a cover story for our North American multinational corporations to move into the Chinese markets and share these untapped consumers.

This strategic globalization plan was supported by all the prominent economists and Western governments, and it was clear: first employ the Chinese population by giving them our products to make, move them out of poverty, turn them into consumers, and supply them with products into the future. In parallel, our Western factories would refocus on complex and higher technology, and any employment displacement would be covered by the huge growth in the Western service industries via this newfound global prosperity.

This all sounded great at the time, and was the prime tenet upon which globalized manufacturing, free trade, and the new world order was founded.

As we will describe in this book, this globalized manufacturing journey will be defined by the history books as the biggest mistake made by the Western world.

Based on my experience at running international manufacturing environments, I was asked in 2003 to go to China to set up manufacturing operations. I spent most of my time living in China between 2003 until 2010 and assisted my clients with many manufacturing projects and technology transfers. We set up a lot of manufacturing capability to ship product in forty-foot containers for North American consumers. I made a lot of lifelong friends in China and came to respect the capability that it and its people continue to offer.

I found the Chinese people and their culture to be capable of learning fast, having a decent work ethic, and being responsive to business opportunities. I am also sad to say that I repeatedly found the Chinese government at all levels focused on the wellbeing and prosperity of their own people, and I saw how superior the Chinese government are at getting the right things done compared to our Western governments. I have many examples, but more about this later.

On my return to Canada from China in the fall of 2010, I reconnected with my friends in industry and caught up on the trade press and the local media. I was horrified with how much my efforts at assisting the offshoring manufacturing had contributed to the decline of the North American manufacturing community.

The Canadian press was full of the realization that we had a double-digit decline in manufacturing jobs, and whole sectors of the manufacturing economy had been hollowed out or eradicated.

For many of us, this was not a total surprise. We had seen the contribution of manufacturing in the Canadian and US economy continue to decline since the 1960s, but the percent decline since 2000 had accelerated, as had the decline in the employment contribution within manufacturing.

It became clear by 2010 that the political promises of an increase in service jobs offsetting those lost in manufacturing—promises made by US President Bill Clinton and Canadian Prime Minister Brian Mulroney when they installed NAFTA with Mexico and opened trade with China—was never going to be forthcoming. In fact, service-sector-employment growth flatlined or declined in some sectors due to the lack of manufacturing jobs, as typically a substantial number of service jobs are dependent on manufacturing jobs. Also, many service jobs got offshored even more than those in manufacturing. These were banking, telecommunications, and commercial back-office jobs such as customer service, technical support, and accounting. Next time you are asking your telephone company some technical issue or asking for a solution on your TV service or computer software, or have a payment issue, ask the nice service representative where they live... it won't be in North America. Maybe India, Bangladesh, Puerto Rico, or the Philippines, or someplace else offshore. This clearly destroys the notion that we can participate and be prosperous in a globalized world as a post-industrialized service-based society.

My first reaction to all this was to feel ashamed of my activities in Mexico at the end of the 1990s, and certainly in China through 2003 to 2010. I could see how the next generation of kids that were then ten or eleven (the same age as me when I became aware of the maker within me) would not have the opportunities to join the manufacturing workforce, develop a career, and enjoy the prosperity that goes with it. I am sadly being proven correct, as now, more than ten years later, I see the ongoing struggle the twentysomethings are having with starting a meaningful and sustainable career, their lack of prosperity and related social issues of low self-esteem, and, as they mature, an inability to afford to start a family in these precarious times.

An article in a Toronto paper published in 2010 grabbed me. It was about Canadian hockey sticks, essential to our national sport. They are all made offshore, so when our kids pick up that first stick on the ice and read where it's made, it won't be Canada, or even North America. This is a great shame, and an ongoing signal to our kids, who will question how many other items around them are not made here: computers, fridges, cars, and most of things they see in the large chain stores. There's no maker thinking needed; they just learn how to unpack, read instructions, and consume.

They don't seem to think about it much at all, and never ask how it is made. It's called "globalized manufacturing," and it's something we have all gotten far too used to. It's clear we have all become brainwashed into the notion that globalized manufacturing is the only state of manufacturing we can have.

I had a strong feeling that we in the Western world were getting it wrong, and that our manufacturing heritage was being destroyed. I started to think about how it could be different and what should be done. I started to form an opinion on how unsustainable the notion of globalized manufacturing was to the world, and I started to ask questions about what had happened to take us there.

The TBM Forum

I reconnected with the Society of Manufacturing Engineers (SME), of which I have been a member since 1983. After a few SME Toronto chapter meetings, I joined the executive committee, and it became clear from the many committee meetings and discussions there that the decline in the manufacturing community had also gutted membership and interest in any SME chapter events, and much discussion on what direction to take to survive in this climate was had. It occurred to me that we were all trying to put lipstick on a pig by carrying on as if nothing had changed in the manufacturing community, and the issue of the decline in manufacturing and its focus as a future part of the economy was best addressed by directly talking about it, rather than avoiding it. It was also clear that other technical and industry-based societies and business associations were feeling the same angst and appeared to have like-minded views, so after some thought and concurrence we decided to pull together a cross-society-and-association event to learn about the issues as a collective, and decide what should we do about it. In desperation, but with a twist of direct frontal assault, we called the initiative "Take Back Manufacturing" (TBM), and the events we held became the TBM Forum. Our aim was to become a powerful advocacy group dedicated to restoring our manufacturing sectors.

The TBM Forum was supported by a range of technical and industrial societies and associations, and it's been a battle cry for the restoration of our manufacturing sectors, with a focus on Canada. We have been raising awareness of the need for a strong manufacturing base for our future prosperity since 2011.

Since its formation, TBM has been well received as a worthwhile cause, and many Canadians we have talked with firmly believe that we must take action on the current state of decline of the manufacturing sectors in Canada and restore them for our future prosperity. This feedback has kept us motivated as advocates, even after many years of less than positive outcomes.

Our TBM message has always been the same: Our manufacturing sectors continue their slow death. We all need manufacturing, and its continuous decline is having disastrous results for our economy and our prosperity.

In the next chapters we will explain the problem, how it happened, and the proposed solution.

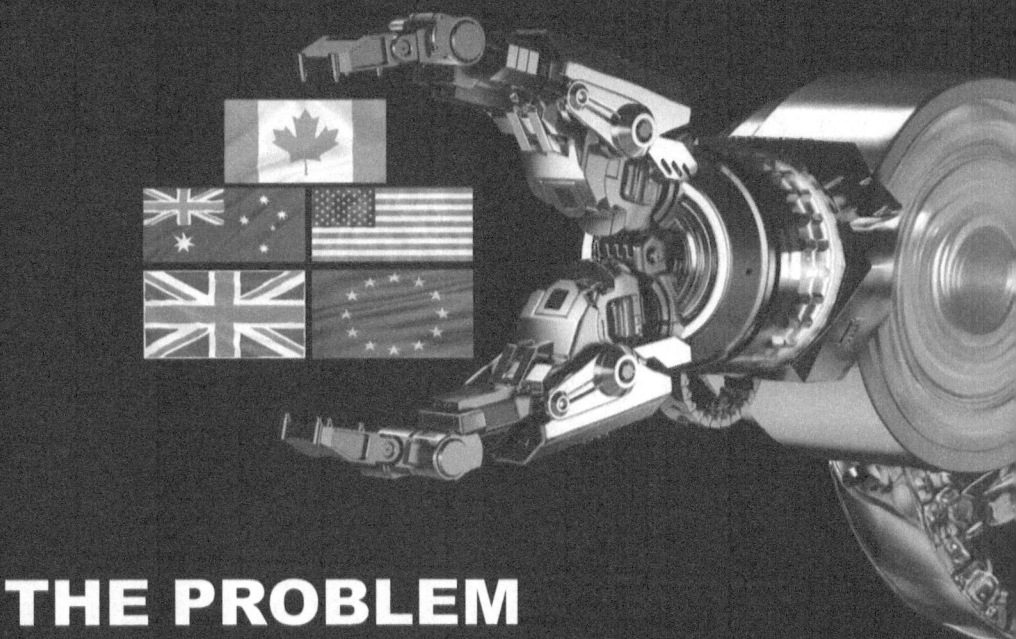

THE PROBLEM

WHAT HAPPENED TO
WESTERN MANUFACTURING?

TO UNDERSTAND HOW we lost a huge portion of our manufacturing in the Western world, we need to review global trade history. From about 1980 onwards, Western governments, especially in the US, subscribed to the liberalization of international trade. The economists termed this "global free trade," and it has increased eight times since 1980. Prior to 1980 imports were mostly essential raw materials and some cheap low value commodity products, with the bulk of manufactured products being manufactured within the western nations.

This globalization of trade was driven by the removal of national trade controls. The economists of the day sold our governments the notion that the liberalization of international trade would be a win-win strategy for prosperity across the globe. These economists used the expression "the rise of global free trade will make all boats rise together." The expression was applied to free-market policies, in that comparative-advantage production and subsequent global trade would theoretically increase incomes for all participating entities. It is said to be a favorite proverb of former US Treasury Secretary Robert Rubin, who served In the Clinton administration. We all now know this concept was either at best a foolish generalization or at worst a dangerous misconception, which has redistributed wealth rather than creating it.

Most consumers quickly sucked up the apparent benefit of lower-cost offshored products, but most now realize the longer-term implications. It's become clear that global free trade is not working for everyone. It is the prime reason for unplanned wealth transfer, precarious employment, increasing inequality, and declining prosperity in most Western nations.

Large corporations, in the rush to enter and benefit from new offshore markets, insisted all their suppliers utilize supply chains that accessed cheap labor in these offshore sources. This dangerous journey went unimpeded due to a lack of interest by the Western nations in controlling their trade balance. This was coupled with a total absence of national trade policy. This free-for-all was enforced by multilateral agreements organized by the World Trade Organization (WTO). The WTO is an intergovernmental organization that regulates and facilitates international trade. Governments signed up the organization to establish, revise, and enforce the rules that govern international trade. It officially commenced operations on 1 January 1995, replacing the General Agreement on Tariffs and Trade (GATT) that had been established in 1948. The WTO is the world's largest international economic organization, with 164 member states representing over 98 percent of global trade and GDP. Recently it has been criticized by many Western governments, including the USA, for not correctly enforcing the rules it had facilitated, and not operating in the best interests of all its participants.

In many business sectors, it has been corporate herd behavior chasing competitors offshore to see how to get to the new markets and the next lowest price, and joining the race to the bottom. I remember sitting in the boardroom of a local supplier with their customer who was threatening them with a statement I heard a lot: "If you guys don't have an offshore source, you obviously cannot be competitive and won't remain on the bidders' list at the next round of contract reviews." This mix of corporate browbeating with contractual pressure and economic brainwashing led to almost total herd behavior, a stampede to go offshore to get that share. In fact, the notion was that we *had* to go on the offshore journey, and that on the upside a new market opportunity awaited us in these emerging markets. Through this process, many suppliers were eliminated if they were unable to join the offshore journey, and were replaced with offshore sources. So, as we moved a lot of our manufacturing value offshore, whole sectors of local manufacturing have been hollowed out.

It is estimated that in the last two decades we have reduced our manufacturing intensity in the Western nations by at least 15 percent. This means we have 15 percent less value-added effort in the products we consume. The products may be repackaged here or have the same label or badge on the front, but within the supply chain we have 15 percent less material and labor contribution from our own economies. The value is being generated by imported products manufactured in low-cost countries. Many products have experienced this "reduced intensity" in everything from furniture to food to automobiles to electronics. (We will show the automobile example later in this chapter.)

Try buying anything with "Made in Canada" on it. When leaving Canada at the airport, it's hard to find anything made in Canada in duty-free, or any of our local stores, for that matter. I don't know about you, but my gift choices of maple syrup and ice wine have worn thin with my foreign friends. (They keep asking for the ice wine anyway.)

Clothes, footwear, plastic goods, and many consumables are almost completely made offshore, as are electronic products. Furniture, appliances, and other consumer durable goods and other specialized industrial equipment are in a mixed state of globalization.

It's also scary how many foodstuffs, medical supplies, and drugs are now supported by offshore supply chains.

Historically, the automotive industry has been a good indicator of the health of our Western industrial economies, and it still represents an important part of the economy in Ontario, where I live. It's now clear we have significantly globalized manufacturing, even in this technology-based industry.

To put this in perspective, below is the supply chain for General Motors, a North American corporation, and it describes the supply chain for a domestically assembled vehicle.

We have listed the major components—tires, trim, electrical, battery, plastic parts, lighting, air conditioning, chassis, glass etc.—and the areas from where they are supplied. It's certainly a global supply chain, and some of these components are large, which require greater effort in shipping.

The map shows that some are sourced from low-cost countries, who mostly do not have any comparative advantage in terms of raw materials.

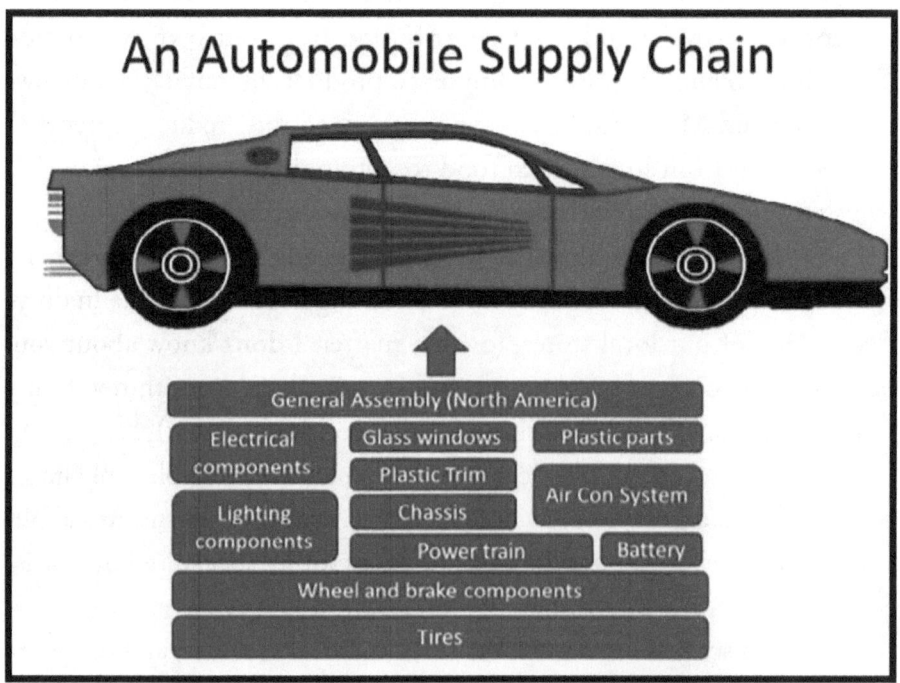

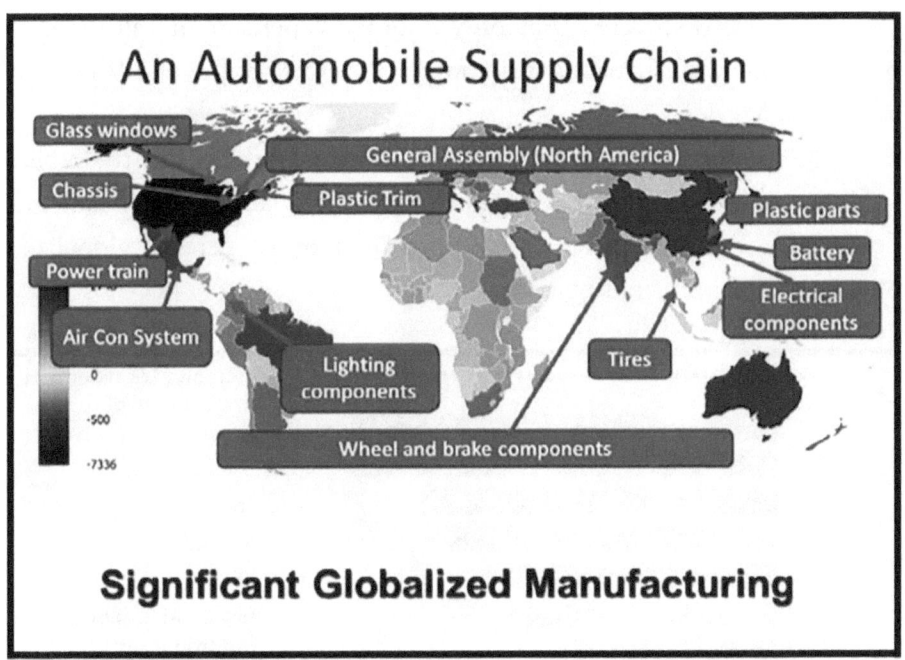

Component	source	$ value%	Labor Hrs %	Supply Travel Miles	Offshore Value %	USMCA Value %	USA Value %	Canada Value %	Mexico Value %	Offshore Lab hrs %	USMCA Lab hrs %	USA Lab hrs %	Canada Lab %	Mexico Lab %
USA General Assembly	USA	15	10	0		15	15				10	10		
Canada Plastics trim	CANADA	7	3	500		7		7			3		3	
Detroit chassis	USA	6	5	25		6	6				5	5		
Chicago glass	USA	7	8	900		7	7				8	8		
New Mexico power train	USA	15	17	1700		15	15				17	17		
Mexico air con systems	MEXICO	8	9	1100		8			8		9			9
South America lighting	OFFSHORE	4	6	1500	4					6				
India wheel/brakes	OFFSHORE	7	8	6000	7					8				
Vietnam tires	OFFSHORE	7	7	5500	7					7				
China electrical parts	OFFSHORE	10	8	4000	10					8				
China battery system	OFFSHORE	4	9	4000	4					9				
China plastic parts	OFFSHORE	10	10	4000	10					10				
Total		100	100	2657	42	58	43	7	8	48	52	40	3	9

We tabulated the value of each of these major components and the assembly activity, and discovered that the final assembly, either in the US or Canada, is only 15 percent of the value and 10 percent of the labor content.

Then we discovered that only another 7 percent of value and 3 percent labor is in Canada, and another 8 percent value and 9 percent labor is in Mexico.

So, the total contribution inside the NAFTA/USMCA trade bloc is 58 percent value, and that includes 52 percent labor. This means our domestic automotive product is approximately 42 percent globalized outside of our local trading zone.

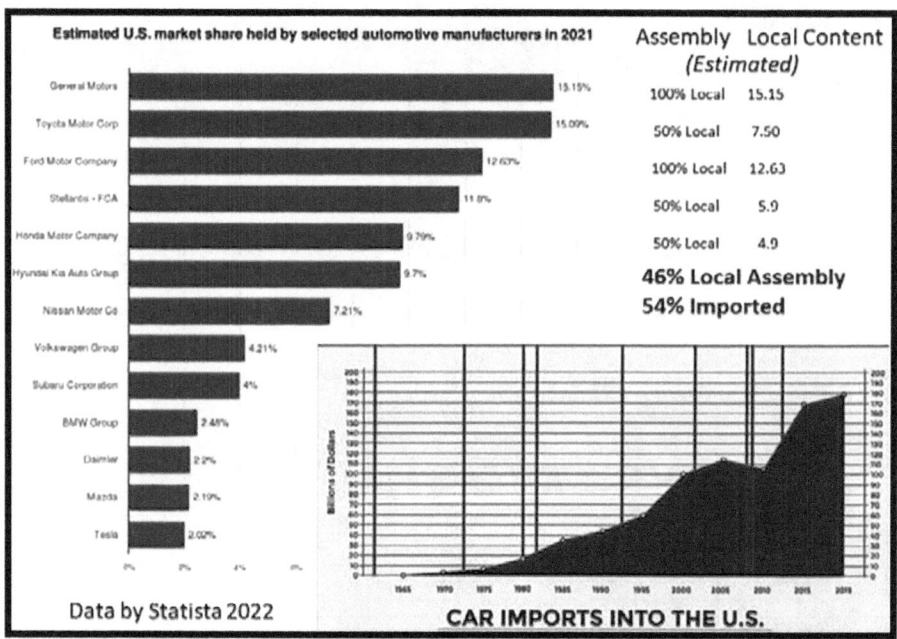

We estimate that, based on the US market share graph, the US imports 54 percent as finished vehicles. This has doubled since 2000, mainly from Asian suppliers since the start of the globalization of manufacturing. The local assembly is estimated at 46 percent of total purchased vehicles. This means that when supply chain offshore content is further discounted, our local industry content for the vehicles we drive on our North American roads is at best only 27 percent USMCA content, and at best 4 percent Canadian content.

Further, when we look at the part and product transportation distances, we find that the average component travels approximately 2,600 miles to get integrated into the assembly.

Although local sales of autos have been positive due to cheap credit, the decline of the local automotive sector continues, with far less value-added manufacturing content and employment that has dropped by 25 percent in the last two decades.

Like many Canadian industries, the auto industry is experiencing under-capitalization and is attracting significantly less than its capital quota with the Northern United States. Mexico is gaining an increasing share of the capital investment to support new products, tooling, and factory plants due to both low-cost labor and operating costs, as well as the local growth market opportunity. Mexico has the opportunity of being the only NAFTA region with mature trade agreements already in place with some other non-NAFTA jurisdictions, so our main competitor for our share of the NAFTA auto industrial manufacturing pie will be Mexico.

The recent retooling of GM's Oshawa, Ontario, plant to produce gasoline-powered Chevrolet Silverados and GMC Sierras to meet North America's insatiable demand for pickups was good news and will help boost Canadian production over the next few years. But auto production in Canada has declined steadily in the last two decades due to a loss of competitiveness when the Canadian dollar reached parity in 2011. The big three US automakers produced only 383,000 vehicles in Canada in 2021, about 240,000 fewer than they sold in the country the year before.

Although the Canadian government hopes to reverse this trend, I predict that we will experience a further 25 percent reduction in the Canadian automotive manufacturing sector's GDP within a decade, unless we make significant changes to trade policy and investments.

The future of Canada's auto industry will also hinge on how successfully it manages the transition to electric vehicles. So far, things are not looking great. In 2021, Ford, GM, and Toyota announced billions of dollars in new investments to build electric vehicle (EV) batteries in several of the United States. GM will invest US$7 billion in Michigan to produce electric versions of the Silverado and Sierra pickups and will build a new battery cell plant in the state. Local state governments are subsidizing many such ventures.

Although some EV battery component factories are planned to open in Quebec and Windsor, Canada is barely on the radar when it comes to the global EV supply chain, which includes everything from critical mineral mining and refining to cathode and anode manufacturing and EV assembly.

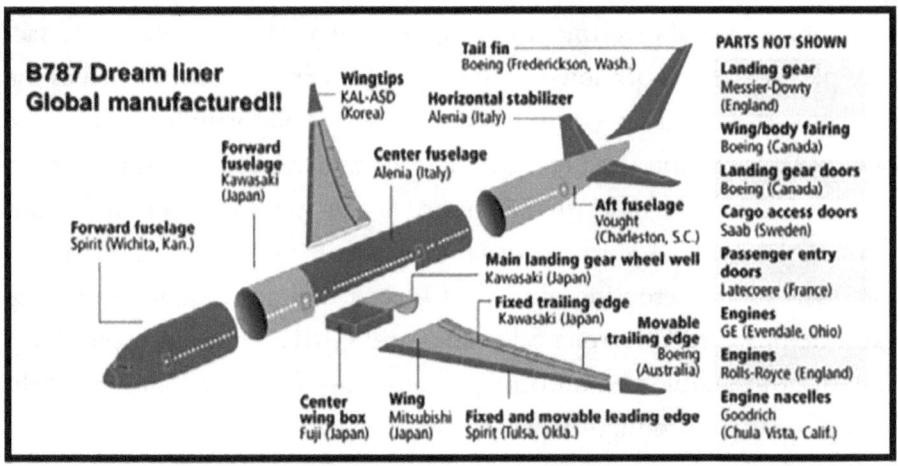

Many other industry sectors have experienced a similarly high level of globalization. The aerospace industry has globalized not only manufacturing activities but many design, R&D, and process technology activities via international consortiums that have enabled many different national supply participants in a single airframe.

But this is clearly not the most productive approach. The new Boeing 787 Dreamliner supply chain breakdown explained in an article in *Design News 25 August 2009* details how the added global collaboration, transportation, and integration costs were huge, and significantly added not only to final product costs but major mistakes and delays.

Other Ontario industrial sectors, such as information and communications technologies, food, pharmaceutical, furniture, footwear, clothes, and appliances, and primary industries such as mining and steel, have seen decline in terms of employment contribution. Some of this is due to technology and automation, but most is due to the contribution of offshore supply chains reducing the manufacturing intensity or value-adding manufacturing contribution to local GDP.

Also, R&D does not stay when manufacturing relocates. Manufacturing and R&D work best when they are integrated and co-located. Manufacturing is an important incubation ingredient for R&D and product development. So, as manufacturing is outsourced and offshored, it should come as no surprise to see large corporations developing the need to move R&D into developing countries while also benefiting from the lower cost of skills. Although these locations may need developing, they will eventually become capable and fully aligned with the offshored manufacturing base. Many industries have experienced this domino effect. R&D has been offshored as the manufacturing migrated offshore for a large segment of the electronics industry; the large pharmaceutical industries; the machine, tool, and furniture and appliance industry; and the associated compliance testing facilities. The notion from economists early in the globalization journey that that the West will keep the high technology products, and that the offshore supply base will only provide the low value products, is now clearly a huge fallacy.

With the internet and other globalizing tools, service and technical resources can be globalized easier than manufacturing jobs. This has raised concerns for associations that are concerned about membership jobs being redeployed offshore. This has already happened in the information and communications technologies and finance-services industry. Just about every telephone service call and technical assistance hotline is being fielded by a representative or technical support person from offshore. Even the publishing support in writing this book is provided for a Canadian publishing company from staff located in the Philippines. I see so much of the services we as consumers are paying to have performed adding no value to our economy or local employment or supporting our tax base. These are jobs most members of our citizen base could very easily perform with limited training.

THE RUST BELT

Many areas in North America continue to feel the pinch of the globalized manufacturing situation and now form a geographical area termed the "Rust Belt."

The Rust Belt runs southwesterly from Central New York through Pennsylvania, Ohio, West Virginia, Kentucky, and Indiana, and then northwesterly through the Lower Peninsula of Michigan and Northern Illinois, and ends in Northeastern Wisconsin and includes New England. In Canada it includes many parts of Ontario and Quebec.

Due to the aftermath of uncontrolled globalization, these regions are continuing to experience the elimination or outsourcing of manufacturing jobs. The term "rust" refers to the impact of deindustrialization, economic decline, population loss, urban decay, and real decay in factory real estate and idle equipment, attributable to the shrinking of the once-powerful industrial sectors. They include steelmaking, automobile, heavy equipment and coal mining, clothing, furniture, pharmaceutical, food products, and food finishing plants, which have all been significantly offshored.

This has contributed directly to the decline in the prosperity of small towns, and human prosperity loss in those regions that were directly dependent on the local manufacturing.

The Great Lakes region was formerly known as the industrial heartland of North America, and it was where wealth was created through manufacturing using the abundance of raw materials and fresh water, and the ability to use the Great Lakes to move materials between states. It leveraged our intellect, investment, and labors, and generated the wealth we had all enjoyed since the industrial expansion of North America. This industrial decline increased significantly due to globalized manufacturing from 2000 to 2010.

This situation has created a huge dent in the firm promises our politicians made with input from our global-orientated economists. They had promised that we would become prosperous in a post-industrialized society by developing our service and financial industries. If that's so, excluding the bloated financial sector pay rates available to a very few due to the increasing financialization of our economy, where are all the high-paying service jobs we were promised for the general population, who have been displaced and badly affected by this economic change?

Looking back, it's clear we were sold a myth by economists and governments, who promised we would only lose the low-tech jobs to globalization but keep the high-tech and R&D content. Well, we have kept the burgers to flip, but have lost many high-tech automobiles, computers, aerospace, and pharmaceutical, and the associated R&D and many technical service jobs. But we still have the burgers to flip.

In the next chapter, we will look at just how these economists and politicos allowed this disastrous form of globalization to happen.

HOW DID ECONOMICS CHANGE
TO MAKE IT HAPPEN?

This book is not specifically about explaining in detail the highly flawed economics of this era, but I will dwell for a while on the economic thinking that confused itself and everyone else with its own brilliance and allowed the over-mobility of capital and trade on a global basis. This destroyed the delicate balance between capital and labor, driven by a flawed ideology of neo-liberalized economics that generated poor global trade policies that, for most Western national economies, forced the destruction, or at a very minimum, the hollowing out of their manufacturing sectors.

WELL, IT'S GLOBALIZATION...

Globalization is not new, with some experts defining that it's the fourth cycle in 500 years, but it's the first time we in the West, through no fault of most of the population, have been on the extreme negative end of global wealth transfer.

The Western world had built wealth from the mid-eighteenth to the mid-twentieth century using a maker model. So how in the heck did we expect to stay wealthy by giving a lot of it away in less than a few decades to recently emerging economies? These emerging economies have queued up to participate in this model of "low-cost-country globalized manufacturing." It has clearly been a negative-wealth-transfer journey for the mature Western economies, who in the same timeframe were informed by economists that everyone would benefit from this journey. We were told that our Western economies were entering an era of becoming "post industrialized nations." Well, good luck with that, as far as the outcome is concerned.

So how did we get there?

After a few earlier economic disasters, the biggest being in the 1930s, the economists appeared to have learned that what is called the "Keynesian economic model" worked best for everyone involved for most of the first thirty years after WWII.

This Keynesian economic model, created by the Bretton Woods Agreement in 1944, generated what some economists call the golden age. This is the prosperity period I and the other baby boomers grew up within. Keynesian economics struck a balance between the power of market capitalism and national government intervention and controls to ensure a balanced economic environment. This also ensured controlled and balanced transfer of import and export trade and capital between nations and used a currency-exchange and transfer-control mechanism called the "gold exchange standard," and it was based on the prominent reserve currency of the US dollar. The gold exchange standard ensured countries fixed their exchange rates relative to the US dollar so that central banks could exchange dollar holdings into gold at the same fixed exchange rate. All currencies pegged to the US dollar thereby had a fixed value in terms of gold, and this option was not available to businesses or individuals.

Although we did suffer from inflation that caused conflict between capitalists and trade unions, we had reasonable growth and prosperity in the Western world through this period, with most international trade in balance.

This was the model up until about the early 1970s, but then a series of geopolitical mistakes that started in the 1950s changed the fortunes and stability of the Western economies.

Firstly, The US national debt to fight foreign wars, support global peacekeeping, and support the post-war restoration had been allowed to pile up, with no significant repayment being provided by those being protected or supported, and these free handouts continue to this day, placing undue financial pressure on various Western economies. A good example of this peacekeeping debt was described by President Trump, who correctly requested European nations pay their fair share for NATO support. Also, the UN always expects so-called rich Western nations to support conflicts with expensive peacekeeping missions, which often have zero to do with Western national security.

This US national debt placed significant pressure on the US dollar, which was the main reserve currency for the gold exchange standard. France has a lot to answer for, as it caused the conflict in Indochina (Vietnam) due to a poor form of colonialism, which started a war that the US got dragged into, which added to the US debt burden. Although France certainly owed their liberation after WWII to the USA, they did little to support the US dollar. It's fair to say that the French government broke the rules of the gold exchange standard and added to the strain on the US dollar and other compliant currencies. The outcome was the demise of the gold-exchange-standard system that had been installed by the Bretton Woods Agreement. This allowed most national currencies to float and, in many cases, destabilized economies.

Secondly, the West allowed other underdeveloped nations to overly control and benefit from oil-resource extractions and other important trade infrastructures it had developed. This eventually allowed the Arab states, and some others, to form a cartel and start a price and resource war, which effectively held the Western world to ransom. Many experts and politicians of the 1950s had warned of this outcome, but the Western governments of the day relinquished ownership of these major oil resources, infrastructure, and transportation systems, which has always been directly linked to our ability to operate our modern economies and create wealth. The penalty was a destabilizing of the Western economies. History shows that the Arab states were not entitled to the full value of those resources. The deal should have been a small fee for the land rights, and clearly, we did not set up the rights of ownership of the resources correctly.

Milton Friedman and many other leading economists of the mid 1970s onwards, with almost religious fanaticism, disregarded and dismissed the hard-earned experience of a more balanced Keynesian system which had lasted from 1945. They started to lobby and get approval to undertake new economic policies that followed a strong free market-based approach, sometimes described as Free market fundamentalism or neoliberalism. This fostered a strong belief by many economists in the ability of unregulated *laissez-faire* or free-market capitalist policies to solve most economic and social problems on a global level. It was described as a return to 18th Century economic concepts by the Scottish Enlightenment thinker Adam Smith. He introduced the concept of the "invisible hand" or "free hand of the market" This refers to the invisible market force that brings a free market to equilibrium with levels of supply and demand by actions of self-interested individuals. More recently Friedman has been criticized as one of the apostles of this "laissez-faire approach" that has dominated contemporary economic policies. It has clearly allowed unfettered Globalization that has significantly damaged our western economies. Alan Greenspan was Chairman of the Board of the United States Federal Reserve and an economic advisor, and with others was instrumental in further allowing uncontrolled globalization and trade imbalance, as well as generating a series of financial disasters due to supporting changes to the US financial system that created its instability.

It's now clear to me and some economists I have talked with, that this free-market ideology was just plain stupid when applied to a global market with a huge wealth and capacity gradient between the Western economies and the emerging economies.

The first thrust at the free-market methodologies was the North American Free Trade Agreement (NAFTA), between the US, Canada, and Mexico. To some extent, this has been less of a concern than what came later, as it was really the ratification of existing local border controls that had existed well before its inception in 1994. When NAFTA was initiated, it was openly recognized by economists and politicians that manufacturing jobs would diminish in some sectors and communities, but they believed that they would be replaced by the growth of service-sector jobs. Also, the hope was that the increased productivity within the NAFTA trade bloc would foster the growth of trade and prosperity, but they have since found out that hope does not pay the rent for their citizens. NAFTA was not expected to change the US-Canada trade relationship very much, as a healthy trade level had always existed between them, with their economic living standards being close to the same. The real change was between Mexico and the other two developed economies. The hope was that the larger economies would be able to absorb the lower-cost labor capacity offered by Mexico, and as a bloc use this to gain additional growth and prosperity. By 1999, many Mexican *maquiladora* plants had been developed along the US-Mexico border, like the one I ran in 1999 and 2000. The impact of adding low-cost Mexican labor was significant in some sectors, and it adversely affected some manufacturing in the US and Canada, but many of us agreed that the proximity of Mexico made the supply chains manageable and, over time, as consumerism in Mexico grew, NAFTA would evolve into a strong and balanced trade-bloc environment.

In parallel with all this, the Soviet Union collapsed in 1991. This allowed the Berlin Wall to come down. It was hailed as a victory for the West and democracy, and it fueled the notion of a new world order. But history shows that it generated Western economic brazenness and risk-taking on a global level. It also generated a bitterness by Russian leadership, with current events in Crimea and Ukraine clearly demonstrating that the vision of a Soviet Union and a return to an East-West iron curtain is far from dead.

All these geopolitical events and new economic ideologies started an increase in the free movement of capital and a move away from the adherence to reserve currencies. This allowed a jag of unstable foreign investments, which resulted in a series of financial crashes from the early 1990s onward.

But what came next did the main damage. In the late 1970s, China moved from a closed communist economy and started a journey in the early 1980s to open for international trade. At the time, this trade opportunity was hailed as a roadmap for future peace and the eventual liberalization of China toward democracy. It's now clear that this is as probable as pigs flying to the moon, as China has evolved into a successful communist mercantile economy that is the second largest in the world.

The opportunity to trade with China was a huge lure for Western multinationals to open and develop a new consumer market. This started in the early 1980s and moved into high gear in the early 2000s. Without any controls or thought of the implications, the US and Canada have extended free trade/free market ideology to China and other non-NAFTA countries, such as South Korea, India, and Taiwan.

Looking back, it is now hard to believe that any sane Western government would allow this to happen.

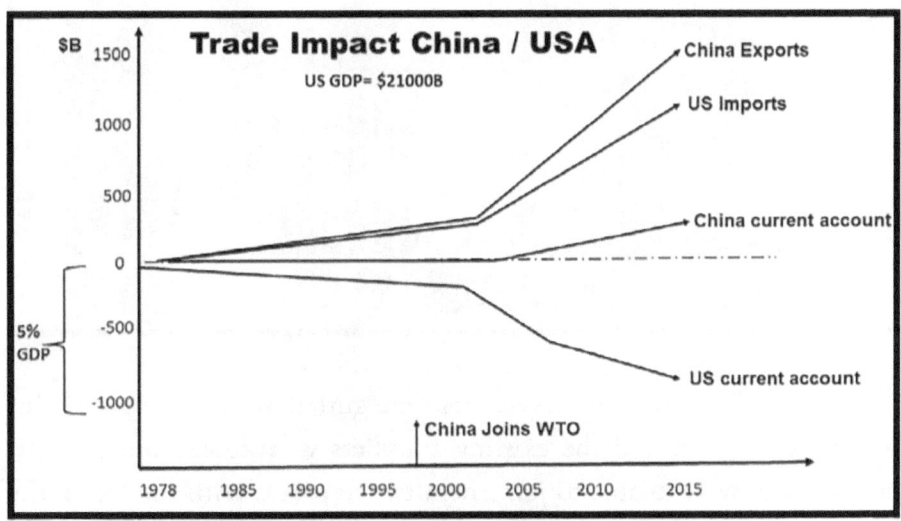

Trade with China accelerated out of balance from about 2001, when China joined the World Trade Organization (WTO). Chinese export to the US increased almost six times in six years from 2000. This quickly created a US account deficit almost four times what existed before the trade with China commenced. What they did in a short period was open our trade borders and allow a huge global labor force (paid no more than two dollars per hour) free and uncontrolled access to our consumers. This access, coupled with sea-freight-container technology, relocated massive amounts of valuable jobs to Asia outside of the recent trade bloc we had between the US, Canada, and Mexico. Canada experienced the same fate as the US with the Canada-China trade imbalance shown below.

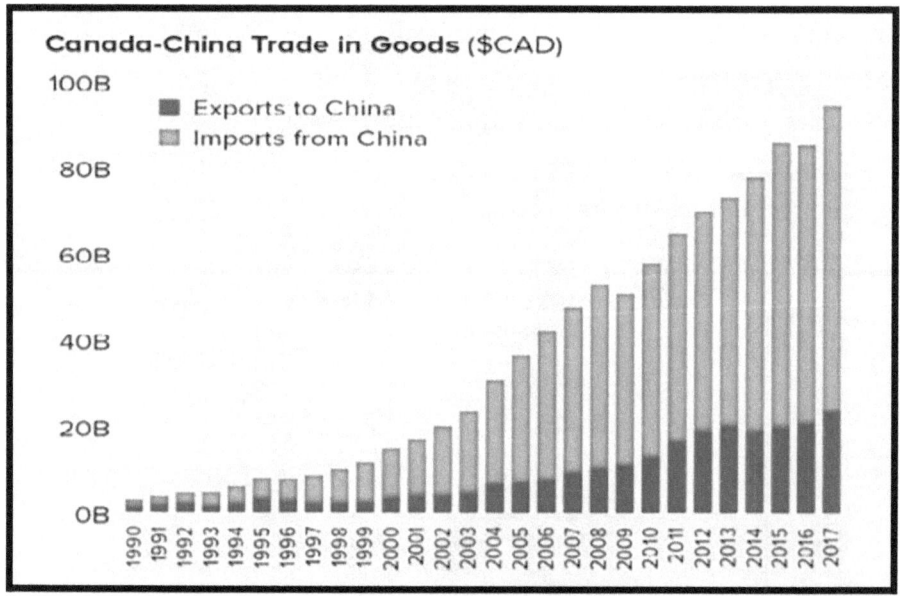

Canada-China Trade in Goods ($CAD)

■ Exports to China
▨ Imports from China

Whole Western business sectors were gutted as some supply chains became disrupted, and the existing suppliers were forced out of business, as they were unable to join the offshore party. With the US in the lead, the stage was now set for an ongoing meltdown of most Western nations' economic balance. Multinational corporations were allowed to follow a free-market liberalized trade approach, with limited tariffs and tax controls, as well as the free movement of capital. This debacle was underwritten and allowed to flourish without much unified objections by six consecutive US presidential administrations, and six consecutive Canadian governments, with the supporting economists of the day 100 percent complicit in this ongoing blunder.

It's interesting to note that, even though this global trade policy (or the lack of any) was to have a huge impact on all its Western citizens, at no time did anyone in government or the public get to vote on the direction taken. It was orchestrated behind closed doors by the mainstream global-free-trade-oriented economists of the time, who followed a neoliberal ideology. They kept telling the governments, the media, and the public that free trade in all forms made sense, and "all boats rise together." They promised that the increased global productivity that would be created would foster the growth of exports to these offshore economies and offset the huge imports from these same emerging economies. They stated that national trade balance "does not matter," as long as we get global growth overall. They diverted many funds into the formation of the International Monetary Fund (IMF) and the World Bank, that, together with their deregulation policies, forced what is termed the "financialization" of many economies and the global markets with disastrous results. (The impact of financialization will be explained later.)

History now shows that this free-trade journey has benefited mostly the Chinese and other emerging economies, their citizens, and the global financial elites. This trade relationship provided a short-term trap of cheap products that Western consumers happily absorbed, but it has resulted in a long-term sustained loss of national prosperity in terms of national wealth transfer, job loss, lower living standards, and the significant imbalance of trade payments for the Western economies. There is no end in sight if this trade model continues, due to the massive wealth gradient between the mature Western economies and the many emerging markets.

These disastrous policy changes and activities affected not only the West, but the emerging markets that joined this grand global free-market debacle. The outcome of this financial deregulation and "giving the market a free hand" was the financial crash of 2008 that destroyed significant middle-class wealth across the globe.

The main point is that, in this period, the whole leadership and the populations of most Western nations got conditioned by the economists to forget the need for strict national economic controls, and they moved to a liberalized and free-trade approach, including the free and uncontrolled flow of capital and reduced trade barriers and tariff controls between the participating countries. This has had an ongoing disastrous effect on the manufacturing sectors and the Western economies.

The Western nations continue to practice global economics like Boy Scouts, with unrestrained and open laissez-faire policies of trade and mobile capitalism, while the emerging economies use modern capitalism, but with a balanced backbone of state-managed economics. They have also wisely invested in developing their economies and sometimes utilized a predatory approach to setting exchange rates and tariffs to protect their industries. Many of these totalitarian governments, such as China's, had the advantage of not needing to carry the added burden of the inconsistent planning cycles of modern democracies. Putting it in blunt street language, we in the Western world kept taking a knife to a gun fight.

The result was a destabilizing of most Western economies that are now unable to deliver a prosperous economic outcome for its citizens, as they had enjoyed in the golden age. Many in the USA say it is the end of the American dream.

Some economists will still argue that free trade and globalization are working. They use data to show it's "not that bad," and we are "better than someplace else," but it could have been "a lot better" without this failed journey. They continue to talk about successfully managing globalization using multilateral agreements, even when confronted with countervailing evidence. They still believe that the perfect laissez-faire worldview will pay off, but they are trapped in an ideology like religious fanatics, and for them it's a matter of faith rather than fact-based science.

I have asked some economists to explain this insane entrenched position within their profession, and they responded that it is a range of things. Some believe that the economic science is locked up with mathematical models that show too much of the perfect rather than the real world. Others declare it is an ivory-tower view driven by an arrogant focus on growth and the financialization of the economies, rather than a real-life focus on value that is important for the prosperity of the citizens at the middle- and lower-class levels. To my mind, it's about the intellectual corruption of the economic profession, with free thought being blocked and suppressed unless it fits the rigid free-market doctrine. A recent front-page special report in the *Economist* in January of 2022 demonstrated that the free-market mindset is still prevalent with the economists of the day. At any cost, they will protect their perfect world models run on neo-liberal logic so they can satisfy their god of economic growth. They believe that any form of government control and oversight is too constraining to the concept of the free hand of the market, and they will insist on applying the failed theories of global free trade and comparative advantage, even if they jeopardize the prosperity and sustainability of most Western nations.

Not all economists are free-trade globalists. Ian Fletcher, the author of *Free Trade Doesn't Work*, is clear in his book that a trade imbalance *does* matter, and that a trade deficit acts as a wealth-transfer system. In talking with him, he explained how he is not against international trade provided it is managed with the correct controls to ensure that a true benefit and balance is maintained. He outlined that it's free or uncontrolled trade that is bad, not trade itself. He comments that free trade is a recent ideology that is only practiced selectively by nations such as China, Germany, Korea, and Japan, at great expense to those that implicitly follow its rules, such as the US, Canada, and the UK. He also declared that the free-trade ideology rests on unsupported assumptions. He maintains that much of the problems in the Western world are caused by the trade imbalance. I agree with Ian, and his books and videos are a must-follow for anyone who doubts the comments we are making in this book.

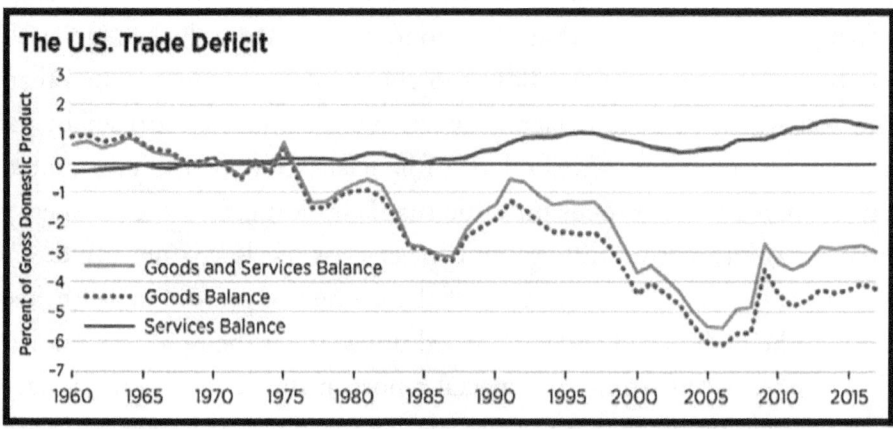

The best indicator to show how free trade went wrong is to review the historical trend of the US trade balance. The US economy had a positive trade balance through the 1960s, and within 0.5 percent through the early 1970s, even though it had significant trade partners, with Canada being one of them. But is now 4–5 percent GDP negative on average. This means that for every dollar in the economy, up to five cents is passed on in wealth transfer to other trading nations or shared with investments in term of government loans and bonds eventually held by foreign powers, who, due to this imbalance, hold the surplus to participate in owning our future wealth. So, the US, Canada, and many Western nations continue to over-import and struggle with an ongoing trade imbalance. This has resulted in huge un- and under-employment, difficulty in getting to a position of self-sufficiency and prosperity and increasing levels of inequity for newer generations. Western jobs and manufacturing infrastructure have been lost or eroded due to this global-wealth transferring machine. A hard lesson for the Western middle class is that citizens need passports, but your job and the capital to send it somewhere else does not. Western governments that were still expected to provide the same level of service and benefits to its under-employed citizens have been forced to defer the problem by borrowing or printing money, which will eventually make the situation even worse.

% Decline in Employment in Manufacturing

	1996	2000	2004	2008	2012
Canada	100	105	85	75	76
USA	100	110	95	83	85
UK	100	95	85	75	75
JAPAN	100	95	90	80	80
EU	100	98	96	95	95

As the above chart shows, most mature Western nation manufacturing sectors have seen double digit decline due to globalized manufacturing. Some of these economies that do not have a strong resource base to prop up their economy are suffering the most.

This global free-market journey has allowed the rich transnational corporations to continue skimming the top, while pushing the Western middle class into a race to the bottom while they have been forced to become over-dependent on a global market rather than their own national sustainability.

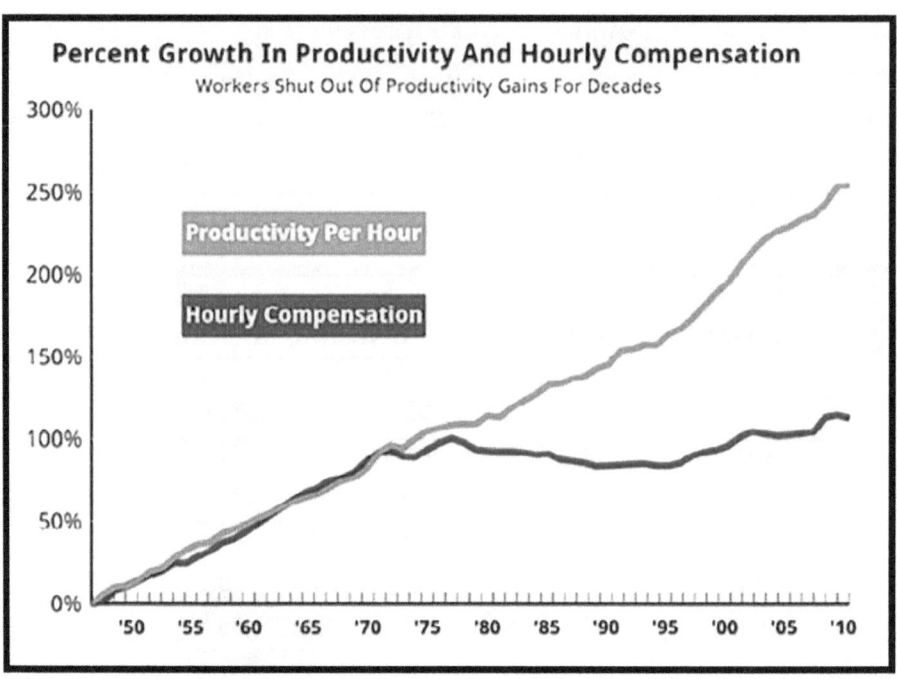

Percent Growth In Productivity And Hourly Compensation

Workers Shut Out Of Productivity Gains For Decades

Corporations, who can now operate on an international basis, continue to find ways to maximize and stash cash by offshore tax avoidance. They have held prices constant or even increased them, even though margins have improved due to the free ride offered by the lower costs due to productivity and the lowest global labor rates. But as this chart shows, they are not compelled to pass these benefits on to the labor force due to a significant decline in the delicate balance between capital and labor bargaining power enabled by globalization.

The emerging economies via these globalized corporations, and through the internet and improved supply-chain technology, have now almost unlimited access to consumers in the Western economies, and they continue to take advantage of their significant pool of low-cost offshore labor.

Further, the free flow of excess capital and cheap money has forced interest rates down, resulting in irresponsible lending and borrowing practices and the ability to hold significant amounts of inventory in these long global supply chains.

Due to globalization, we have experienced an unparalleled age of oversupply of labor and capital with little balance between them.

Unless things change, the Western economies will not enjoy the recapitalization cycle needed for self-sustainability. Most of the Western capitalization that was available has been misappropriated into rent-seeking purposes such as real estate, etc. Also, capital investment in Western manufacturing and infrastructure will be limited, as fresh capital will be attracted to offshore investments that offer sustained growth and payback.

Global free trade was driven by the unrealistic and misapplied economic concept of comparative advantage, with many economists and multilateral organizations such as the WTO conditioning us to believe that global free trade is the only solution, and that free trading is a God-given right for one nation to expect from another. This has now been proven to be absolute nonsense. Nations must always maintain independent trade sovereignty and controls. Each nation must have the right to choose with whom and how it trades and must have the right to control all trade activity. Their real goal is national self-sustainability, and their priority must be the welfare and prosperity of their own citizens.

THE DAMAGE OF FINANCIALIZATION

The outcome of this free-trade ideology and neoliberalism has been the uncontrolled adoption of globalized manufacturing. But another bad outcome of this ideology has been the growth in financialization, which on balance has been a major problem for overall prosperity and equality in Western economies.

Financialization is a term that refers to the increase in size and importance of a country's financial sector relative to its overall economy. This took effect after the fall of the Bretton Woods system, which was replaced with neoliberalism and the free-market principles of Milton Friedman in the 1980s, which contributed to financialization in the United States. As the US paid off its debts for excess imports to other countries by printing more money, there was a huge surge in global liquidity. This allowed banks to extend more credit to consumers and opened up additional opportunities for profits in the private lending market, which inflated the value of global financial assets from $56 trillion in 1990 to a staggering $219 trillion in 2010. Financialization has also led to significant job growth in the financial sector, which is expected to continue.

Deregulation and new financial technologies have had a major impact on the financial sector, and the laws regarding the methods and amount banks are able to borrow are relatively lax, creating further liquidity and a massive increase in financial instruments such as "securitization," which occurs when an originator packages various financial assets into one group, then sells this group of repackaged assets to investors. Such financial instruments have grown diverse and unstable.

Financialization has also enabled international trade by moving capital and cash around the globe and allowed large corporations to dominate economies. This has affected and inflated the cost of housing due to making it an investment asset rather than a utility and a human necessity. The food industry has also suffered from over-financialization, such as the failed push-investment for the introduction of plant-based meat products. Also, the educational system has become a business for profit due to financialization, which has forced up the cost of tuition rather than it being an affordable service to our citizens, and we will discuss this in a later chapter.

Financialization generates a focus on short-term profits that can disrupt a company's long-term goals and negatively affect product quality, and has led to "unproductive" capitalism, in which profits come not from production, but from financial transactions. Put another way, using the stock market and the financial institutions, they focus on the transfer of wealth rather than making it.

My view is that financialization has been an enabler of the wrong form of globalization due to the free and uncontrolled movement of capital, which has contributed to the demise of our manufacturing base, and one of the major sources of inequality and loss of prosperity for the bulk of the citizens in the West.

In the next chapter, we will focus on the impact of free trade and globalized manufacturing on the Canadian economy, and the slow death of Canadian manufacturing.

THE SLOW DEATH OF CANADIAN MANUFACTURING

Over the last thirty years, we have been witnessing the slow death of Canadian manufacturing due to global free trade that has enabled the rampant globalizing of manufacturing, resulting in a dismal outlook for prosperity.

These are historical trends for our Canadian manufacturing economy from Canadian Manufacturing and Exporters (CME). We have seen no improvements or significant change in trends since these reports were produced in 2019.

From 1980 until about 2000, we enjoyed a stable trade balance of resources, manufacturing, and services, with our manufacturing trade being in balance with our main trading partner, the USA. But since 2000, the manufacturing trade deficit has trended ten times worse to more than $100 billion.

Our current trade balance with the USA remains in balance or slightly positive, with most of the trade imbalance being with emerging nations. We have far less ability to balance our national trade using resources due to their recent decline. We show the latest trends for the overall Canadian trade balance later in this chapter, which shows no improvement.

We continue to see an almost 20 percent decline per decade in the domestic share of our own market for manufactured goods, and our share of the global manufacturing market has been reduced by at least half since 2000.

The real issue is that Canadian manufacturing sectors continue to decline and lose market share and trade balance.

It's clear when you look at the countries where trade is out of balance and adding to our deficit that it's mainly emerging economies taking advantage of the significant wage differential, or perhaps leveraging their national industrial policies that have a far better focus on supporting their manufacturing sectors than we have in Canada.

This is an ongoing disaster. We continue to lose ground, and although we hear some talk, we see zero government planning to halt this decline. Canada continues to lack the correct political will and focus to support its manufacturing sectors and develop a balanced and sustainable economy. We also lack strong federal government direction and commitment to recover an ailing and under-managed resource sector, illustrated by the lack of planning and direction in building pipelines to get the product to markets.

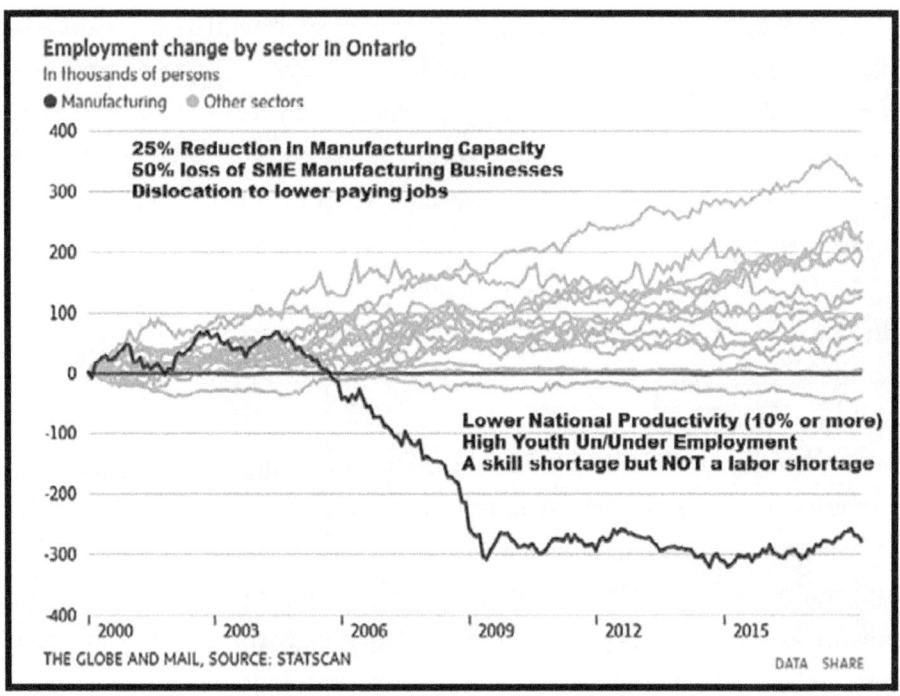

Employment change by sector In Ontario
In thousands of persons
● Manufacturing ● Other sectors

25% Reduction In Manufacturing Capacity
50% loss of SME Manufacturing Businesses
Dislocation to lower paying jobs

Lower National Productivity (10% or more)
High Youth Un/Under Employment
A skill shortage but NOT a labor shortage

THE GLOBE AND MAIL, SOURCE: STATSCAN   DATA SHARE

Between 2000 and 2008 (prior to the 2008 financial crash), we experienced a reduction of our manufacturing base as a percentage of GDP from 15 percent to 11 percent, with 10,000 plants forced to close in Canada. These operations constituted about 50 percent of our small and mid-sized enterprises, with most of them in Ontario, the Canadian manufacturing heartland. These were mainly small operations that could not easily join the offshore supply chain, and they were replaced by offshore capacity as their supply chain relocated offshore.

This resulted in a 25 percent reduction in the Canadian manufacturing workforce, about 500,000 citizens, 300,000 of which were from Ontario. Other than a small segment that relocated to the Alberta oil fields, many struggled to find full-time employment, with many remaining under-employed in precarious part-time employment. Those who remained in manufacturing have seen wage values decline, with many jobs at almost minimum wage. A high percentage are temporary, even though they demand significant knowledge, skill, and experience.

Many economists and politicians tried to blame this employment change on the 2008 financial crisis, but all this change happened before 2008.

This unplanned globalization of our manufacturing base is the prime reason for adverse employment change, unfair wealth transfer, increased inequality, and declining prosperity in Canada, and most other Western nations.

LOWER PRODUCTIVITY IS NO BIG SURPRISE

After this rapid decline in our manufacturing base from 2003 to 2008, our national productivity dropped by about 10 percent. In general terms, this is easy to explain: we had real manufacturing demand rapidly extracted from our manufacturing capacity because of globalization, so due to this demand reduction, we were carrying more overhead and attracting more cost per output. As these plants and their equipment went idle over more shifts, an overcapacity was created, so it is no surprise we have a huge productivity problem. This was not an efficiency issue—most plants in Ontario have been as competitive in hours applied to standard work as others in NAFTA—but we had a utilization shortfall, where whole production shifts were idle, with equipment capital and facilities unable to be utilized due to reduced demand. Also, we had under-utilized indirect labor in supervision engineering and office staff.

This was exacerbated by the smaller scale of our Canadian plants compared to those in the US, so our ability to consolidate was less than in the larger American plants. So, the main cause of the productivity loss has been a lack of demand effecting utilization, not processing efficiency. As we continued to struggle to utilize the existing capital, it became difficult to apply new capital to move up the technology and productivity curve by using efficient processes and technologies that used the latest equipment tooling and systems. So, as we lose manufacturing, we will suffer with declining productivity. All in all, this isn't a healthy outlook.

Also, service and resource sectors are inherently less efficient than the manufacturing sectors, so the decline of the manufacturing sectors has reduced average national productivity even further. This has created a vicious cycle of even worse competitive performance, further attracting the move toward offshoring manufacturing.

DID WE LOSE THE JOBS DUE TO OFFSHORING OR AUTOMATION?

Some economists will argue that the prime driver of job loss was automation and new technologies, but in the last two to three decades the significant and growing contributor has been offshoring in many industries. The economic numbers show that over the same timeframe we have seen a significant decline in investment in Canada for automation and innovation, with most of the investment and recapitalization for new technology and automation going offshore, so very little capital was spent on local manufacturing. So, offshoring of manufacturing was the prime contributor to the rapid decline of our manufacturing base, not automation. When we look at these trends, it's clear that the downturn in manufacturing happened in early 2000s, exactly when globalized manufacturing started to displace our domestic capacity.

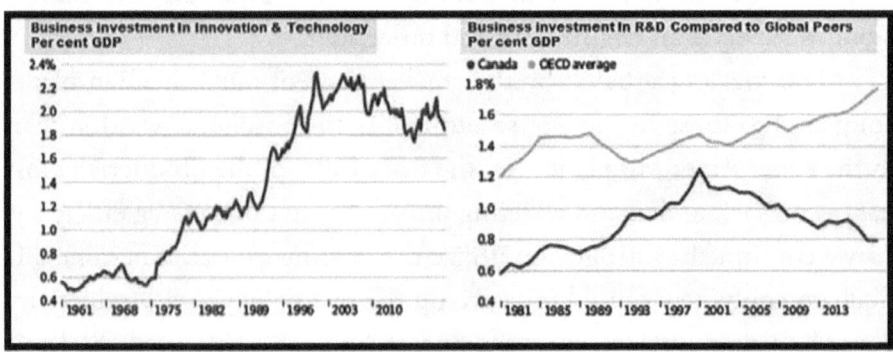

This is supported by Jim Stanford, an economist representing the Centre for Future Work.

He has published a report…Canadian Workers Need More Technology, Not Less—Centre for Future Work https://centreforfuturework.ca/2022/04/25/where-are-the-robots/

The report declares that the typical Canadian worker uses 11 percent less machinery and equipment to do their job today than they did in 2014. This supports the argument that we did nor lose most of the jobs due to automation, but more to globalization.

Many of us consider offshoring to be far more destructive to an economy than automation. With an offshoring transaction, we end up with no jobs at all, added import debt, increasing wasteful logistics and inventory costs, and negative cashflow. With an automation transaction, we retain some jobs even if we must retrain, we retain the utilization of our manufacturing multiplier effect on resources and services, and the opportunity to retain economic autonomy within a national economy. Automation can improve productivity and can also ensure our economy becomes less susceptible to labor arbitrage from offshore. Also, automation can free us from the trap of needing to retain or import cheap labor via immigration to continue to perform manual tasks and may also be a mechanism to require increased skills that should allow wages to rise.

The public is quite correctly becoming far more sensitized to offshoring than automation, as they perceive automation as an inevitable journey of technology and the elimination of menial tasks. But they see offshoring as a bad option that eradicates jobs and government revenue. This is illustrated by a recent objection to a system installed at a chain of restaurants in Ontario. These restaurants adopted a system operated by a third-party company that connects customers to a live video-calling service at the payment point that connects to an offshore person who takes their orders and processes payment. The public's response to this approach has been highly negative, with many believing we need jobs that pay taxes in Canada and help boost our economic activity. Down the street we have many 100 percent automated teller systems at food marts and gas stations without any complaint.

As we will explain later in this book, more investment in automation will be necessary if we are to become entitled to take back manufacturing.

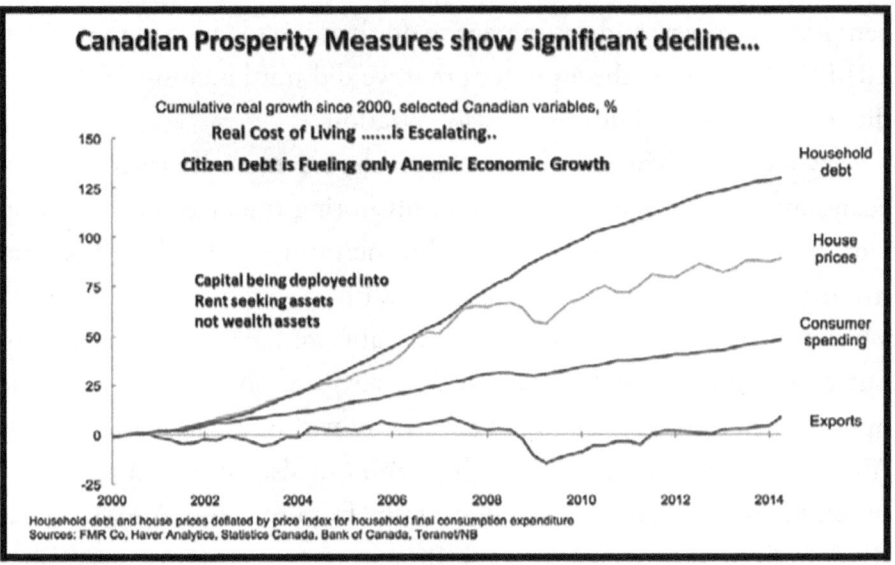

Due to this economic shift away from manufacturing, the real cost-of-living index is escalating, and, as we have shown, our economic prosperity index is trending worse for most of the population. Our bankers show growing concern about citizen debt having to fuel consumer spending and only achieving anemic economic growth. Any hard-earned capital is being deployed into wasteful rent-seeking assets, such as inflated housing prices, rather than manufacturing and infrastructure that would far better assist the economy.

We are also seeing foreign capital and stock-market speculation contributing significantly to this rent-seeking and forcing demand and prices up without any real value to our economy. Federal and local governments are slow to react to this debacle.

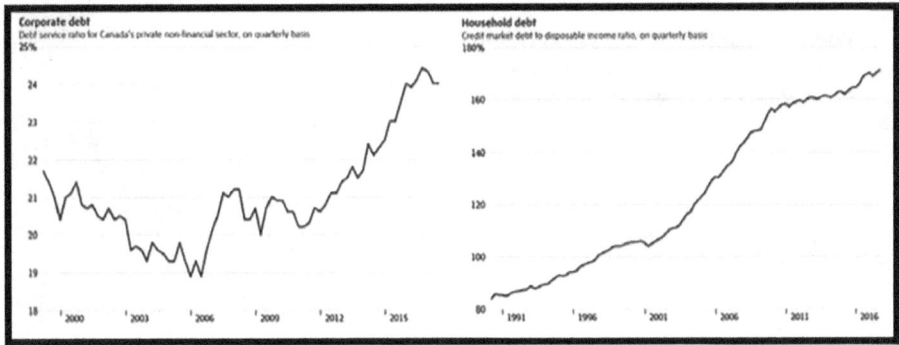

The problem is that globalization is not working for our govern-ments, for a high percentage of our corporations, small and medium enterprises, a large part of our citizen population, or for our younger citizens. Debt is increasing on all fronts. For Canada and most Western nation-states, it's a going-out-of-business plan.

The wealth of the North American middle class has been eroded, with flatline wage growth and a continuous increase in living costs. Social unrest and anger with national government policies is spreading, provid-ing a strong signal that the populations of Western nations are reaching a threshold of dissatisfaction.

Due to this bad journey, Ontario continues to struggle with gov-ernment debt due to the growing imbalance between public and service jobs. It's no wonder the province has so much debt, with tax-paying employment lagging the expenditure on services.

Public vs. private sector job creation in Ontario
Percentage change since January, 2000
● Public sector employees ● Private sector employees

THE GLOBE AND MAIL, SOURCE: STATSCAN

This is not a pretty sight, and a common issue across many provinces and states in North America. Many in government have tried to rationalize it as "not as bad as other places in the Western world, so get used to it." Well, I fervently hope we don't get used to it.

THERE GOES THE TRADE BALANCE

We explained how the US, our largest trading partner, has a negative balance of trade, and has dug a deep fiscal hole for itself with liberalized free-trade policies. We are fast shedding our manufacturing base, which continues to lose traditionally well-paying jobs and continues to offer jobs at close to minimum wage or sub-par wage growth against inflation. We are becoming ever more dependent on resources, which, based on the recent projections, may see decline and reduction in some types of resource demand in the world market. This places us in a precarious position.

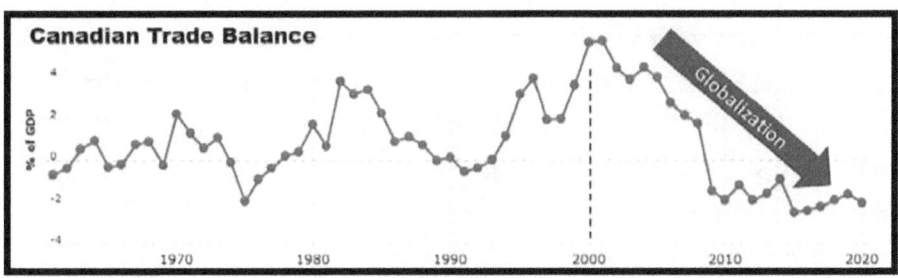

Historically, Canada's resource sectors have assisted with maintaining an overall positive trade balance, even with our declining manufacturing sectors. Without our resource sector staying healthy, we may see a negative trade balance of as much as 4 percent, which would make it as bad as the US. Currently, the resource sectors are a shadow of their former selves and seeing a net decline in investment and employment opportunities, especially in the oil production in Alberta. Although the service sectors have shown some growth, we may soon have an uncontrollable negative trade balance with the rest of the world.

EMPLOYMENT TRENDS

All this past disruption, dislocation, and lack of renewal and maintenance of the core manufacturing population has created an ongoing skill shortage, as any sudden increase in demand for skills cannot be met by the depleted labor pool. It is not by any stretch a labor shortage, as many citizens are under-employed or have given up looking for work, but it is a skill shortage, even further exacerbated by employers who have neither the budget nor the timeframe or stability to offer retraining programs. The skill-training system is a shadow of its former self. The outcome is a weird inversion of "some jobs but no skills, and some skills but no jobs."

Our overall workforce, including manufacturing, has experienced a race to the bottom, with ongoing employment pay-equity issues in many sectors, some of which are operating well below the suggested living-wage levels with insufficient career opportunities, a disadvantage to our younger generations. The recent COVID-19 situation has amplified the fact that our food service and related sectors are underpaid, with a significant segment of that workforce being paid below government-legislated minimum-wage and experiencing temporary work levels that make it difficult to maintain a living wage.

The engineering and technical employment statistics also reinforce the concern about the decline in manufacturing employment opportunities. Past statistics from the PEO (Professional Engineers of Ontario) show a severe under-employment of the technical skills we are preparing in our schools and universities. It indicates that engineers end up holding less meaningful positions within their profession, with many engineers working outside their field of study at about twice the rate of other professions.

The reduction in the above opportunities results in any sudden demand forcing businesses to look for only fully trained and work-ready experts, as they do not have the stability to invest in developing such technical skills, which reduces the ability to bring new entrants into the profession in any significant numbers. This also means the baby boomer generation has been retained longer, blocking new entrants, which will eventually deplete the base of experience further.

It is true that currently, post-COVID, we have a perceived overall labor shortage, but it is expected that once that pent-up demand dissipates, we won't have a real labor shortage by any stretch.

Participation Rate (% Average for 3 Decades)

	Average 1990 to 1999	Average 2000 to 2010	Average 2011 to 2018	Change 1990 to 2018
Total, all education levels	92	92	90	2% worse
0 to 8 years 5	76	70	71	5% worse
Some high school 6	88	83	75	13% worse
High school graduate 7	93	91	87	6% worse
Some postsecondary 8	91	89	85	6% worse
Postsecondary certificate or diploma 9	95	94	93	2% worse
University degree 10	96	94	94	2% worse
Bachelor's degree	95	94	94	1% worse
Above bachelor's degree	96	94	94	2% worse

Unemployment rate, participation rate and employment rate by educational attainment, annual (statcan.gc.ca)

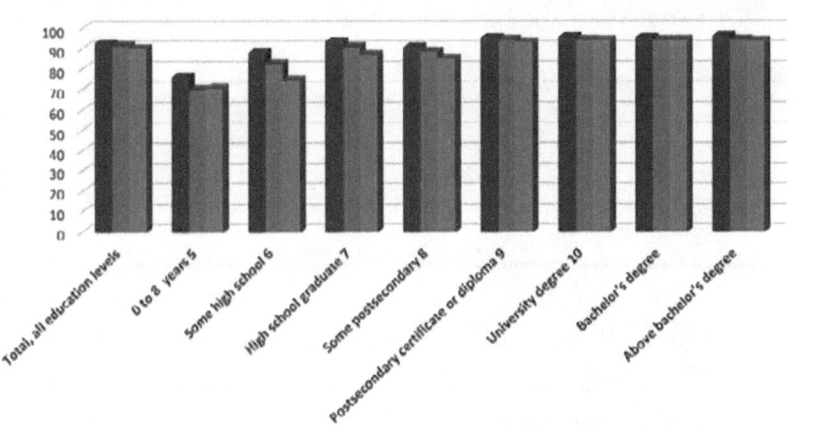

The best way to understand the employment situation is to look at labor participation rates.

The participation rate chart is based on the population of Ontario aged between 25 to 55 and reviews the data across three decades.

The participation rate varies depending on the age and education range but shows a significant gap in full participation at the lower levels of education.

It also shows a wide spread of 2–13 percent decline across the education range, due to the reduction in manufacturing jobs through globalization since the early 1990s. We assume these lower education ranges will experience jobs that are temporary and transient. This paints a dismal picture of under-employment, under-training, and lost employment opportunities.

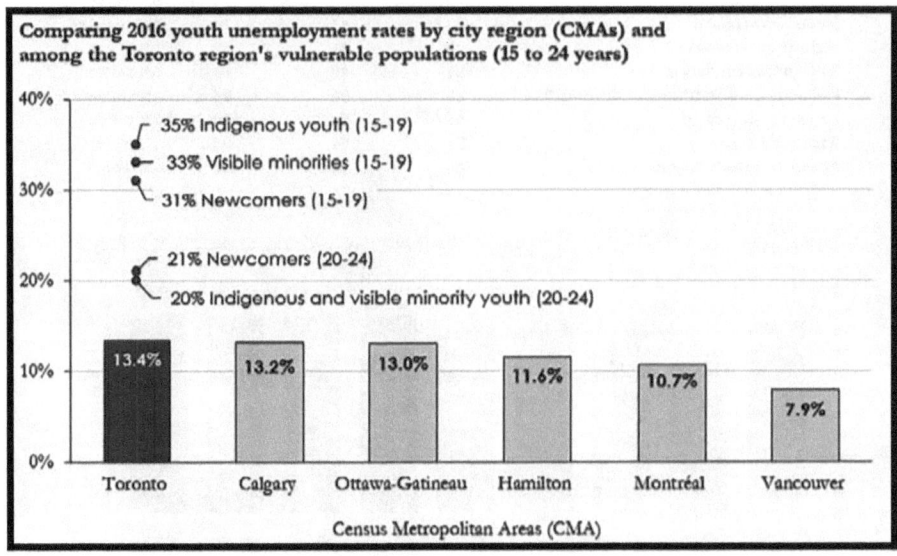

Further, since 2010 we still have about one million young Canadians under-employed or unemployed, or not able to correctly follow an effective career path. Our youth unemployment rate is in double digits in the Greater Toronto Area, which is our area of densest population and traditionally the center of our industrial base. (See Report: 2018 Issue Briefing: Youth Employment—City of Toronto)

The young immigrant population aged between 20 to 24 has an unemployment rate of 21 percent, and the younger immigrant's population below 20 is unemployed at a staggering rate of 31 percent. These numbers should certainly force a strong discussion about immigration and the success of multiculturalism. The number for Indigenous youth shows how much more needs to be done within our own communities before we assume we can afford to support any form of refugee activity.

Due to these low youth workforce participation rates, many that can make such a choice are staying longer in post-secondary education and falling further into debt. Many end up being over-educated and under-trained, and light on the early-life industrial or business experience they need to take their place in the workforce to replace the industrial knowledge and experience as the older working population plans to retire. In other words, it's a huge, unplanned mess.

This situation even exists with post-secondary-educated youth from our best universities, who are unable to follow meaningful careers as they have followed educational journeys that are badly mismatched with the education, skills, and experience needed to become employable with the current jobs available. This is mainly due to poor career planning, with too many arts and social-science graduates who have taken "hobby courses" and not enough science, technology, engineering, and mathematics (STEM) courses to be able to effectively engage in the job market. One appropriate joke often used is.... *STEM students qualify and get employed and are asked to solve complex business and engineering problems, art and social studies students graduate and ask... would you like fries with that?*

This employability problem will always be far worse for those outside of the university or post-school educational system who have fewer skills and training and will have even greater problems with gaining stable employment status. Due to a lack of clear industrial policies, the youth have difficulty engaging in the correct career goals that are aligned with the economic direction. We need better policies to direct these career goals so that the investment in educational programs is better aligned with future employment needs.

Further, we have a significant shortfall in the level of knowledge and skills in the current industrial workforce. The European baby boomers who immigrated to Canada already well-trained, qualified, and ready to fill the industrial gap forty years ago are now retiring. The industry-based workforce remaining have experienced a significant decline in available retraining programs. They are significantly under-educated and under-trained on the latest advanced manufacturing technologies and business operating concepts and tools.

If we will have any hope of recovering our manufacturing sectors, we will need to rethink our educational system so it becomes aligned with future employment needs. It must also improve the balance between education, training, and industrial experience, especially for those wishing for a meaningful career in industry or within business in general.

Apathy for the future of manufacturing has had an effect

The reduction in manufacturing and lack of vision for the future has created apathy for both employers and employees. This means business becomes reluctant to invest in manufacturing, and leads to a population reluctant to start or study for a career in manufacturing.

Manufacturing's decline forces the flatlining of services

The reason the dream that service jobs will replace manufacturing jobs did not come true is that some service jobs depend on manufacturing jobs. Many economists believe that every manufacturing job generates and supports up to three service-sector jobs. So, it is foolish to have an unbalanced economy that tries to survive on services only. Also, less manufacturing and industry will mean less demand for infrastructure projects that demand engineering and technical skills and create employment across a range of engineering disciplines. Therefore, a pure service-sector society is going to be difficult to sustain.

Our economy needs manufacturing

So far, we have painted a bleak picture of the decline in our manufacturing activities. Almost everybody we have talked to and shared the facts with agrees that Canada needs a balanced economy for our future prosperity.

Although we as a country are blessed with natural resources, it's clear that just selling them straight off the land will not make us rich, and such a practice is fraught with commercial risk and instability, as oil-price fluctuations over the last twenty years will illuminate.

Also, building a society around service and resources is risky and won't work at all if we have significant levels of imports, with only resources to trade with. It's now clear that we need strong manufacturing as well as resources and services blended together in a balanced economy, so we minimize our reliance on imports and are able to reduce the need for exporting resources to pay for them.

So, the conclusion that seems irrefutable is that our economy needs manufacturing and a balanced economy for its success.

When primed with facts, the population always agrees with this conclusion but has a low level of confidence and a high level of apathy that the situation will change. A strong feeling of helplessness exists in Western societies, and I agree that it's a challenge.

How are the Canadian manufacturing-based provinces doing?

Ontario, the historical heartland of Canadian manufacturing, experienced a massive impact on its prosperity due to globalized manufacturing, with a negative impact on the overall job market. It's now clear to many citizens that they will never see any benefit from this ill-conceived global trade experiment, the consequences being lower prosperity and sustainability of their economic well-being for them and the next generation.

The truth is that Ontario is now a "have not" province with a difficult future, as we are facing the greatest decline in our provincial well-being in memory due to the decline in our industrial base. The manufacturing base has declined 15 percent, with the contribution to GDP eroded by 13 percent since 2000. Ontario has been the main participant in the overall national numbers of manufacturing decline. In the same period, it has sustained a large and unbalanced provincial trade gap of about 15 percent. Ontario now has far more imports than can be supported with its exports. These are all indicators of poor economics and reflective of the challenges Canada faces to pay its way.

The Ontario provincial government struggles to make ends meet and afford the infrastructure and services to sustain our communities. The main issue is not expense control, as, in fairness, Ontario is one of the better provinces at cost control and the operating efficiency of government services. The issue is income revenue due to the decline of the industrial base. This is shared with many Canadian provinces and states in the US who have seen revenue decline as they lost huge sectors of manufacturing to globalized manufacturing.

WHERE THE HECK IS OUR GOVERNMENT?

We are extremely lucky to live in Canada, a country with a broad base of great provinces to choose to live in, and it sure beats out many other countries in comparison. But many of us wish for a government that can wake up from its complacency and focus on what is important.

We have become complacent with the status quo, spoiled with new technology and drugged with low prices from offshore, and we have found ways to adjust to the lesser job market and reduced government services by adjusting our own and our kids' expectations. Some have been further anesthetized with low interest rates to be able to not feel the pain of the massive debt and wealth transfer that is happening in our society.

Our government at all levels appears asleep at the switch or preoccupied with other issues. They have plenty of time and our tax dollars to waste on media-attracting social topics such as race and multicultural differences, distinct societies, Indigenous rights, abortion, religious rights, political correctness, sexual inequality, and sexual orientation, and are far more concerned with "who we are" than "how we are doing."

One downside of democratic governing is that they are forced to consume effort on social topics that are only important to some minority groups. These can be serious cultural and social distractions from the prime goal of government, which is to provide the correct environment for a prosperous economy and citizenship. Such social topics can have no real value or meaning unless we have the prosperity at a certain level to afford them. For this reason, I question whether government of all kinds and levels are focused enough on doing the correct things to manage the industrial policy of North America to maximize the benefit for its own citizens.

In the next chapter we will explain why many businesses are now, at last, questioning the use of global supply chains.

LEAN COMPARISON OF GLOBAL VERSUS LOCAL SUPPLY CHAINS

In 2011, the very early days of our TBM advocacy, we struggled with how to provide a reasonable and logical argument against the complicit acceptance and herd behavior for globalized manufacturing by just about everyone in positions of power and authority. We eventually decided to compare global (long supply chains) versus local (short supply chains) using the concepts of LEAN thinking and sustainability. We could then explain with facts the extensive waste in all forms in the globalized manufacturing environment versus a local manufacturing environment. We were able to build a case that such a direction defied common business sense, taking us way off course for a balanced economy and a sustainable future for all of us on the planet, and in fact the planet itself.

In this chapter we are going to share our LEAN comparison and show you that these long global supply chains have forced our business and our economies to install and operate business systems that share considerable global waste rather than real wealth.

First, let's understand what globalized manufacturing is. It's a bunch of container ships moving material from a resource-rich area to another area to grab the lowest labor cost, and then reshipping the semi-completed or completed goods using long-distance supply chains to deliver to customers somewhere else.

The prime focus of globalized manufacturing is to leverage "labor arbitrage," which is the practice of searching for and then using the lowest-cost workforce to produce products or goods. However, there are many other costs that may outweigh any advantage of low global labor rates.

Container and cargo ships are the world's biggest polluters

Global trade in products and materials has increased 8 times since 1980, and this is creating significant global pollution. newatlas.com produced a report in April 2009, "*Big polluters: One massive container ship equals 50 million cars*". (See link in appendix)

Container ships burn expensive and dirty bunker fuel that we spend extra effort to extract as a resource. We burn it to move non-value-adding inventory to another place, where labor value eventually gets added. There is no manufacturing performed on these ships; they are just a mechanism to move the inventory of material to and from one center of low-cost labor to someone who can afford to buy the product. These container ships account for 90 percent of the global world trade by volume and have a large carbon footprint. It has been calculated that the low-grade bunker fuel used by the 90,000 container and transport ships that traverse our oceans create a pollution footprint six times that of all the automobiles in the world. A single ship emits pollutants equivalent to 50 million cars during its annual usage. They are rated at emitting 2,000 times as much sulfur as all the diesel automobiles in the world. These ships could be cleaned up with better engine technology, but this would significantly increase the costs of transportation. Oil prices are projected to continue to rise, and this will make burning such oil increasingly prohibitive economically.

Jeff Rubin, who authored the book *Why Your World Is about to Get a Whole Lot Smaller: Oil and the End of Globalization*, predicts in the long term that "We will not run out of oil or stop using it... but... we will certainly run out of oil we can afford or want to burn!" Many people are concerned about the notion of a climate emergency brought on by humanity's use of carbon-based resources, while others are less concerned, but it's safe to say that all of us should be focused on reducing pollution, and container ships are a strong contributor to global pollution and are far from what anyone would reasonably call "green." These expensive and dirty container ships full of wasteful inventory are going to "Low-Cost -Countries" (LCCs) to grab that low-cost labor, but the problem is that over time these LCCs will not actually be low cost. China, for example, was the classic LCC with direct labor rates at about 1/20 of North American labor costs, but with escalating wages the rate has moved up to about 1/5 that of a typical comparative skill in North America. China has seen almost double-digit wage escalation per year in some past boom times. In the same timeframe, material prices in China have become on a par or even higher than those in North America due to rampant demand and the increased cost of Chinese labor, and by many resources and raw materials needing to be imported into China from other parts of the globe.

These three escalating operating costs—transportation, labor, and materials—have raised fundamental questions about whether globalized manufacturing is the best solution for a future manufacturing trading model.

To put these questions in perspective, we have used LEAN thinking principals to compare globalized versus localized manufacturing that is closer to the consumers. LEAN thinking is a powerful business imperative that is all about eliminating as much waste as possible from any business process.

After almost four decades since it was introduced as a business improvement imperative, LEAN thinking is still a hot topic for most management teams, as it assists with business innovation and evolution and can improve product development with the goal of keeping business processes and their products as competitive as possible.

LEAN theory states that every process is composed of either parts or steps that add value to the product or customer, compared to parts or steps that are non-value-adding and waste. "Waste" describes activities and states in a process, such as wait times and delays, inventory in all forms, unnecessary processing steps, and scrap and rework. One measure of LEAN is the ratio of "value" to "non-value-adding" elements in a process. The other measure of LEAN is business process cycle time, where the shorter the cycle time, the more LEAN the business process. "Business cycle time" is defined as "the elapsed time from when a customer expresses a demand for a product or service to when it is delivered, and the business gets paid." For more on LEAN concepts, read Cycle Time Management by Northey and Southway, published by Productivity Press.

Unfortunately, LEAN has historically been perceived by most business leaders as only applicable to the factory floor and some white-collar support areas, rather than the holistic business process. It has not been effectively applied to review supply chains and the degree of waste and cycle time trapped within them. Clearly this was not a consideration when we started the globalized manufacturing journey, but it's a powerful consideration for us to review as it relates to our future supply chains.

So, using LEAN concepts, let's compare global supply chains with localized supply chains.

THE GLOBAL SUPPLY CHAIN

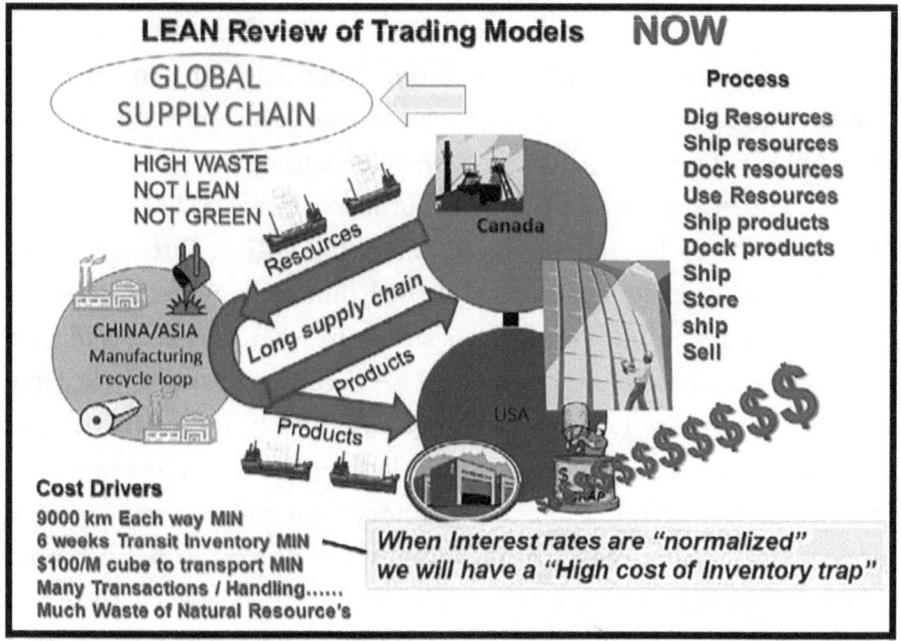

For illustration, we will use a product-trading cycle that starts with resources dug out of the ground or harvested in Canada and sent by sea to China by container ship. This typically involves many transportation transactions before the resource gets to the Chinese manufacturing site that converts these resources into product, and it then undertakes the return journey to Canada and the US as products. Sometimes, due to the long supply distance, this includes holding safety stock and requiring sorting and grading and reworking for quality issues. It's then distributed with further inventory stocking points to support the end consumer.

If we look at the process, we will see that many steps have no added value, such as shipping by sea, docking at both ends, and the extra quality and inventory holdings needed to manage the long supply-chain delays. If the business is build-to-order or seasonal in nature, then significant inventory and customer-delivery risk exists with such a long supply chain. It's clearly high in wasteful steps that don't add value, as are the potential quality-control issues that many offshore processes experience, with less tactile feedback possible due to distance and the extra effort needed to manage different time zones, language barriers, and maybe cultural challenges.

One of the reasons businesses were able to contemplate an offshore or globalized approach to manufacturing using long supply chains was the adoption of efficient supply management tools. This has happened in the last thirty years with the introduction of technology, such as internet-capable supply management systems to control worldwide inventory through complex logistics hubs and seaports, using automated material handling and distribution systems. These were enabled by the introduction of containerization that uses a system of intermodal containers (also called sea shipping containers). These containers are organized into effective consignments that are carried on large and fast container ships and offloaded onto compatible rail and road transport systems.

Unfortunately, none of the above technologies add value to the core manufacturing process, but they do enable long supply-chain networks, even if it is far more wasteful than local supply chains. At the time of writing this book, the cost of container services has almost quadrupled due to oil prices and pent-up demand due to the COVID crisis as well as adding weeks to the delivery cycle. It remains to be seen if these logistics costs will return to pre-COVID levels.

This global supply chain approach, which relies on cheap offshore labor to trade off with other costs, is inherently not LEAN, and, for the reasons mentioned above concerning the container ships, not at all green and now looking non-cost-competitive.

Also, emerging economy suppliers typically operate manufacturing processes that are far less productive and create much more waste of materials and energy when compared to the mature Western operations. Their advantage is typically derived from their lower cost of labor and not their process productivity.

THE LOCALIZED SUPPLY CHAIN

An alternative approach that offers a far more LEAN solution is to return to localized supply chains. The wasteful non-value-adding process steps get eliminated, and we end up with a leaner and shorter supply chain.

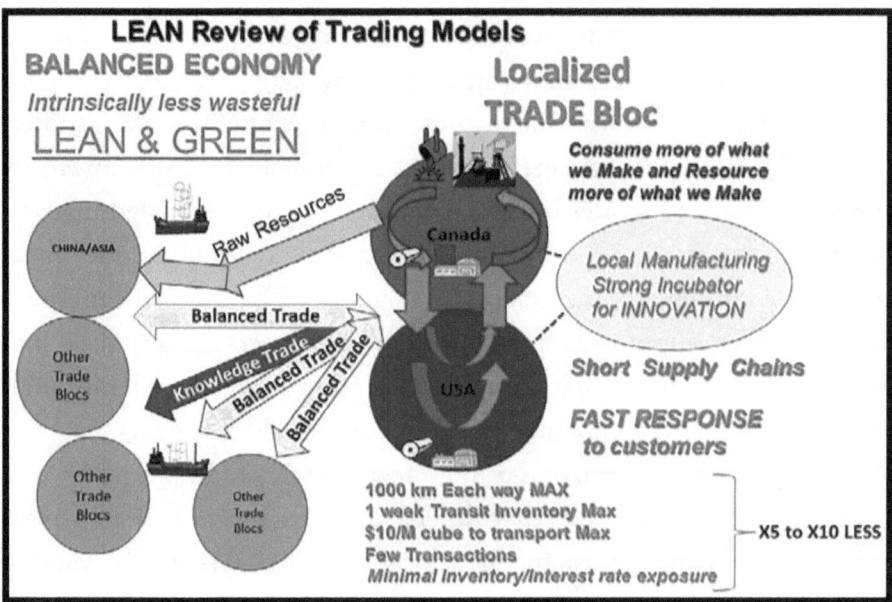

If we use the same product trading cycle as above, the materials and the supply chain stay within a localized trade bloc. The process steps are reduced, as are the cost drivers which reduce by an order of magnitude. One significant benefit of this approach is far shorter delivery lead-times, and that on its own may be strategic reason enough to keep the supply chain short. This leads to a much smaller inventory footprint and less exposure to cost of inventory and interest rates. Also, there is less risk of inventory waste and seasonal demand problems, as supply chain lead time is far shorter and offers less forecasting and inventory risk. Also, the reliability of a shorter supply chain will be far higher than a long supply chain that may have to cross borders and be subject to different time zones and weather conditions, etc. Also, any early delivery expediting in a long supply chain will attract far more cost when compared to a short supply chain.

Manufacturing and its related supply chains and support infrastructure will be far more localized, shorter, and closer to the consumer, and can better provide a faster response to the customer for products.

THE INTRODUCTION OF BALANCED SOURCING MODELS USING LEAN PRINCIPALS

To better define the economic trade-off between long and short supply chains, many of us started to develop a ***Balanced Sourcing Model (BSM).*** This includes LEAN thinking parameters and all the other costs involved in operating and "owning" supply chains.

It was clear that a shorter and locally integrated supply chain should always provide a more LEAN and intrinsically less wasteful supply chain, but that the cost drivers will determine the lowest overall total cost.

To provide a fair comparison the total supply chain costs per product must be run through such a BSM with predictions for future cost trends. This can then compare offshore LCC labor cost advantage against the higher mature economy labor costs, and be balanced with material, logistics and support costs within the supply chains.

An example of a basic BSM for a product offshored to Asia from Canada is shown.

EXAMPLE. Balanced Source Model	Onshore 2005	Offshore 2005	Offshore 2022	Onshore 2025
Inventory time (weeks)	2	5	8	2
% Carry cost of Inventory	24	24	24	24
$1000 cost of goods	1000	1000	1000	1000
Container Cubic M useable volume	65	65	65	65
Container cost $	2000	4000	13000	2000
2 cu Meter space for shipment	2	2	2	2
labour hrs	10	10	10	6
Labor rate	20	2	5	25
Tariffs	0	0.07	0.07	0
Labor cost	200	20	50	150
Shipping cost	62	123	400	62
Inventory cost (24%PA)	9.6	24	38.4	9.6
Tariffs	0	70	70	0
Total	271	237	558	221
%	100%	87%	206%	82%
			Reshore	Reshore

For a product with a $1000 factory cost value

Shipping space per unit is 2 Cu M

2005 offshore plan saved 13% cost

2022 Increase in global supply chain costs now well past tipping point and offshore is a loss of 100%

2025 reshore plan will be lowest cost solution with an 18% saving against constant 2005 dollars and a 5% improvement from best 2005 offshore solution

Note

Sea shipment costs will not return to 2005 levels

INDUSTRY 4.0 will continue to reduce labor differential

The product had an onshore factory cost of $1000 and a unit shipping volume of 2 cubic meters and a labor content of 10 hours when offshored in 2005. Offshoring provided a 13% cost improvement in 2005. Recently, escalating wages offshore and massive increases in the cost of transportation and shipping time in the long sea supply chain has reversed all the advantage. The current plan is to immediately stop further offshore production and manufacture the next generation of product onshore. In 2025 with the incorporation of onshore automation to remove labor content we should see a further cost improvement that will be 5% below the original offshoring plan. In this balanced sourcing model we are comparing labor, transportation, cost of inventory and tariff differentials.

It became clear that the low-cost labor advantage gap in many LCCs has been rapidly diminishing in some economies such as China, which has experienced double digit wage escalation.

We could also include the opportunity costs associated with how the closer coupling between demand and supply can better act as a natural incubator for customer-focused product and process innovation.

Also, we could include the social impact of emerging economies undertaking manufacturing with potential safety and environmental issues, and the opportunity for child- and slave-labor exploitation. Many corporations have been criticized for being participants in this aspect of globalization, and although the real responsibility for such issues must reside with the governments of these emerging economies, it's yet another reason for mature economies to separate their economic interests from other nations.

Also, we can use the BSM to explain to our governments how a localized supply chain can retain far more value adding contribution to the local economy and generate revenue that can be far better collected and channeled back into the local economy. This localization of the trade process also offers the opportunity for a far more balanced and stable economy, as it's far less dependent on the struggle to manage a global trade balance with large ratios of imports and exports. Also, it can be used to justify import tariffs to maximize the economic contribution to the local economy.

OUR BUSINESS LEADERS MUST RUN THE NUMBERS

Based on the work done on developing these balanced sourcing models, it was clear that the economic advantage gap between offshore and onshore supply chains was very small, so we recommended business leaders develop balanced sourcing models and continuously run the numbers to ensure that their choice of supply chain remained optimized, especially with the trends we started to see developing. They appeared to show a firm swing toward the advantage of local supply chains for many commodities. This was due to the cost of labor in LCCs significantly rising, as well as the surfacing and better visibility of many hidden costs in running a long supply chain, as well as the risk of increasing transportation costs that have recently been confirmed. We also declared that if interest rates went back to 2008 levels or higher, it would be a no-brainer that long supply chains will be far too expensive for many products.

At the time of writing this book, many industries have rerun their balanced sourcing models, and are now beginning to understand that these long global supply chains they have allowed into their businesses are, in many cases, not working for them and are translating into significant and tangible added costs to their businesses.

Also, many geo- and eco-political factors are forcing new reports by government advisors to declare long supply chains, and the over-reliance on such foreign trade, to be a threat to national sovereignty, security, and economic stability.

The advisory reports now being published explain how brittle and unreliable long supply chains are now a risk!—This has been my viewpoint for a decade—shame it took so long for the "experts" to wake up, and a huge shame they did not listen to the position Trump was undertaking in his term as president.

Further, as inflation rises, due to pent-up demand from the COVID virus, plus the growth agenda many governments are following as they try to pay for the virus debt, we will see interest rates forced to rise. This will make the cost of the significant inventory levels trapped in the long supply chains far more expensive. This will further suggest a firm opportunity to move toward shorter supply chains.

This will also make the printing of money by governments and long-range government borrowing a huge instability factor. Reducing imports by moving away from long supply chains will assist such a situation by reducing the need for the working capital to support the high levels of inventory trapped in these long supply chains, as well as assisting with any trade deficits, which so far have continued to rise. Also, reducing imports and generating productive tax-bearing local output will assist with the government debt, and better support the local economy.

This new "geo-eco-political" awareness and major updates to some business-cost parameters is significantly affecting the direction of our manufacturing journey, and in certain cases they both resonate and amplify a move back toward a localized and "closer to the customer" form of manufacturing. It's called the "reshoring tipping point," and we will explain this in the next chapter.

THE RESHORING TIPPING POINT

At the beginning of the North American globalized manufacturing journey, no real economic or financial arguments appeared to counteract the herd behavior that moved relentlessly in the offshoring direction, with sector after sector of manufacturing relocating their capacity and capital offshore to mainly China.

The United States and Canada had been losing factory jobs through the early 2000s, with many observers writing off manufacturing as a part of America's economic future. The mass exodus of manufacturing following China's 2001 entry into the WTO deepened this pessimism.

But by about 2015, the tide started to turn. Some businesses started to move product back from offshore to benefit from shorter supply chains. This is termed "reshoring."

As we explained in the previous chapter, many of us advocates for manufacturing, including Harry Moser of the Reshoring Initiative Group in the US, had been reviewing the economics of supply-chain decisions and revisiting the total cost of ownership assumptions for offshoring by using the balanced sourcing models. As I had spent some years operating manufacturing projects in China and Mexico, I had contacts who were able to collect real data, and over time we built a significant database of cost comparisons between offshore and onshore, which included the detailed breakdown of logistics and any hidden support costs. We were able to share this data with many industry experts on both sides of the border, with the joint aim of bringing clarity and realism to the global sourcing journey. I produced a reshoring report for the Canadian market for Export Development Canada (EDC) that is used in part in this book. (EDC provides Canadian businesses with risk-management services associated with foreign markets.)

In August 2011, the Boston Consulting Group's first report in the series (*Made in America, Again: Why Manufacturing Will Return to the U.S.*) explained how rising wages and other economic forces would steadily erode China's overwhelming cost advantage as an export platform for North America. BCG predicted a tipping point by around 2015, when supply chain and logistical costs and other hidden cost factors (now much better understood than when we started the offshore process) would tip the balance in the favor of onshore costs. BCG suggested that, for certain industry groups (that accounted for $200 billion in goods), rising costs in China would make it economically viable for these goods to be reshored to the U.S.

This "reshoring" initiative has forced a fresh thought process to better discuss and manage a balanced sourcing strategy that takes a much more informed look at the total cost of ownership for all manufacturing and supply chain activities, including the optimization of internal and external manufacturing processes and the supply of components, materials, services, and capital to support the business. This added awareness and major updates to some business cost parameters, such as LEAN and sustainability, started to significantly affect the direction of the globalized manufacturing journey, and they continue to resonate and amplify a reshoring direction as a firm option in certain cases. It has generated a counterargument to offshoring, where the advantage of localized manufacturing that is closer to the customer makes much more sense for many business sectors.

In general, it's clear that offshoring using long supply chains will continue to get increasingly more expensive. This includes increased inventory and transportation costs, as well as greater-than-anticipated hidden costs in supporting a remote and emerging supply chain in the low-cost labor jurisdictions. Also, double-digit wage escalation in China, which will certainly become a common trend in other emerging economies due to growth and better prosperity expectations, will continue to color the source decisions.

This has fostered a new belief that local manufacturing can offer more cost-effectiveness and stability, as well as provide the ability to innovate at home more effectively. Being closer to the customer also offers reduced inventory exposure and flexible delivery capability.

Based on all the above, a study done by Boston Consulting Group in 2016 found that 40 percent of global corporations were taking action on the reshoring option for the next generation of products so they can be closer to consumers, and a further 40 percent of them continue to seriously evaluate such a journey in terms of the next capitalization cycle.

Corporations responded in different ways. Most listened and re-ran the numbers using these balanced sourcing models and included staying home or reshoring in their future supply chain options. Those businesses that had bitter experiences offshore with significant cost due to delivery and quality issues quickly justified reshoring their capacity to be close to the customer without any significant cost penalty. However, businesses that have significantly invested in capital offshore are going to have to wait for a new capital investment cycle before they can consider a reshoring option. Many corporations with a manufacturing presence still intact in North America are now consolidating or expanding their local capability to remain within the USMCA region, as they have come to realize that, at the very least, local manufacturing—with far shorter and more sustainable supply chains in a stable and mature economic trading bloc that is much closer to the customer—is now considered a firm option.

Many large manufacturing organizations are already redeploying capital toward regionalized forms of manufacturing and agile supply chains by selecting suppliers or redeploying capital and reshoring to local supply locations. For these reasons, reshoring is now happening in many manufacturing sectors, with some declaring that the great globalized manufacturing journey that was driven by out-of-control corporate herd behavior is now ending.

The journey to reshoring must be data-driven, and a balanced sourcing model must be used that is dynamic, up to date on the current situation, and supportive of the outlook for the relative economic factors of exchange rates, wage rates, labor productivity, total cost of poor quality, energy,-related transportation costs, border tariffs, insurance, brokerage costs, and offshore support services, as well as interest rates that will have a bearing on inventory costs, etc. Other factors, such as IP protection and the of ease of doing business, will affect the balanced sourcing model and the source and supply-chain decision process. It will be important to use current information, as the situation will be continuously changing. Of course, the balanced sourcing model will not always favor a local supply chain, as products with significantly high labor content and/or the utilization of resources remote from the consumers may still support a long and more global supply chain. This may mean utilizing suitable LCCs and just relocating to the next LCC as the more mature LCCs develops and its manufacturing costs escalates.

Most businesses must look at the next generation of products and review where they should be sourced against their balanced sourcing model. The types of new products that will be most likely to benefit from short supply chains and should be reshored are those that:

- do not need significant capital reinvestment to reshore.
- attract significantly large bulk-shipping costs as a percentage of value.
- have low- to mid-labor content, so LCC labor advantage will be less.
- Can employ high-tech solutions for product design or manufacturing automation to reduce labor content to eliminate any advantage of low-cost labor.

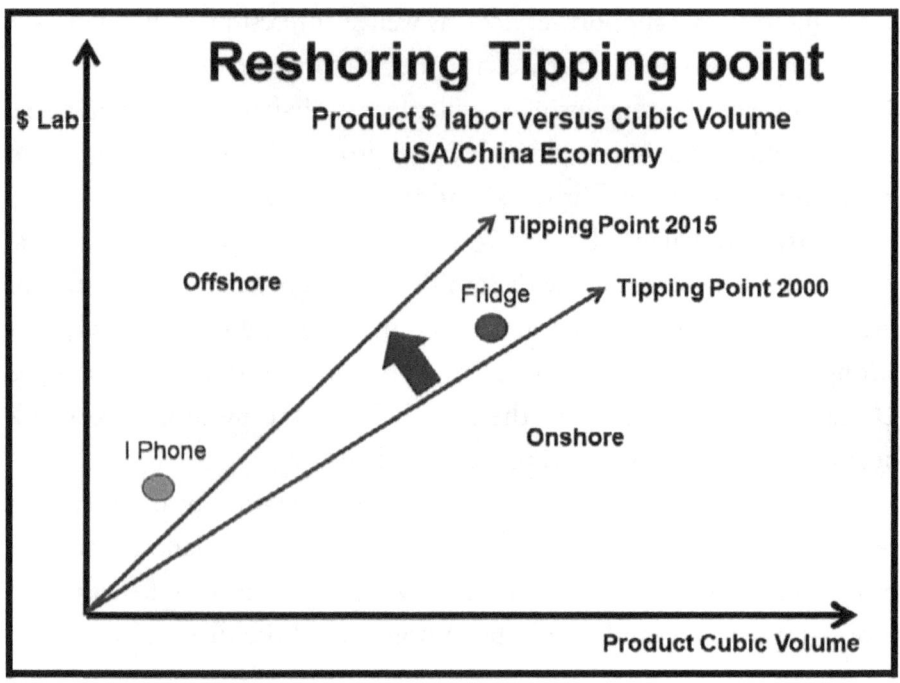

The reshoring tipping-point simulation chart explains how the tipping point has changed over the start and the height of globalized manufacturing (2000 to 2015), due to escalation in both offshore labor and transportation costs from an LCC, and how different products are affected. This demonstrates how the balanced sourcing model depends on the physical parameters of products. Key factors such as product cube shipping volume versus the unit cost of labor are typically the main drivers of where the product will be on the tipping point. Examples shown are large household products such as refrigerators. Although they have a degree of technology and smart electronics, they are physically large in relation to the current labor-cost differential between onshore and offshore, and so the significant shipping costs to support sea transit creates a strong incentive to manufacture them close to the consumer. Contrast this with an iPhone, which takes up far less volume for an equivalent labor cost differential, so it has a less attractive reshore tipping point to move closer to the consumer and can better sustain the global supply chain costs. Other suitable candidates for reshoring are heavy plant and large industrial equipment. These manufacturers will be looking to reshore next-generation products destined for the home market, although many have cloned a manufacturing footprint in other emerging markets, and in some cases offer different products to support those offshore markets.

The logic of reshoring may be strongly modified by the impact of capital investments. For example, the consumer-level electronics industry—which should be an obvious reshoring candidate, with its low level of labor content—is fully invested in high capital levels of facility and manufacturing processes offshore, and to redeploy or repeat that "sunk capital investment" to support reshoring for a substantial part of the supply-chain activity is prohibitive in the short range, although some reshoring of lower-capital-intensive final integration and test of complex and technologically advanced products may take place in that industry. This "sunk capital trap" will be relevant in many highly capitalized industries, and it will mean a reluctance to reorganize the supply chain, as reinvestment will be needed to duplicate capital, but it's still important to run the numbers and keep making the correct decisions, and this stresses the need for correct capital deployment within future supply chains.

The local manufacturing site that has local raw material, or a strong and well-clustered supply base, may also be a reshoring candidate. If that is coupled with a close-to-customer requirement, then many other factors need not be as important. This has been the situation with some local food industry manufacturers. But we still see a significant part of the food industry that is globalized, and it may take significant effort to reshore.

The other reason we are now experiencing a growth in reshoring is that whole business sectors have been sensitized to the reshoring trend and have taken an effort to better understand the hidden costs of supporting long supply chains in offshore manufacturing locations and their negative impact on profitability—kind of herd behavior in reverse.

Some businesses have realized that with only a small amount of improvement in their local business processes, including applying LEAN principals, can close the small offshore-to-onshore cost gap and start to leverage underutilized local capacity. This is because many businesses had stopped focusing on local improvements in the rush to follow the herd to go offshore, but now they find that, with only small improvements in their local capability, they can reach the tipping point and get a clear advantage by reshoring.

Supply-chain logic should dictate that easy access to energy, resources, and raw materials should determine the location of the supply chain and manufacturing process. On this basis, past globalized manufacturing decisions were made very badly, as one of the main resources needed to support most manufacturing industries is fresh water, and lots of it, and it's ironic that the North American industrial rust belt states and provinces that have suffered the most from being hollowed out by the move to offshore are Michigan, New York, Wisconsin, Illinois, Indiana, Ohio, and Ontario. These economic jurisdictions border the Great Lakes, the largest fresh-water supply. Their manufacturing industries were hollowed out and sent to China, which is starved for fresh water.... Go figure.

Yep, many early offshore sourcing decisions flagrantly avoided LEAN principals and were made purely on low-cost labor logic that has forced wasteful transportation and waste into our business models. Canada sends significant raw timber to China, who processes the wood and sends back semi-finished products and finished furniture products. This is a candidate for a strong reshoring effort.

Some products that must be manufactured or integrated closer to the customers, or are highly customized, or fully integrated with customer service at the customers' location, can only be processed using short supply chains. This may mean that some standardized sub-assemblies or sub-systems can be manufactured with longer supply chains, but the final integration must be close to the customer.

The environmental impact of globalized manufacturing must also affect reshoring decisions. The high pollution levels in China and India, and recent deaths due to poor safety in South Asian factories, also point to future global policies that must factor in higher financial and socio-political consequences. This may be to the advantage of mature economies that have developed better controls over pollution and safety due to social balance than an early emerging economy, who may treat pollution and safety rules as secondary to output and short-term economics. These safety-litigation costs are now raising concerns and getting added to corporate cost models when operating such long supply chains in some emerging economic sectors. The increase in corporate responsibility for sustainable supply chains is placing emphasis on better management and optimization, avoiding the impact of long and poorly controlled supply chains.

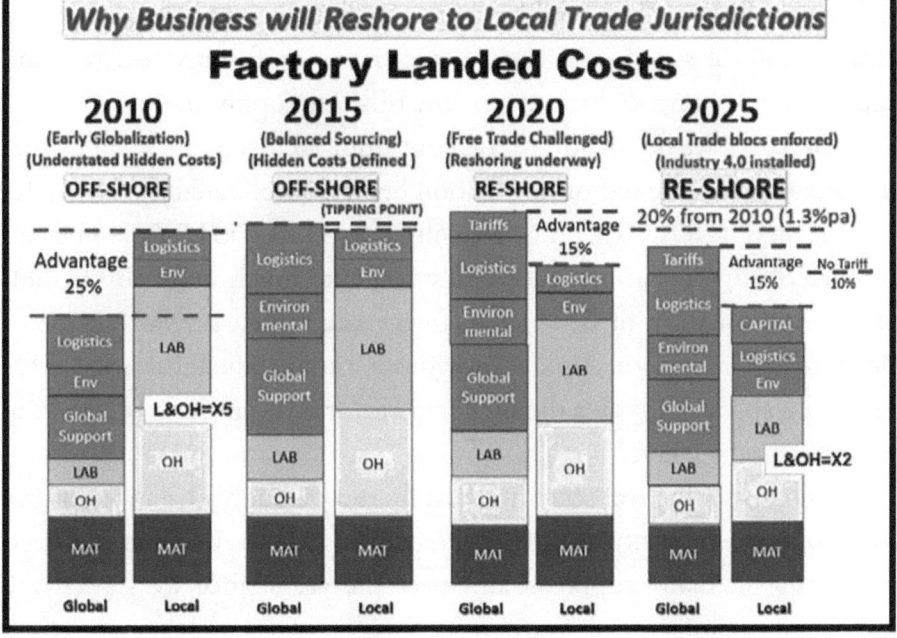

Above is a time chart of how a typical supply chain may evolve from offshoring to reshoring.

In 2010, globalization was getting into full swing, and we were still learning the degree of hidden costs embedded in the supply-chain process. Offshoring was yielding a landed cost advantage of up to 25 percent, and the view was that the labor differential would always carry the decision.

Then, in 2015, much analysis was done across manufacturing sectors, and we started building balanced sourcing models and better understood the hidden costs. We found that, with all costs included, the gap closed to a tipping point, with Boston Consulting Group reporting that reshoring would be an option.

In 2020, tariff adjustments have pushed us toward reshoring. Also, many onshore operations have improved productivity and have earned the right to reshore the next generation of products, with better automation technology, tooling, and business-system solutions. Also, it became clear that local supply chains would attract significantly less working capital than that needed to support the offshore supply chains.

By 2025, we predict this trend continuing across many manufacturing sectors, with the reshoring position being consolidated by the implementation of INDUSTRY 4.0. We will explain INDUSTRY 4.0 in detail in a later chapter, but it will certainly facilitate much more automation and the elimination of labor in all forms and reduce any advantage of offshore low-cost labor. Also, even without a trade bloc tariff, the LEAN reshoring approach avoids the high logistics and inventory cost of a long offshore supply chain.

Of course, the real scenario must be run through a balanced sourcing model, as each situation is different. But this shows what has been happening in many supply chains over the years since we started the globalized manufacturing journey.

It is a real shame we had to learn the hard way by taking this wasted offshoring journey, although the prosperity and capacity built offshore at our Western citizens' expense has made those offshore nations very happy.

These balanced sourcing factors and trends will shape the future decisions each business will make with regards to where to locate manufacturing and the shape of the supply chain, and such factors will need to be prioritized, depending on how they attract cost in the specific business situation.

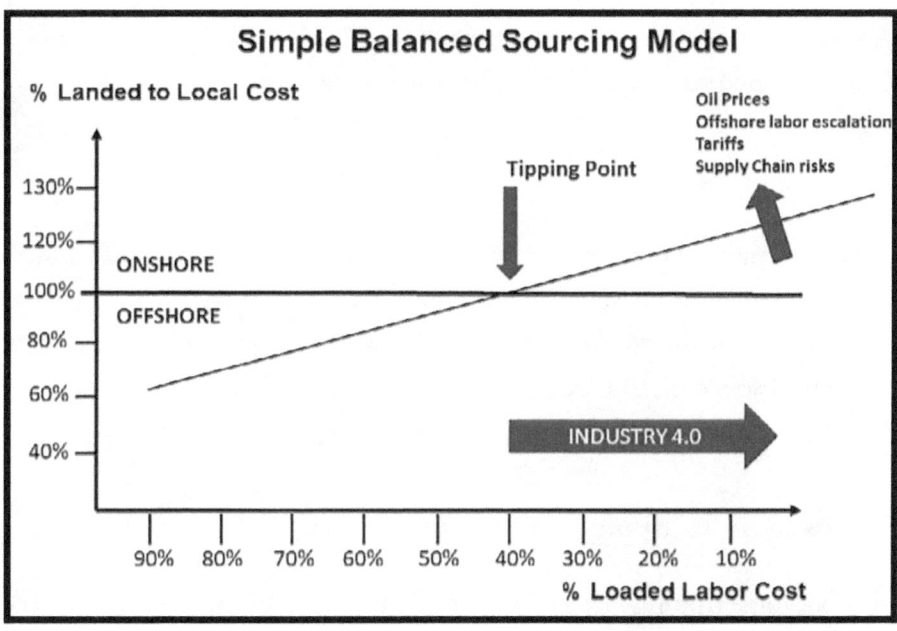

Another way to illustrate the significant factor that loaded labor cost makes on a balanced sourcing model is the simple version of a balanced sourcing model shown in the diagram. The vertical axis defines the tipping point, where above the horizontal line the tipping point of offshore landed cost is exceeding local cost. The slant line defines at what percent of labor cost content in the product will allow the reshoring tipping point. The slant line assumes a certain set of economic conditions. If the local business can reduce its labour content with INDUSTRY 4.0, then it will enjoy a reshoring position. So, the goal is to employ INDUSTRY 4.0 to reduce labor content and eliminate the sensitivity to low-cost off-shore labor. Any increases in supply chain cost, such as oil prices, offshore labor-rate escalation, and added tariffs, will push the slant line up and allow a higher percent of product labor content to be at the tipping point. The intangible risk of long supply chains when calculated into the cost equation will add to this tipping point moving up to support a higher percent of local labour content. Clearly this is a simple illustration, and as already said, a far more detailed balanced sourcing model must be used to run the numbers, but it's clear that the more INDUSTRY 4.0 is deployed, the less a long supply chain will make sense.

GETTING SOME HELP

There are many experts that have balanced sourcing tools and can assist, and the best place to start is to connect and review the work done by Harry Moser at the *Reshoring Initiative* who are early experts and have a balanced sourcing tool called TCO (Total Cost of Ownership).
Total Cost of Ownership Estimator | Reshoring Initiative (reshorenow.org)

THE PROFOUND IMPACT OF INTEREST RATES ON RESHORING

Another huge tipping factor that must be included in the balanced sourcing model is interest rates.

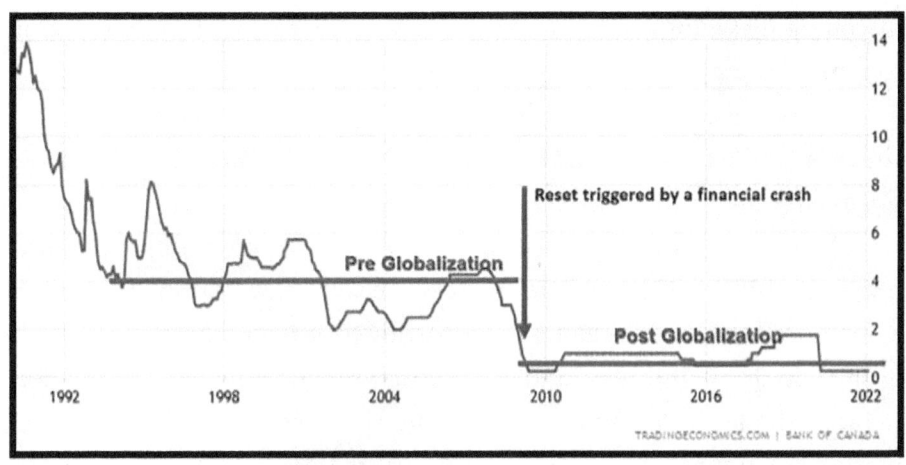

In the BSM charts already shown we assumed current ultra-low interest rates that have existed since 2008. If the interest rates were to return to normal pre-2008 levels it would add at least a 5 percent advantage toward reshoring. This is because as our corporations set up global suppliers it was clear that these offshore suppliers were astute. Most of them refused to ship out product until they were paid in full. Some even requested a significant pre-payment before they would start the production cycle. So, the burden for the many weeks of production and supply chain inventory has been placed on the working capital of Western corporations. This means that the current ultra-low interest rates are enabling our businesses and corporations to afford to operate significant levels of inventory within long global supply chains. Higher interest rates will make this long supply chain working-capital inventory far more expensive and suggest a reshoring option.

Since 2008 we have experienced almost zero interest rates that are both a cause and a symptom of the issues our western economies face via globalization and the financialization that accompanied it. The low interest rates are creating "malinvestment" which is badly allocated business investments due to artificially low cost of credit. This is also a symptom of an unsustainable increase in the money supply. This is discouraging savings and structured investments that we should be using to rebuild our ailing economy.

Economists continue to be "puzzled" about this sustained low-rate situation and have suggested a range of reasons. *The Puzzle of Low Interest Rates—The New York Times (nytimes.com)*

Some suggest that its due to a monetary trap of too much investment capability with nowhere for it to be deployed within the mature economies that no longer have industries to attract investments. This decline in local industry and infrastructure due to globalization has reduced the local demand for new capital investment. This has further pushed down interest rates and has also created painful speculation in the real-estate markets.

Others maintain that as income inequality has risen over the past few decades, resources have shifted from poorer households to richer ones that have higher propensities to save, so more money flows into capital markets.

More likely is the notion that the advent of globalization has exposed us to the Chinese economy, which has grown rapidly in recent years, and as China has a high saving rate a vast pool of savings flows into capital markets forcing interest rates to fall.

There are believed to be some so-called advantages of low interest rates, with a past belief that low rates should assist first time home buyers, but good luck with that, as it has inflated the house prices to send them completely out of reach of anyone but the speculators. Also, low interest rates allow government to borrow more. But with government debt now at the highest point as a percentage of gross domestic product, it has just ensured we may stay trapped in the low interest rates for ever.

Whatever the reason, our governments and financial institutions must better manage the economy and figure out how to fix the dangerously low interest rates back to pre-2008 levels. This would solve many problems if we could redeploy such "loose capital" including the working capital trapped in these long supply chains into the rebuilding of our manufacturing base. It will need a strong political will, a stiff talk with the central bankers, and of course, an appropriate trade policy to encourage the industrialist's and investors to join the recovery process.

Currently the biggest economic issue in most western countries is the onset of inflation. This happened due to governments releasing massive stimulus into the economies due to economic decline due to Covid that has triggered more longer-term economic instabilities. This should be no surprise as we have had almost 15 years of ultra low interest rates to keep the unstable, unbalanced, over financialized, and clapped-out economies of the west propped up. This means that increasing interest rates to manage inflation will probably force the western economies into a deep recession, as they have become over-dependent on cheap capital and credit.

It's yet another good reason to migrate out of a heavily globalized trade environment as quickly as practical and move back to a more local-ized trade bloc environment, so we can gain back productivity to become entitled to a more equitable level of capital and credit return. Further, the "puzzled" economists need to rebuild their economic control models, and quickly.

ULTRA-LOW TARIFF RATES?

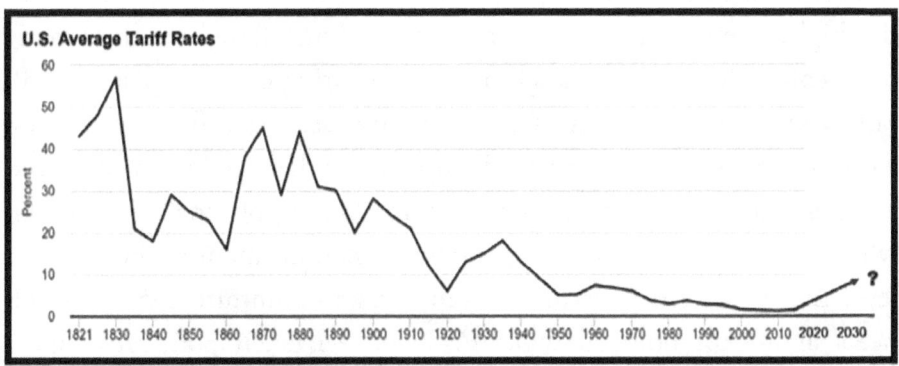

It also remains to be seen if import tariffs will remain ridiculously low. We anticipate that one direction future governments could take would be to maintain high import tariff rates against nations outside of the USMCA trade bloc. This would add to the reshoring advantage and allow some industries to recover. It would also eventually reduce the need for imports, and better drive prosperity in the economies within USMCA, as Trump had intended.

A good suggestion would be to maintain the high tariffs Trump has setup on China, and do the same for imports from other countries outside of the USMCA. Any revenue generated by tariffs earned from such trade outside the USMCA should be used to fund and redevelop the local industries and the economy. As we reshore our manufacturing capability we will see if the need for import tariffs can diminish.

RESHORING MAY NOT HAPPEN NATURALLY FOR EVERYTHING

Unfortunately, in many manufacturing sectors reshoring is going to be a challenge, as the structural damage to the local North American manufacturing supply chains is significant and will struggle to find investment to rapidly recover, as a whole cycle of capitalization has already been deployed offshore. Although some of the product-finishing plants may still be able to undertake reshoring, the smaller, lower-tier suppliers were eradicated from the supply chain, with whole plants closed when the higher tiers sourced their capacity offshore. Based on this, many of us concluded that, although natural reshoring can take place, it will only work for supply chains that have not seen significant structural damage. For those significantly disrupted and damaged we would need a much higher level of capital undertaking and supply chain rebuilding, which will demand a business-sector-wide commitment at the national level that will need government support and commitment. This will need significant political will. We have seen such political support developing in some sectors of industry in the Unites States, but much more is needed.

We will explain the reshoring situation in Canada in the next chapter.

RESHORING IN CANADA?

Many experts are certain that a significant amount of manufacturing capacity is in reshore mode back to the USMCA regions. This will be full products, or at least final assemblies, being placed into shorter supply chains onshore to support the USMCA consumer base and offset the issues of expensive and long supply chains. This is a total shift from the prior offshoring herd behavior that would have seen them shipping in products from outside USMCA.

Unfortunately, as we have mentioned in earlier chapters, the Canadian economic environment does not stack up at all well as a manufacturing reshoring destination compared to its USMCA competitors, with an expert prediction that limited reshoring into Canada will occur compared to the USA and Mexico.

The current Canadian federal government, after a struggle, eventually closed a new USMCA trade agreement. But the future trade relationship with the USA is far from correctly aligned, and this is necessary if we are to benefit from the reshoring efforts happening in our closest and largest trading bloc partner, who has an economy ten times our size.

The reasons for "why not Canada?" are many, and the expert prediction is that the decline in the Canadian manufacturing sectors will continue unless the issues mentioned here are addressed.

INEFFECTIVE INDUSTRIAL POLICY

For many decades, we have had Canadian governments who were in total compliance with the worldview of globalized manufacturing, and that local manufacturing was not key to the success of the Canadian economy. But if we are to gain back prosperity, we will need a government with the correct political will to develop and execute a winning industrial policy. This must be effectively communicated and aligned with our business and financial sectors and major trade partners, so that it supports the recovery of our industries and addresses national competitive factors such as productivity, exchange rate, taxation, and tariffs, etc.

So far, we don't see the current government facing up to this challenge.

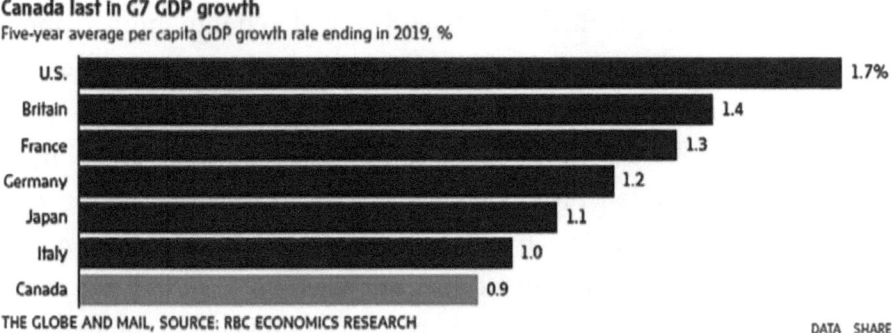

Canada last in G7 GDP growth
Five-year average per capita GDP growth rate ending in 2019, %

U.S.	1.7%
Britain	1.4
France	1.3
Germany	1.2
Japan	1.1
Italy	1.0
Canada	0.9

THE GLOBE AND MAIL, SOURCE: RBC ECONOMICS RESEARCH   DATA SHARE

Although the government keeps touting strong economic growth, it finishes last against its G7 peers.

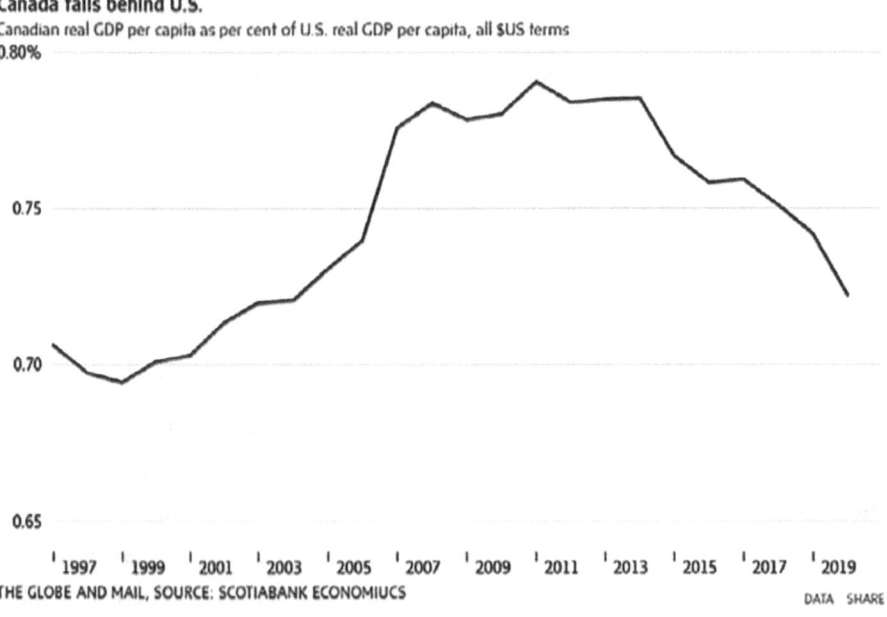

Canada falls behind U.S.
Canadian real GDP per capita as per cent of U.S. real GDP per capita, all $US terms

THE GLOBE AND MAIL, SOURCE: SCOTIABANK ECONOMIUCS   DATA SHARE

Canada's GDP per capita, which is a measure of economic productivity, has been slowing for years, and it's now falling farther behind the United States.

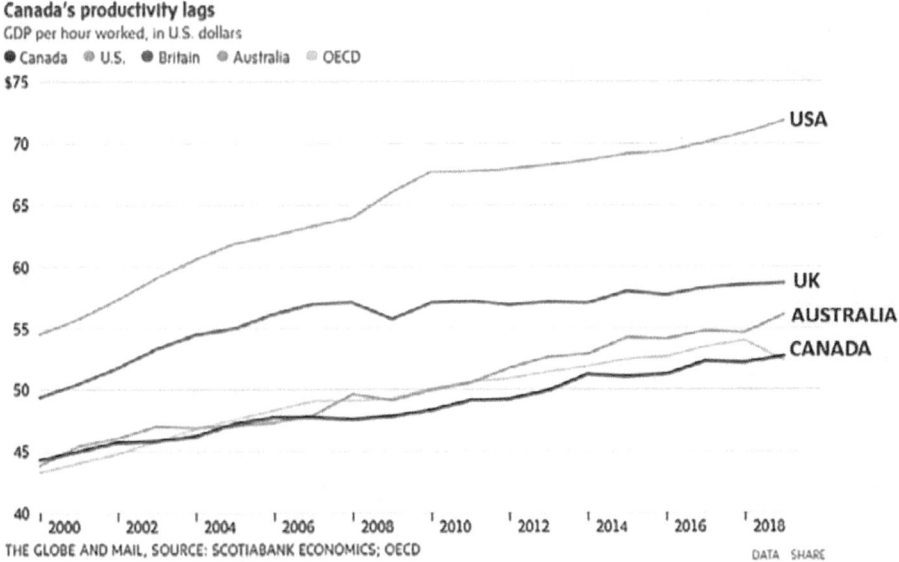

Canada's productivity lags
GDP per hour worked, in U.S. dollars
● Canada ● U.S. ● Britain ● Australia ○ OECD

$75

70 — USA

65

60 — UK

55 — AUSTRALIA

— CANADA

50

45

40
2000 2002 2004 2006 2008 2010 2012 2014 2016 2018
THE GLOBE AND MAIL, SOURCE: SCOTIABANK ECONOMICS; OECD   DATA SHARE

Canada's overall labour productivity measured by hourly output trails the US, the United Kingdom, and Australia, as well as the Organization for Economic Cooperation and Development (OECD) average, and the gap with the US is widening. This is partly because Canadian businesses haven't been investing in machinery, equipment, and commercial buildings at the same rate as their peer nations since the Liberals took power in 2015. This has resulted in a wider gap in productive investment rate between Canadian and US companies. The federal government appears fixated on improving inequality by redistributing wealth, rather than creating it. In fact, the current federal government is not even in sync with the Bank of Canada (BOC) as far as fiscal control of the economy is concerned, with many experts declaring a dichotomy between the latest government high-spend budget and rising debt while the BOC is trying to rein in inflation. This is not a good situation, with all three of the power brokers—the business world, the central bank, and the government—all on different pages. These economic facts and the way the situation is being managed indicates that we will see little increase in living standards in Canada without increased productivity, and that won't happen without focused investment planning, solid prioritized fiscal control, and a strong and supportive Industrial plan to reverse the decline of our industries.

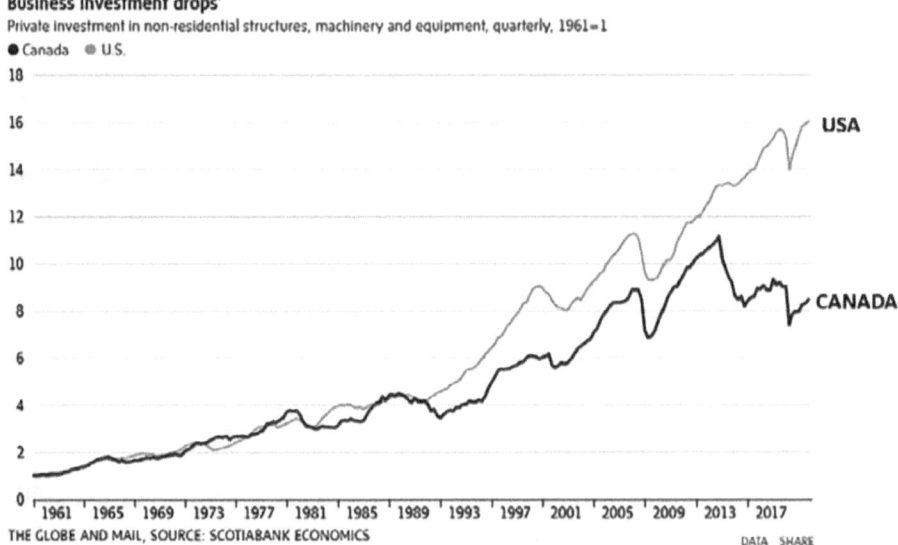

Business Investment drops
Private investment in non-residential structures, machinery and equipment, quarterly, 1961=1
● Canada   ● U.S.

THE GLOBE AND MAIL, SOURCE: SCOTIABANK ECONOMICS   DATA SHARE

THE EXCHANGE-RATE

Canada has the reputation of having an unpredictable resource-driven exchange rate. It was the result of an inflated and badly managed petro-dollar due to significant growth in resource extraction in the early 2000s through to about 2013. This significantly disadvantaged the manufacturing sectors that were, at that time, under extreme pressure to be offshored by globalization. Although some business sectors found ways to adjust, most remained at a global disadvantage using a total loaded manufacturing-cost model. The increasing dollar strength was definitely not achieved by productivity, which would have been an acceptable reason for a stronger dollar. To the contrary, we saw a significant weakening of our overall productivity due to the under-utilization of our diversified and smaller-scale production assets in most sectors due to manufacturing globalization.

The federal government has done little to assure business leaders that the Canadian dollar will never again get over-inflated by resource growth. This is a significant ongoing concern for most manufacturing entities in Canada.

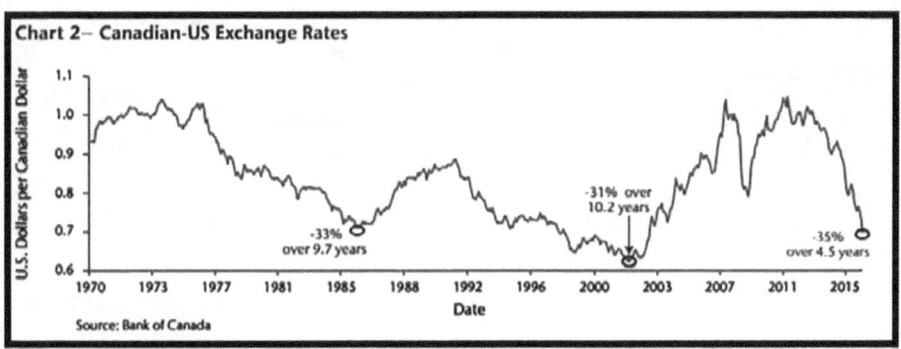

The recent Canadian dollar downward reset is good news for manufacturing competitiveness, and in theory should assist in halting the decline in investment in local industry. But so far, even with the advantage of the Canadian dollar at what many economists consider below purchase price, parity in the sub-80-cent range versus the USD, we may still struggle to compete with the competitive Southern USA and Mexican jurisdictions.

LOSS OF CAPITALIZATION

A further impact of not being intrinsically competitive is the adverse effect on recapitalization per industry in Canada. As already mentioned, capitalization has been in steady decline, with corporations taking stock of the total loaded manufacturing costs being projected and firmly deploying most new capital and manufacturing facilities south of the border, or into Mexico, or going offshore for any new manufacturing capacity for some components.

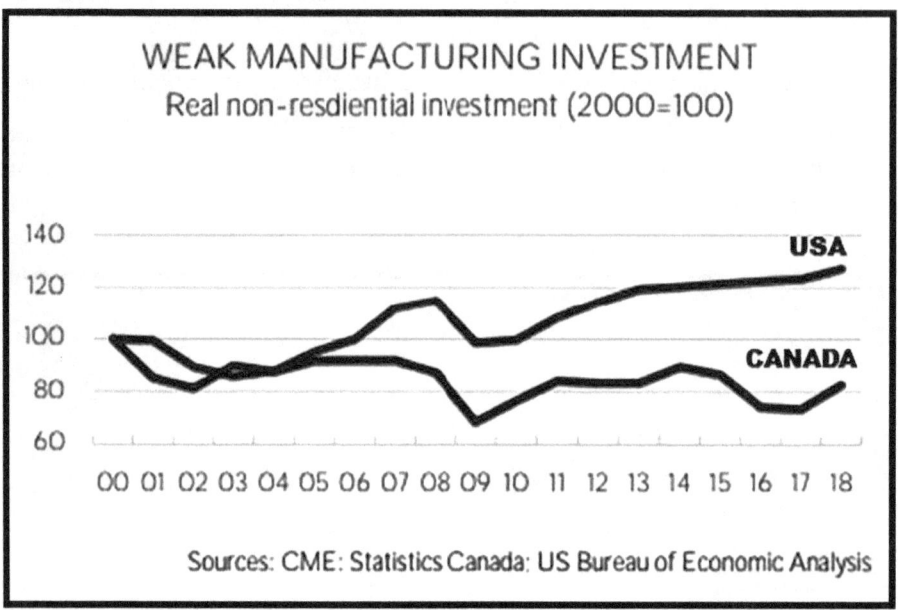

WEAK MANUFACTURING INVESTMENT
Real non-resdiential investment (2000=100)

Sources: CME: Statistics Canada; US Bureau of Economic Analysis

The graph shows the GDP-to-capital-investment ratio between the US and Canada, and illustrates the decline in Canadian manufacturing investment in relation to the USA.

CARBON TAXATION AND SUPPRESSION OF THE ENERGY SECTORS TO REDUCE CARBON EMISSIONS

The adoption of a carbon tax by the Canadian Liberal government supporting the climate change agenda will make our already non-competitive manufacturing footprint even worse.

Political commitment to this approach is divided in our parliament, with some suggesting a far more conservative approach. It's also worth noting that most of the national governments that support this climate-change agenda are multilateral-minded Western governments that can ill afford to be competitively disadvantaged, while other governments of so-called emerging nations, such as China and India, are wise enough to slow-peddle on such a journey to ensure they maintain a competitive trading position and do not disadvantage their economies.

Further, Canadian government legislation, including limiting investments through the banking system on any business that does not toe the line on carbon reduction, appears to be a self-destructive act.

It's hard to believe that the government of an energy-resource-based nation such as Canada would trade the prosperity of its citizens for a few brownie points at the international level for a climate change agenda that will most probably achieve nothing. We can only hope that more realistic and responsible political decisions are undertaken soon. We will discuss this climate-change issue in a separate chapter.

Lower corporate tax rate

Our advantage of a lower corporate tax rate is now diminished due to the USA lowering their rate.

Skilled workforce

Although strong in the past, our skilled workforce is diminishing as the baby boomers retire, and it is not being maintained, as we will explain in the chapter on the need for an Integrated Industrial Learning System (IILS). We will explain that many businesses lack direct access to talent and the education support needed to take the industry sectors to the next level of performance.

Regulatory and compliance bureaucracy

All areas of government have failed to improve regulatory efficiency and remove waste from product and process compliance requirements.

Ontario has one of the most punitive, stringent, and least realistic safety and environmental standards in all of North America.

INEFFECTIVE BUSINESS ENTITLEMENT FUNDING

Little has been done to better manage ineffective business entitlement funding. New technology development funding does exist but must be far better planned and driven by industry, and better integrated into local academic centers to jointly undertake R&D projects. Small business continues to struggle with complicated methods to access development funding and tax credits.

HIGH OVERALL ENERGY COSTS AND READINESS GAP

We still suffer from a large penalty in Ontario in terms of non-competitive cost of electrical energy. This is due to both taking the wrong road toward wasteful renewables and not focusing on moving forward on plans for nuclear power.

We certainly need to rethink our energy plans if we are to recover our industries that will demand much more energy at an affordable price. A recent report in the *Globe & Mail*, 24 May 2022, describes that "Canada has a crisis of electrification readiness," which could mean that Ontario may lose a $2.5 billion investment in a new Windsor manufacturing plant to make key components for electric vehicles. This is due to the inability to provide the power requirements for this facility. This is a signal that we have a real gap in energy readiness. We need a total rethink of our energy plans if we are to rebuild our industrial base. We certainly won't get this done with renewables like wind and solar. It's going to need a nuclear power solution, and quick.

NON-COMPETITIVE TRANSPORTATION AND
BORDER TRANSACTIONS.

The current transportation-cost disadvantage due to the US/Canada border has increased over the last fifteen years due to enhanced and additional security and COVID checks at the border, with customs red tape and added fees to cross and further time delays.

HIGH LABOR EXPENSES

Here is an example of the depth of this challenge, with a quick summary of the relative loaded-factory-footprint cost for equivalent technology in the auto sector, which is where we in Ontario would want to be competitive.

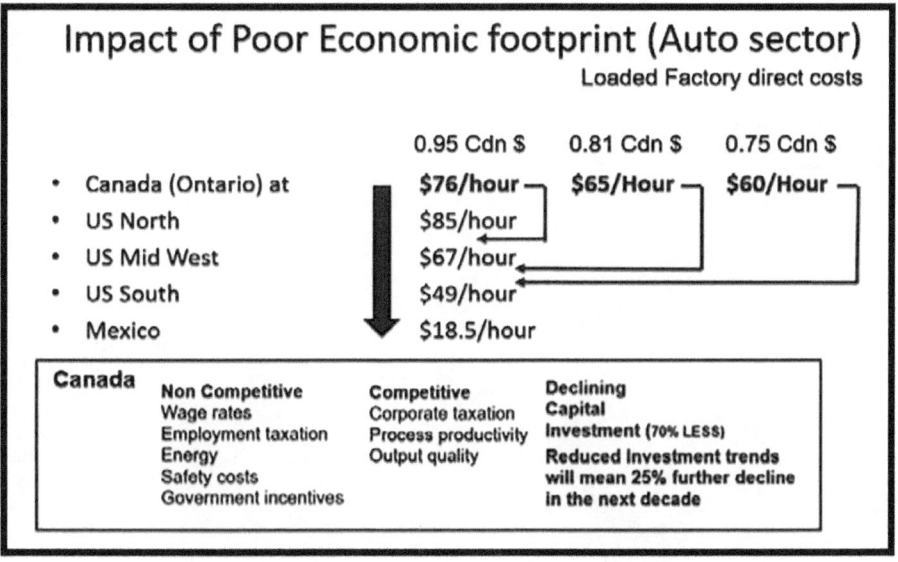

What it shows is that, even with a favorable exchange rate, we cannot compete with the Southern USA or certainly Mexico on loaded labor costs. It reinforces why many auto-sector facilities across all tiers of the supply chain are moving south to these lower-cost jurisdictions, and closer to the growth market of Mexico.

The scorecards below show the Canada manufacturing advantage/ disadvantage versus other USMCA countries for reshoring on several major factors and by sector.

CANADIAN MANUFACTURING ADVANTAGE/DISADVANTAGE VERSUS OTHER USMCA COUNTRIES

Factor	Past	Present	Future	Trending
CDN/US Loaded Factory Cost Comparison	Par	Higher	Delta	Disadvantaged
CDN/US labor rate differential	High	Higher	Major Delta	Disadvantaged
CDN Energy cost competitiveness	Low	Low	Lower	Disadvantaged
Corp tax rate advantage	Lower	Lower	Unknown	Advantaged?
Can $ exchange rate value	OK	Improved	Unknown	Advantaged
Local technical skill level	Higher	High	Declining	Advantaged?
Local Tech skill availability	Ok	Ok	Declining	Disadvantaged
Local region financial support	Weak	Weaker	Unknown	Disadvantaged
Cross border transportation	Par	Weaker	Major Delta	Disadvantaged
Mexico as a Manufacturing Partner	Low	Strong	Stronger	Opportunity
Mexico as a Manufacturing Competitor	Low	Strong	Stronger	Threat

Scorecard of key industry sectors in Canada and how they relate to this competitive USMCA environment and reshoring.

	Past	Present	Future	Trending (Can)
Automotive	Competitive	Non-competitive	Relocate US/ Mexico	Decline
Aerospace	Competitive	Competitive	Sustain	Maintained
Consumer products	Offshored	Offshored	Reshore US/ Mexico	No change
Electronics consumer	Offshored	Declined	Declined	No change
Electronics Hi tech	partial offshore	further offshore	Declined	Niche growth only
Food	Competitive	Semi offshored	Reshore possible	Recovery possible
Pharmaceutical	Competitive	semi offshored	Semi offshored	maintained
Furniture	Offshored	Partial Reshore	Reshore US/ Mexico	No change
Clothes and apparel	Offshored	Partial Reshore	Reshore US/ Mexico	No change
Medical equipment/ devices	Local	local	Relocate US/ Mexico	decline
Resource extraction equipment	local	local	Relocate US/ Mexico	decline
Heavy plant and equipment	Local	partial offshore	Reshore US/ Mexico	No change
Natural wood products	local	partial offshore	Reshore possible	Recovery possible

Some outliers and exceptions will always exist, but comparison studies performed on various sectors of manufacturing find that this is the predominant outlook. It demonstrates that

Canadian manufacturing corporations will face significant challenges to manufacture within their home nation. Many may have to adopt a USMCA-wide manufacturing strategy and relocate manufacturing into the best location within the USMCA region.

In situations where a strong and highly capable Canadian manufacturing capacity already exists, or leverages on localized natural resources with low transport costs, or where support to local customers or product development can be leveraged, certain Canadian sectors will sustain better. But where duplicate manufacturing sites within USMCA exist with equivalent spare capacity, and where no raw material or product delivery supply-chain differentiation or other leverage exist, these will be candidates to relocate to the US or Mexico, who region to region still offer a significant lower operating cost. The specific business situation can only be determined by using a balanced sourcing model and developing directional business plans.

Summary

In general, Canadian balanced sourcing costs in most sectors are still far from the same reshoring tipping point currently being enjoyed by some parts of the US and Mexico, such that any reshoring decisions involving recapitalization and investment in new facilities will be directed toward those cost-competitive locations. Further, Mexico is fast looking like a strong consumer-growth-market opportunity in some sectors, and the future close-to-customer preference will further drive an interest in Mexico as a strong choice as a manufacturing destination.

The challenges for Canadian manufacturers have been to understand these disadvantages and make plans to mitigate or adapt to the reality. Unless things change, Canadian manufacturers will continue to face significant challenges in operating home-based manufacturing facilities competitively.

Our governments, manufacturing sectors, and educational-support organizations have failed to respond to these challenges, and do not work cohesively enough to reverse this outlook. Some local governments are trying to focus on industry support, including upgrades and maintenance of energy, logistics, and communication infrastructure, but much more effort will be required.

I believe that there is now growing citizen concern that the over-liberalized federal-government agenda appears to be far more focused on "who we are" in terms of our social image to the rest of the world than "how we are doing as citizens."

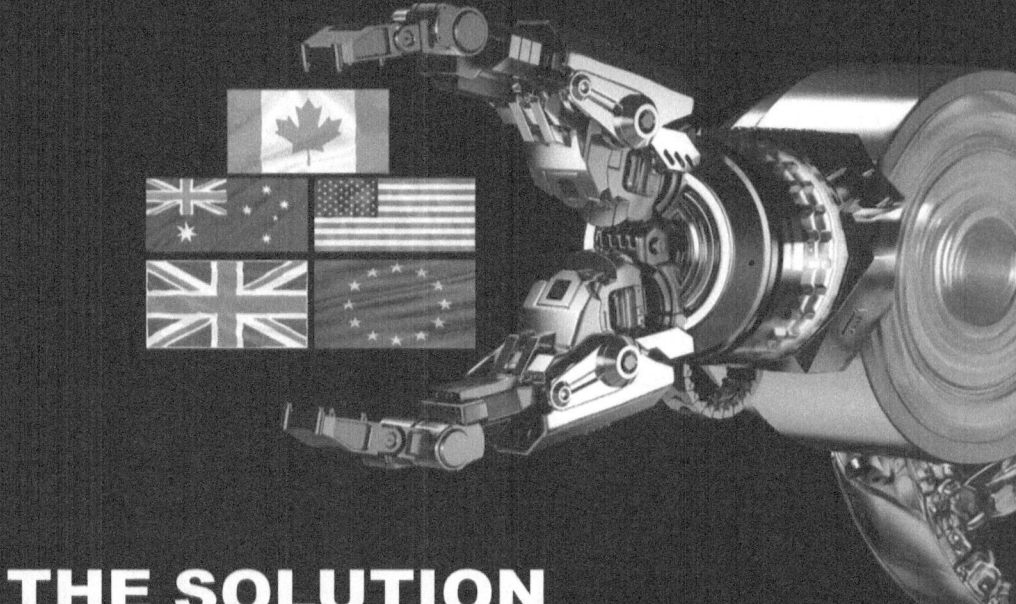

THE SOLUTION

THE GLIMMER OF HOPE

ALTHOUGH THIS IS not a book about politics, I must comment on how it has badly shaped the economic situation for manufacturing in our Western economies, and how we recently had a glimmer of hope for a better future.

In the Western world we have done a lot of things right, but in the last three decades we have lost the political plot in terms of the economic balance between nationalism and globalism and the delicate social balance between capital and labor. As we have explained, Western governments adopted a direction that allowed out-of-control globalized manufacturing to hollow out our home industries and destroy our national prosperity.

Although many people in all levels of society have agreed we have a problem with our manufacturing sectors and prosperity across North America, many are powerless, and those with the power to act have simply chosen not to do so. Even though some reshoring may take place through business-driven balanced sourcing of the supply chains, the industrial infrastructure has been significantly damaged due to the past hollowing out, and so in many cases will not just reset naturally to allow total recovery. So, it just won't be "Welcome Back Manufacturing" through natural reshoring. It will certainly have to be a "Take Back Manufacturing" approach with far more direct intervention and deliberate effort by everyone. Even with compelling evidence, economists refused to grasp the issue of the dangers of global free trade and the imbalance between capital and labor. They have continued to badly advise our governments, who have not reacted to the issue much at all. Between them they have been complicit in the globalization debacle, either by following the wrong and flawed neoliberal ideology or by being overwhelmed by the corporate elites and their lobbyists or being distracted by near-term social or geo-political issues, rather than the more important national economic threats. I will agree that that some individuals in the North American political environment on both sides of the border have tried valiantly to raise the correct issues affecting manufacturing, and to those I apologize if this is a harsh generalization, but as a collective they all looked asleep at the switch.

This all changed in late 2016 with Trump in the White House. Yes, Trumpism was a good thing for a manufacturing renaissance. The excellent book… *The case for Trump…* by Victor Davis Hansen explains what caused this unlikely event to happen. It was a long-term flaw in the evolution of most Western Political parties. Everywhere in the western world politics had historically been segmented left to right. The left, linked to trade unions, represented the interests of the industrial working class and most of the middle class, while the right spoke for small and big business. These democratic systems worked because these parties held each other in balance between capital and labor. It was clear what they stood for, and most voters felt that they had a stake in the fortunes of one side or the other.

The left's shift away from class-based politics and failure to maintain the balance between capital and labor, coincided with the right's harsh union-busting era. This was followed by the introduction of free market economics by US President Ronald Reagan and UK Prime Minister Margaret Thatcher. When the left's got back into power the US Democratic Party under Bill Clinton and UK's formerly socialist Labour Party under Tony Blair took no real action or priority interest in restoring or managing the Capital-Labor balance, and continued to embrace free-market economics. They both forgot their roots. They became implicit in the damage to the Capital-Labor balance and continued to support the neoliberal policy agenda of unfettered globalism. This process allowed the untethering of capital at the national level without any concern for the disastrous implications on the working and most of the middle-class labor (their citizens). Many of these voters thus felt betrayed by both the left, which they thought no longer represented their economic interests, and the right which took no notice of them once in power. Trump exploited this opening and turned it into a populist cult and promised to work hard to reinstall the balance of capital and labor and better manage the issues with global trade.

Trump got it right about the globalization issues, and his policies were designed to focus on reversing the problem. He is also one of only a few political leaders who undertook to carry out exactly what he said he would do at election time. Also, he is the only recent president or leader of a Western nation who has been crystal-clear that he puts his nation and its balanced economy first. All the other Western leaders in the last twenty-five years have waffled and wallowed in some mixed level of multilateralism and internationalism, and in some cases rank globalism, that has clearly not been working for their citizens. I can hear those purest "free trade economists" now.... They will be yelling about "comparative advantage" and the sin of "protectionism" etc.... Well, it's high time these economists moved on and stopped referring to 19th century books and papers by Adam Smith and David Ricardo and face the fact that "comparative advantage" is a failed perfect world concept. One of the rank assumptions in comparative advantage theory is that full employment of resources and trade balance is maintained, which for many years to come will be impossible to obtain on a global basis, and therefore it's just not the concepts we should apply in a modern world with rampant global over-capacity and significant wealth gradients between national economies. These concepts are a gross and dangerous over-simplification, and not in the best interest of national economies, whatever their state of emergence. But the good news is that slowly over the last decade some honest economists, such as Krugman, Ha-joon Chang, and Ian Fletcher to name a few, have declared that global free trade and the other tenets of the neo-liberal free market theory was a plain bad idea for western economies.

Trump is not the only president in history who correctly pushed back on global trade. Abraham Lincoln was once advised to buy cheap iron rails from Britain to finish the railroad across the US, and he replied, "It seems to me that if we buy the rails from England, then we've got the rails and they've got the money. But if we build rails here, we've got our rails and we've got our money." You said it Abe!

Trump's personal style was either loved or loathed. He said what many of us were thinking, and other senior politicos were too scared to say. His political incorrectness and brash ego-driven energy was refreshing to many voters, who had for a long time felt disenfranchised by almost all the politicos of the past. But he infuriated and alienated some of the left-leaning media, some of whom were clearly aligned with the global elites, who were very happy with the current self-serving status quo of unfettered globalism. Trump suggested that in their current form the institutions of global multilateralism and internationalism worked against the interests of the Western nations. He argued that liberalized global free trade was clearly unsustainable and not in the best long-term interests of citizens of most national economies. He believed all these relationships needed a firm reset or were to be avoided.

Trump was correct in moving the political agenda back in a national direction, as globalization was not working. Trump has been criticized by the liberalized democracies on many topics, but he made valid points concerning global free trade and reinforced the issue that it was not free nor fair and not balanced.

Trump started to engineer the practical suppression of imports to avoid unfair labor arbitrage and force much more closed-loop national trade and economic sustainability. He wanted to encourage business and consumers to make more of what they consume, force the localization of manufacturing supply chains, and utilize more local resources if practical. The new USMCA was part of his approach. He wanted these localized trade blocs with shorter supply chains so they would utilize local manufacturing closer to the consumers, enabling faster and more flexible response to demand and employ less process steps and wasteful inventory. This would mean trade will be far less sensitive to inventory so that interest rates can be normalized upwards to drive investment and prosperity. Also, the increased local demand would generate increased GDP and wealth within the North American economies. It would reduce wasteful labor arbitrage and the harmful free flow of capital between economies. It would also force a better balance of imports and exports. This required firm national controls via a better organized and enforced North American trade bloc to minimize wasteful global trade; resource waste; and environmental pollution; gain energy independence and enforce better controls on unplanned migration.

Trump was correct that some emerging nations such as China had continuously broken the free trade rules at the expense of the west to achieve an ongoing trading advantage. They had maintained strict controls on currency, imports and all forms of foreign investment and capital transfers to protect their local economies. It's also clear that in the future many emerging economies will follow a similar path to protect their industries, and gain growth at the expense of the more mature western economies. He, like many of us, had no confidence in the Multilateral organizations such as the WTO to control the situation. The only certain way to avoid this issue was to develop and enforce the local USMCA trade bloc and start to restrict trade from others outside of this trade zone as much as practical.

Trump did not imply that global trade should not exist, but due to the consideration mentioned above it must be considered more as an option of last resort. If undertaken it must add more value and be rationalized, balanced and waste-free, rather than the duplicitous, redundant, wasteful, and destructive free-for-all we see now. The best approach to manage and better control global trade is to group nations into regionalized trade blocs that will generate sustainable economies. The trade bloc approach is not a desire to create national isolationism, but it is a plan to modify the existing overall global free market and "partition" the global markets with localized trade blocs to better manage the rules of free trade within those trade blocs. This will avoid over exposure to large global wealth gradients, and better control the unplanned movement of capital and created wealth. The theory of comparative advantage, if it is to work at all, could actually operate in such a trade bloc environment with limited excess capacity and less mobile capital.

It should be remembered that until 1997, before the national economies started to move to global free trade, more than 50% of all world commerce was conducted within regional trade blocs. Economist Jeffrey J. Schott of the Peterson Institute for International Economics notes that members of successful trade blocs usually share four common traits: similar levels of per capita GDP, geographic proximity, similar or compatible trading regimes, and political commitment to regional organization.

Scholars and economists continue to debate if Trade blocs obstruct the "perfect model" of global free trade or assist in preventing massive unentitled wealth transfer. The advocates of global free trade insist that global free trade is in the interest and the right of every nation to expect from another. Well, its clear to me that any debate is totally over, as any kind of trade is an option only if its in the best interest of a nation and does not distract from the sovereignty of that nation. It is certainly NOT a god given right for one nation to expect from another. So, enough of this perfect world nonsense… global free trade is out, and regional trade blocs are back in!

When we investigate the feasibility of such blocs, we find that for example a North American trade bloc would only need to import a very small number of goods or resources that could not be provided in any other way inside the local economic bloc.

In North America, a localized trade bloc would equate to the USMCA trade bloc and in Europe it would equate to the EU zone. However, both the USMCA and the EU zone do not currently operate as true trade blocs as they do not vigorously enforce trade rules to ensure almost all trade stays within the bloc's borders. Currently they allow free trade to be undertaken with many other trading entities outside of the trade bloc zone, such as China and other Asian nations, which creates an over complex and duplicitous trading environment. A true trade bloc model would allow trade outside the bloc, but much stricter trade rules would apply, such as import and export tariffs, to ensure that such external trade provides a benefit to the participants of the bloc. Such exceptions could be the importing of resources and materials or products that are not available currently. Or, it might be productive and equitable export trade with other blocs to support their resource or raw material needs for use in their own economies, and for their own consumption.

If we are serious about reducing global pollution and waste then manufacturing should not continue to move wasteful, dirty, and environmentally destructive container ships around the world to chase a transient labor advantage. Also, we should avoid trade with countries that are ill-equipped to manufacture in a safe and ecologically compliant manner. Manufacturing must use sustainable supply chains with a lower pollution footprint to satisfy escalating ecological concerns. We must focus on gaining productivity closer to the customers, through LEAN business practices and using new manufacturing technologies.

The above reinforces the principle that all that should be traded outside of a trade bloc is non-indigenous raw materials or products that we have no capability of providing or producing now or in the future.

Trade in transfer of ideas and knowledge and technology must be far better controlled with well documented and enforced intellectual property (IP) transfer rules. In the past we have experienced product or process IP being stolen or transferred at no value through the panic to globalize manufacturing.

FUTURE GLOBAL TRADE BLOCS

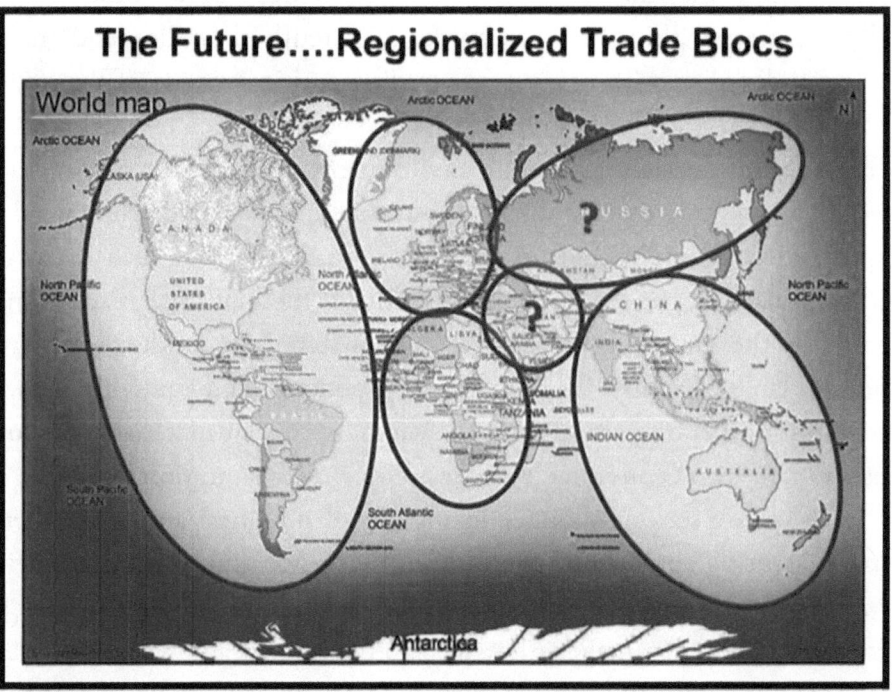

Future global trade blocs may eventually look like this diagram. These will still be nation states, but they will operate in trade blocs with strict controls on trade and human migration. The EU-style economic union approach may have to be redefined and rebuilt into a true trade bloc of self-contained nation states. NAFTA is now redefined as USMCA and may be extended into the future to add the South American nations. Asia, Australia, and Africa may develop into a separate bloc. In some manner this is already underway but needs to be better negotiated. The unknowns will be Russia and the Middle East.

The recent global strife caused by Russia trying to re-absorb Ukraine demonstrates how the 1990s fall of the Soviet Union will be a transient of history, and that the post WW2 iron curtain will now certainly return to the global scene. Also, some parts of the middle east continue to demonstrate why their culture and stability is incompatible with western values. In both cases isolation from our global trade bloc environment is a firm option being expressed by some experts.

The final regional trade bloc solution will demand a suppression of unnecessary imports and exports external to the trade bloc to avoid unfair labor arbitrage, and encourage consumers to make, grow, and mine, more of what they consume within their own trade bloc. This will drive economic sustainability, rather than global wealth transfer and local inequality. The regional trade bloc solution avoids the free-for-all of the global village based on free trade, that some globalists dream about.

A trade bloc far better supports important national controls that we have sadly lost with the alternative of global free trade. A trade bloc allows a large enough trade zone to provide balanced economies of resources, manufacturing and services.

A BIG SETBACK

Unfortunately, Trump's strength was also his weakness. He was not a politico, so he was not trapped in past mistakes and could speak out. He got a lot more done in his term than many expected, and he was certainly showing positive economic results that were unfortunately curtailed by the COVID crisis. But he was not accepted by the political machine to allow things to get done in a sustained manner or generate a level of ongoing support at the administrative level, and not getting a consecutive second term has meant that some of his policies are being easily reversed.

Based on the disaster and fallout from the January 6th 2021 capital insurrection, it remains an open question as to if he will return as a US presidential candidate in 2024.

But, thanks to Trump, we now have a large part of the US population successfully sensitized with a new critical mass of awareness that globalization is not working for them. Further, many citizens believe that their current government is not listening to their issues or managing their interests. It is not yet clear if others with similar agendas to Trump will be positioned to take his place as the US democratic machine grinds onward. Let's hope we can return to the correct level of political will and economic agenda necessary for the Western world to prevail.

In other nations in the Western world, discontented citizens are voting for more nation-minded leadership that may force a direction back to a national rather than global position on economics, trade, border control, immigration, ethnic and culture preservation, and national security.

These new leaderships will be questioning the level of globalism and should force action to slow things down, if not reverse some of the wrong paths we have taken on economics. For this reason, in many Western societies we had better be undertaking a realistic political dialogue to ensure our democratic process moves with the times. Significant discussions and debate will be necessary so that the Western nations can take a road that steers away from the over-liberalized global order that we have allowed ourselves to be drawn toward. Let's hope we all get it right soon.

HOW CAN CANADA TAKE
BACK MANUFACTURING?

The Canadian economy has been in reset mode for some time, with an ailing resource sector and a hollowed-out manufacturing base.

Disregarding the impact of the COVID epidemic, which has made things worse, we have an economy out of balance. The worldwide price fluctuation in oil and the inability to build the correct infrastructure to distribute it has devastated this export-oriented resource sector. We are also experiencing instability and change in our saturated service and retail sectors. Some of this is due to e-commerce migration.

This situation has prompted some political parties to recently ask my advocacy group what it would take to rebalance our economy by recovering our manufacturing. Well, our first reaction was: Please... don't expect a fast recovery. Manufacturing has been neglected, with indifferent industrial policies, under-capitalization, and poor development funding. It's been outpriced with an over-inflated exchange rate for decades and allowed to be hollowed out by globalization. So don't expect it to just spring back and do much to assist in the short term. And, unless you provide a rock-solid political will and focus, don't bother.

But let's assume we did get the political will and focus to get it done. Let's review what our manufacturing sectors will need to become entitled to take back manufacturing. We believe it will be a significant challenge for some sectors of manufacturing to naturally reshore in Canada based on the economic situation and our position within USMCA, but we believe some manufacturing can be stabilized and sustained and some could return, but only if we take it back. We did not call our initiative "Welcome Back Manufacturing." It won't be that easy. It will demand a focused and coordinated road map that is embraced and followed by all involved: our political leadership, our industries, our education system, and our society.

It's clear that such an integrated national game plan to focus on the well-being of the local manufacturing base is far from new, and many other nations are either starting this journey or are ahead of the rest. Ian Fletcher, author of the book *Free Trade Doesn't Work,* shares my concern that much will need to be done to set up an effective manufacturing environment to support reshoring in the USMCA. He briefly explained the steps being taken in the USA:

> The American government has taken recent steps to ensure that its local manufacturing succeeds in the coming decades with a range of programs. These include foreign-oriented policies, from a dialogue to set a competitively priced dollar to counter-mercantilist tariffs, as well as the need for domestic policies designed to support development and deployment of manufacturing technologies and what I would describe as assisting a technologically aligned maker culture of education and training programs.
>
> They have recognized that inventing technologies is not enough, and America needs to become better at technology deployment. Although the US has had a strong governmental commitment to pure science and a reasonable process for technology development, its institutions for the deployment of manufacturing technology have been weak.
>
> Thankfully, solutions to this weakness are already emerging. One is the "Manufacturing USA program" which should be greatly expanded. But this program, though it has a deployment component, is centered on developing technologies. Deployment at national scale, reaching many manufacturers, raises sufficiently different issues, and requires sufficiently different skills and institutional capabilities so that it merits organizations of its

own. This is where the federal Manufacturing Extension Partnership (MEP), a small program that may be ready for significant expansion, comes in. This program is explicitly devoted to transmitting technology, and related business skills, to firms to enhance US global manufacturing competitiveness. The focus is on small and medium manufacturers (SMMs) as they typically lack organizational capacity to embrace new technologies and need help finding or training employees to use new technology.

Other nations that had already defined manufacturing as an important part of their economy have already installed national solutions to these problems. Japan has the keiretsu families of companies and the long-term business relationships of mittelstand ("small or medium sized") firms in Germany, Austria, and Switzerland. And these nations have government institutions, such as Germany's Fraunhofer Gesellschaft and Japan's Kosetsushi, dedicated to such issues.

Thanks to Ian's input, I compared what others are doing to upgrade their manufacturing. My contacts in the UK indicate that their government is reinstalling their once highly capable apprenticeship system to rebuild the maker culture, and many other associations are integrating to emulate the successful German industrial support system, which is one of the reasons Germany has retained its industrial base. I reviewed the situation in Canada, and we do have some similar organizations, as mentioned by Ian, but they are less focused and not supported by a cohesive government industrial policy.

For many years in Canada, we have had silos of technical societies and industry sector associations that contribute to the communication of industry knowledge and improvement, but they are typically underfunded and fight for membership between each other, and they create considerable duplicated effort. Examples of these are PEO and OSPE for engineers, OCEPTT for technicians and technologists, ASQ for quality practitioners, SME for manufacturing engineers, and APICS for supply management practitioners, to name a few. Each of these organizations are divided into regional chapters and most struggle to develop a cohesive impact for their membership.

Businesses have been encouraged since the mid-1980s to embrace R&D by participating in **a** Scientific Research and Experimental Development Tax Incentive Program (SR&ED), **supported by the federal tax system**, that encourages Canadian businesses of all sizes, in all sectors, to do R&D in Canada. Unfortunately, the system is complex and highly bureaucratic, and it requires support from consulting experts to extract the tax rebate that adds to the effort to earn the rebate. Its program has been revised over the years but is still considered bureaucratic. Many small businesses have legitimate R&D rebate opportunities but lack the effort to take advantage of them. Many of us have suggested a change to the tax-code system to set corporate tax rates per business types based on the expected level of R&D needed to be competitive in that sector. This would save the effort in collecting taxes, and the huge effort of justifying and auditing a rebate claim, and then giving it back in a tax rebate. This would free us of the bureaucracy and leave the earnings in the companies where it belongs, rather than use it as a hard-to-get carrot, which does not achieve any real improvement for the industries.

The longest-running support funding for industry was from the CME, who provided a range of support for industry with training and educational packages. Recent funding efforts provided free consulting to SMEs on topics such as business systems, productivity improvement, and skills training. One recent focused-assistance program is the Canada Makes program, introduced in 2015. This is a network of private, public, academic, and non-profit entities dedicated to promoting the adoption and development of advanced manufacturing in Canada. The network covers a broad range of technologies, including 3D printing, reverse-engineering 3D imaging, medical implants and replacement human tissue, metallic 3D printing, and more.

Many of us have complained and campaigned for more government action to support industry, with only minimal results. However, one positive outcome came in 2018, when the Canadian government announced a focused spending effort within various industrial sectors on innovation in five regionalized superclusters. The plan is to spend $950M over five years to incentivize large-scale collaboration among industry leaders, large and SME companies, researchers and academics, not-for-profit organizations, and accelerator and incubator organizations.

The federal government predicts that when companies of all sizes, academic institutions, and not-for-profits come together, they can generate bold new ideas that wouldn't have otherwise come to light. The goal is to help build first-rate and productive innovation ecosystems.

The five superclusters are defined by the public government website as follows:

- The **Digital Technology Supercluster**, based in British Columbia, is focused on unlocking the potential of data. Through bigger, better datasets, and cutting-edge applications of augmented reality and cloud computing, to name a few, this supercluster is improving service delivery and efficiency in the natural resource, precision health, and manufacturing sectors. Ultimately, the Digital Technology Supercluster is arming Canadians with the best data to drive decision-making and connect the digital and physical worlds.

- The **Protein Industries Supercluster**, based in the prairie provinces, is increasing the value of key Canadian crops—such as canola and wheat—and serving growing markets for plant-based meat alternatives and new food products. Through plant genomics that improve nutrition, novel processing technology and digital solutions from farm to fork, this supercluster is helping Canada capture premium markets for its agribusiness and feed the world.

- The **Advanced Manufacturing Supercluster** is based in Ontario. NGen is the industry-led, non-profit organization leading this supercluster to build the next-generation manufacturing capabilities, such as advanced robotics and 3D printing. Ultimately, the Supercluster is positioning Canadian companies to embrace industrial digitalization and INDUSTRY 4.0.

- The **Scale AI Supercluster** is based in Quebec and spans the Montreal-Waterloo corridor, and is bringing the retail, manufacturing, transportation, infrastructure and information and communications technology (ICT) sectors together to build intelligent supply chains. Links between businesses is becoming faster and easier as new tools see and predict where and when products are needed, ensuring Canadian made products and services are first to market.

- The **Ocean Supercluster**, based in Atlantic Canada, is tapping the combined strengths of the industries operating in Canada's oceans, including marine renewable energy, fisheries, aquaculture, oil and gas, defense, shipbuilding, transportation and ocean technology. By harnessing emerging technologies, this supercluster is digitizing and optimizing marine operations, maximizing sustainable approaches to resources, and increasing safety for those operating in marine environments.

Although I am thankful something has been done, and I highly respect the hard work by all the participants, it's still a disappointment to see such a modest budget of $950M over five years. It is only 0.01 percent of the nation's GDP. To compare the level of commitment, culture spending by Canada's municipalities is about 3 billion a year, **the federal government spends about $4 billion** a year, and the provinces and territories spend $3 billion a year. This is a total of $10 billion a year for culture topics or O.6 percent of GDP, which is sixty times more than we are starting to spend on innovation and technology. I am sorry, but it's another example of a misplaced focus on "who we are" rather than "how we are doing."

Many of us are hopeful yet somewhat skeptical of how well these superclusters will work, and how productive they will become to assist the industries. They will struggle with alignment and consensus and will conflict as they try to focus on the funding priorities. The risk is that the multinational corporations who will probably put more effort into the program will benefit the most from the intellectual property developed, and the technology and solutions may not be deployed within Canada and so will not end up benefiting Canadians, who funded the effort. It has been recognized that it may be far more difficult for the many small businesses to undertake technology deployment, which is the issue the US has experienced with its own programs.

Also, the academic institutions who will be involved are rife with globalized funding and foreign sponsorship that places any IP they are involved with at risk of being transferred to these foreign actors.

To many of us, it feels like the government is doing this to keep us happy and off their back. They are throwing a small amount of money at the problem with various grants, training subsidies, tax rebates and the supercluster funding. In no way does this constitute strong political will or a firm focus to get the TBM job done.

A recent update on this federal Supercluster program in the Globe & Mail 29ᵗʰ June 2022 confirms my pessimism. The article states that we have seen little measurable progress with only limited results. Its also clear that there is much government confusion s to its goals and intended results. Some experts are declaring the program an overall failure.

Our TBM forum has firmly advocated that, to recover and sustain our Canadian industrial capability, our governments must have far more political will and commitment and must work closer with the educational organizations, and industry.

Also, they must follow the three parallel imperatives we outline here.

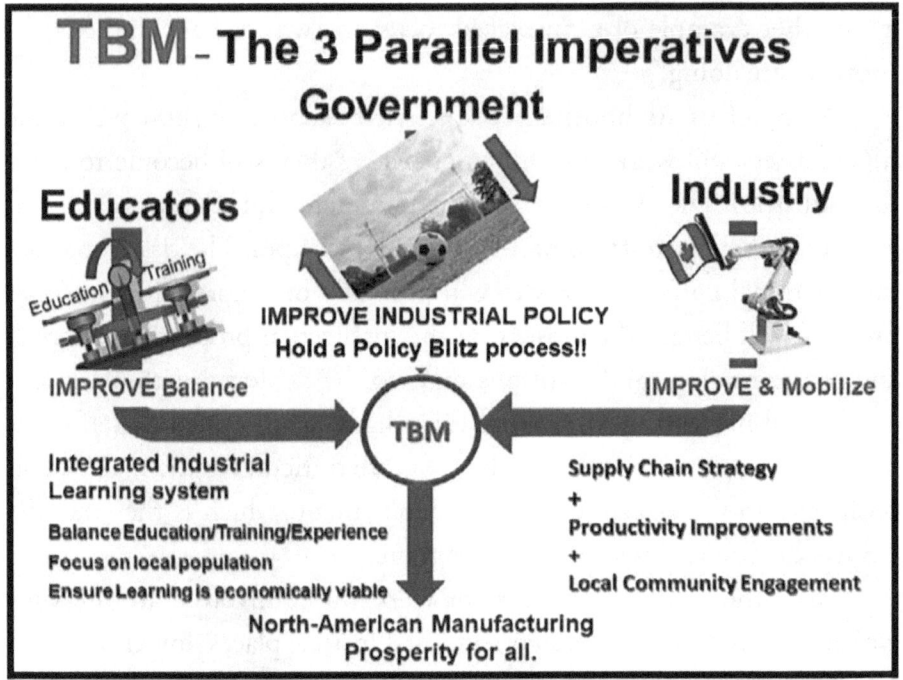

TBM − The 3 Parallel Imperatives
Government

Educators

Education Training

IMPROVE INDUSTRIAL POLICY
Hold a Policy Blitz process!!

Industry

IMPROVE Balance

TBM

IMPROVE & Mobilize

Integrated Industrial
Learning system

Balance Education/Training/Experience
Focus on local population
Ensure Learning is economically viable

Supply Chain Strategy
+
Productivity Improvements
+
Local Community Engagement

North-American Manufacturing
Prosperity for all.

TBM IMPERATIVE #1: NEW GOVERNMENT POLICIES

We continue to struggle to enact industrial policies in our nation and at the provincial level, and this pressure is building as we come to realize that the post-industrial age is not going to work for us.

Manufacturing things, including leveraging our natural resources as well as our ability to support them with highly functional services, is the only way to achieve a balanced economy to guarantee prosperity.

We need the federal and provincial governments to work closer together and increase the level of political will and focus to improve economic policies. This must include a productivity improvement plan, not just a growth policy. It needs to also integrate the ideas and commitment of the industrialists and business leaders and the educational system if it is to be successful.

TBM Imperative #2: Integrated Industrial Learning System for Success

We need our educational system to reset its focus to provide an Integrated Industrial Learning System (IILS) with the correct balance of education and training and experience in an integrated manner, as we have far too many young Canadians and existing members of our workforce over-educated but under-trained, and without enough experience to support Imperative #3.

TBM Imperative #3: Industrial Improvements

We need our local industries to realize and rediscover that they can and must improve and mobilize themselves if they are to be effective in the future Canadian economic environment.

In the next chapters, we will discuss each of these three TBM imperatives in more detail and discuss how to get them started.

TBM IMPERATIVE #1:
NEW GOVERNMENT POLICIES

THE CURRENT GOVERNMENT PLANS

Our current Canadian government is banking on economic growth to outrun the enormous debt burden incurred before and during the COVID-19 pandemic. Finance Minister Chrystia Freeland asserted in her economic and fiscal budget update in early 2022 that, "Above all, our national focus must be growth and competitiveness through productivity." Sounds like the correct thing, but it's easier said than done. This is because Canadian productivity growth has been on a continuous decline over the last fifty years as shown in the following chart.

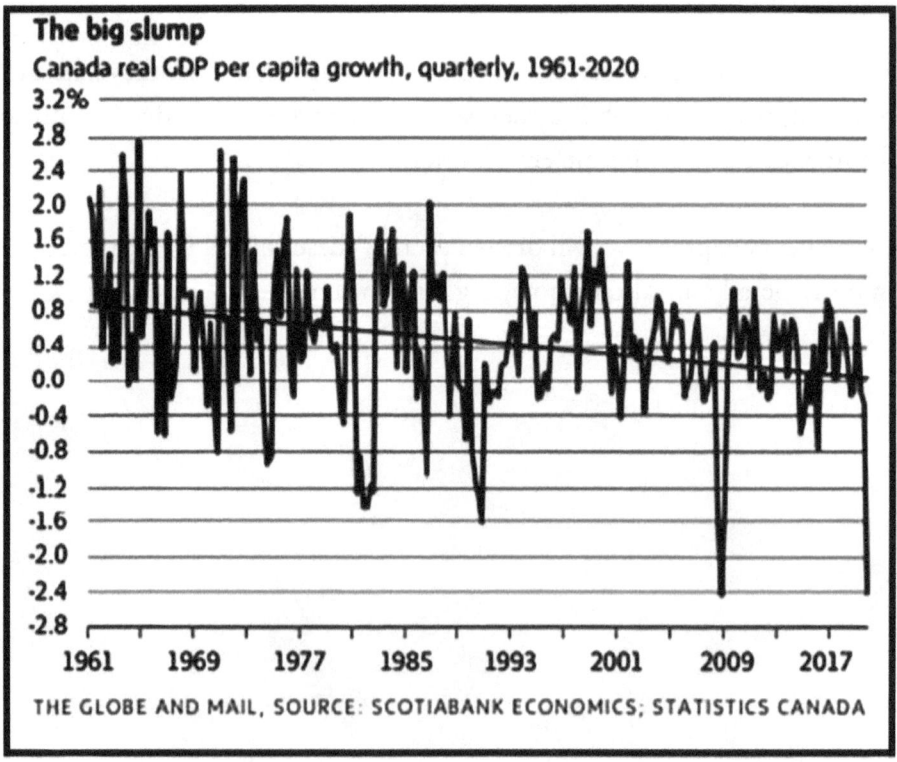

THE GLOBE AND MAIL, SOURCE: SCOTIABANK ECONOMICS; STATISTICS CANADA

Canada also finished in last place in a recent study from the Organization for Economic Co-operation and Development on projected growth in per capita gross domestic product from 2020 to 2060 among its thirty-eight member countries. Canada is a leader in creating jobs among developed countries, but we remain last at creating real wealth. Canada needs a productivity plan, but the federal government keeps focusing on social-infrastructure spending, including higher levels of immigration. The biggest initiative is child-care expansion, which the government portrays as a catalyst for increased productivity, but economists say this won't have any real effect other than costing the taxpayer more debt. There is small funding in the budget aimed at boosting the rate of technology adoption by small- and medium-sized companies via technology superclusters, but it's too little, too late to make a difference. There is no mention by the government of any plans for a manufacturing renaissance.

It's clear that rising productivity is what is needed to cope with the federal debt, but federal plans fall far short of what's needed to reverse Canada's decades-long slide in productivity to better achieve wealth creation and improved prosperity.

We need a strategy now, and it's got to be a cohesive plan from both federal and provincial governments. They need to develop a "get things done" attitude more in keeping with how the Chinese government plans change. Of course, we need to learn how to do this within our democratic framework, but let's make sure it does not keep getting in the way.

PROPOSED FUTURE ROADMAP

The federal and provincial governments must work together to improve economic policies to include a definitive industrial policy to rebuild, grow, and sustain the manufacturing base across industrial sectors. They must develop a combined roadmap with business and industry leadership and the educational organizations to make it happen.

We have governments and opposition parties that appear continuously distracted and unfocused by many issues other than supporting industry in a structured way. Also, we have many members of the federal government who still hold a misplaced notion, still reinforced by some economists, that a post-industrialized society is an inevitability. We must educate them, so they realize we won't get rich on services or shipping raw resources out of our economy without adding value to them and still bringing in vast amounts of imports.

Even if we did have a high level of political will to act, we have government organizations that don't understand manufacturing in enough depth, and have difficulty developing such an industrial policy, so they react to the need for this plan by reaching out and asking for paid expert studies, positional reports, and commissions. The result is that, over the last few decades, we have had many and mainly academic-based policy study groups getting paid to perform analyses and generating reports about the health of manufacturing and what ails it, and sometimes they even suggest a fix. They publish many of these reports regularly, which hardly get read, and almost none are acted upon.

Due to all this, we lack a well-coordinated national and provincial planning process to shake us out of this eternal reporting tailspin. They have a significant lack of team focus to productively get on with such a planning process at all levels within government, industry, and the various technical associations, societies, and relevant academic institutions. We have special interest groups, such as engineering and management associations, operating in debilitating silos, who are contradicting each other's directions, policies, and proposals and who then engage in confusing government lobby activities. They get locked into political-level conflicts with no positive outcome possible. So, what we have is a huge waste of collective talent and energy, and a resulting dysfunctional manufacturing or industrial community that has great intentions but badly needs to get organized. All this wasted activity is happening in a critical time window to move on any reshoring opportunities.

PLANNING PROCESS

For the reasons mentioned above, we must convince our political leadership that, before we can apply any solutions, we need a strong unifying planning process to solve the lack of the focus mentioned above, and then manage the selection of the solutions, and get on with it so we can take back manufacturing.

First, we must define the members of the planning community who are best positioned to represent and assist such a planning process. Once defined, they need an active planning team structure with key members who will be fully tasked to meet on a focused basis to engineer the solutions. The plans must be set against timed deadlines and supported by the best strategic planning facilitators money can buy to generate consensus and ensure a resolution is reached.

At the completion of this planning process the output will be presented to Parliament, and it is suggested that it should be a cross-partisan coalition approach, with limited disruption from extraneous lobbying to ensure rapid concurrence at the political level. The results will be the formation of a policy and detailed implementation plan for our manufacturing sectors. Then key team leaders must be appointed to lead various elements of the plan, and the journey needs to be one of continuous planned evolution that must sustain long-term through any government changes.

SUGGESTED PRODUCTIVITY SOLUTIONS FOR CANADA

The plan must contain bold new ideas formulated into solid policies with aggressive prioritization to galvanize growth. This will set Canada on a clear path to greater prosperity that must include the return of its manufacturing sectors. Many economic experts have suggested specific solutions for productivity and prosperity improvement, and I have incorporated some of those suggestions.

Some readers may struggle with these solutions and call them unconstitutional or too right-wing. They are not intended to be either of those, but I do agree they are pragmatic and Trumpian, as President Trump's policy direction—once you cut through the rhetoric from all sides—was mainly correct for where we are at in North America.

Of course, Canada lacks the economic clout to undertake such bold policies mentioned here without the USA, but if Trump, or a Trumpian-style leadership, returns to the White House, and with the current geopolitical outlook of deglobalized trade, these may well be the kind of policies discussed within the USMCA trade environment.

All this may be wishful thinking, but it would be nice to see! Anyway, who knows what will happen in the next American and Canadian elections?

POLITICAL LEADERSHIP

Such plans can only be conducted by a political leadership using a strong democratic but focused government that undertakes the plans for the good of the citizens. We need to appoint a leadership team that better understands and will undertake the installation of streamlined, unified, and connected national policies that will support business, sustainable economic growth, and more localized trade. Also, the leadership will need the ability to navigate around what some are calling "The Great Derangement," and we will cover this risk in a later chapter on socio-political risks.

BETTER GOVERNMENT PROCESSES

The preference over the long term must be to simplify our political systems to avoid the many wasteful levels and division. In most places in our nation, we have at least four layers of government: federal, provincial, regional, and local. These are duplicated across the political spectrum and create a huge waste of effort and bureaucracy. This will require a purge and a migration of employment from the public sector toward the planned growth of the private sector so that more citizen resources have the opportunity to add direct value to the economy. This will take time and require a huge government re-alignment and re-budgeting process.

BUILD POLICIES TO REDUCE IMPORTS

Past events provide a strong lesson that must be considered for future trade policies. As we have stated throughout this book, globalized trade has been mismanaged by most Western nations. Now we need to learn from the inability to control pandemics and manage any recovery due to long, unsustainable supply chains. It's yet another reason to localize our economies in all forms and improve national economic borders and controls.

We need to learn to avoid so-called multilateral free-trade agreements that are never followed by the emerging nations, at great expense to the mature nations. These agreements have promoted unfair free trade, providing uncontrolled access to the Western consumer base with cheap labor and subsidized dumping, or duplicitous product offerings that add no value to our economy. If such trade is still desired, it can be undertaken with an associated tariff.

The solution is to form a rigid, localized trade bloc with our USMCA trade partners to avoid the current high level of imports outside of that trade bloc. This must force reshoring and make the need for some exports unnecessary, so we can better balance trade. Unnecessary trade outside this bloc needs to be highly discouraged by tariffs and other forms of control to force the localization of supply chains and resources. Throughout this book we have defined how obvious and attainable this approach can become. We just need to align the correct political will across all three partners of the USMCA. If Trump or someone similar takes the next US presidency, this will be an essential approach for Canada to get behind. If undertaken correctly, the population will not see this approach as an economic burden. The landed price differential between imports and local goods is now typically less than 10 percent. So, it has been calculated that most Western economies need to shoulder a 10 percent increase in the price of only some goods to reshore, and so gain back all the much-needed value-adding jobs and the associated prosperity. Most citizens would happily trade a stable, well-paying job and be prepared to pay the extra 10 percent on most luxury goods rather than the alternative of no job security and the inability to afford such goods anyway. I believe this concept will need to be carefully explained to the population, but it will be accepted, as many are now sensitized to the downside of the current level of globalization. Of course, this reshoring can only happen when local alternative capacity and products are available, but we need to start this journey.

This means that many emerging economies will have to depend on organic growth rather than the "instant economy" provided via free trade with a mature economy using excessive labor arbitrage. In other words, the China story of massive exporting to the West to fund internal Chinese growth must not be repeated. Everyone must learn that trade is not a God-given right to expect from another economy, and that the WTO's rules will need to be rewritten. We can still assist these emerging nations with aid and support, but it must be structured as a loan that must somehow be repaid in the future.

MANAGE NATIONAL TRADE

Dismantle trade and regulatory barriers between the Canadian provinces to accelerate growth and create a unified national economic space for the national good, rather than provincial protectionism. It's estimated that the removal of these barriers could liberate a fiscal dividend of between $13 billion and $15 billion if there were more free trade within Canada.

ENERGY POLICY

We must eliminate the unnecessary and untenable climate mitigation plans and the associated expense and economic pain it is creating for an oil-resource-based economy such as Canada. We need to restart balanced dialogue and expose the climate-change-emergency myth that is promoting an agenda that threatens our civilization. This will mean backing out of the Paris Accords—Trump was right when he did that. The national focus should be to manage any national climate-change adaption deemed necessary and move toward practical conservation and sustainability of the environment by reducing pollution and resource depletion. This is discussed in detail in the chapter Managing the Climate Emergency.

We must work within the USMCA to gain total energy self-sufficiency inside our North American trade bloc. This is possible and should be accelerated by government directives. This should be a strong thrust to improve local output on oil and gas and eliminate imports from unstable foreign actors. The Canadian oil sands must be a key national focus to accelerate output to support the solution. It is not a perfect oil-source solution, but it *is* part of the solution, although we need to review localized Canadian refining capacity to reduce the waste of distribution and wasteful pipeline activity.

We need to accelerate the use of nuclear power, and this will be paramount to support the growth in the demand for electrical power. Forget the crazy notion of wind and solar unless it is planned for remote-area usage. W&S is not a viable thrust for a North American energy plan.

FISCAL POLICY

We need to ensure that the Canadian dollar is maintained at the same trade tipping point with US currency.

Simplify and consolidate income tax in personal and corporate taxation, as it has grown in complexity since its introduction more than a century ago. As a minimum, prioritize to eliminate a few complicated tax measures each year, so that over a few years we create a transparent, simple, effective, and fair income-tax system.

Install new tax benefits for investments, with accelerated depreciation for certain sectors and limited to Canadian-controlled corporations. By making accelerated depreciation a permanent measure, we can spur investment by the private sector while avoiding the peril of cutting corporate tax rates. This could include tax benefits on new products, technologies, equipment, education, training, pollution reduction, etc.

Adjust the ultra-low interest rates upwards to a normalized level close to pre-globalization levels to make investments worthwhile. This will require a total rethink and a long-range effort. Taking back manufacturing will liberate all the cash trapped in inventory in the long supply chains and can assist this process greatly by reducing the working capital burden on businesses so they can better afford higher lending rates.

A global transportation tax (GTT) must be defined and enforced so the true cost of long supply chains and the associated waste will become apparent. This will further drive the demand for shorter supply chains and reduce low-cost labor arbitrage. This will become a controlling factor in how supply chains are defined and utilized. The motivation for the tax will not be climate change, but it will reduce the pollution of the oceans by container ships and the wasteful consumption of scarce oil resources in the future.

Corporate cashflow and taxation will need to be controlled with legislation that will be possible once the national governments, via trade blocs, wrestle control of their economies back from global financialization that has gorged for far too long on the Western middle class. It will also mean a refocusing and better national control of the financial and corporate sectors to better serve the national good rather than the globalized agenda.

Eventually, some discussion will be needed to plan a return to the gold standard of global balanced trade and currency management, or something equivalent. This would control globalization and dampen the dangerous ability for capital to slosh around between economies, and it will far better control wealth transfer gradients. It is unlikely that any single national reserve currency will be an acceptable future solution. But removing national currencies as a tradeable commodity on the stock market casino should be a worthy goal. It is going to be an exceedingly long but worthwhile endeavor to design such a system, and reverse the damage done by past neoliberal ideologies and the over-financialization of our economies.

INVESTMENT POLICIES

Simplify industry incentives (SR&ED, etc.) Instead of a complex tax-ation-and-funding-release system that increases bureaucracy project by project, release an R&D tax break every year to each business based on a simple audit of their type of business sector, their business activity, the local content the business provides, and the amount of R&D they are deemed to undertake.

EDUCATION POLICY

Generate a formal national plan for the implementation for an industrial learning system. This is explained in the chapter on Integrated Industrial Learning Systems (IILS)

IMMIGRATION POLICY

We must reduce immigration rates significantly, as it's clearly not the solution to improve productivity. We do need to combat an aging popu-lation, but we already have a significant level of excess labor capacity that is not being utilized effectively. This labor under-utilization is obvious from data showing a declining employment participation rate, significant youth under-employment, and a bloated public sector that should be redeployed to the private sectors to add more value to our economy. Further we will need far less low-paying jobs when we implement INDUSTRY 4.0 and we will need to retrain and redeploy those jobs. We need to do much more with less to get productivity, not keep adding to our workforce capacity by bringing in more untrained labor from mainly under-developed countries. Also, adding to the population will just add even more burden to our already over-stressed housing, education and support infrastructure. Any investment in improving the national work-force should be employed in retraining and re-deploying the existing underutilized citizens, rather than adding expensive immigration.

We must ensure that only essential immigration is undertaken. We should reinstate the rule that only immigrants with firm job offers can be admitted to our nation. Let's place our energies into making any such immigration recruitment processes highly effective to support the future business needs. Let's also minimize the back-door approach offered by student visas to ensure these educational processes are effective and always add solid economic value to our nation. Let's also constrain any type of refugee programs and unplanned border immigration, as it's clearly been abused and has questionable benefit to our national prosperity and social well-being.

We must start making citizenship a distinct privilege by implementing a "citizen jobs first" process. We must also ensure that Immigration is not some kind of "human right" that others from elsewhere expect us to support.

INFRASTRUCTURE & REGULATIONS

Fix our declining infrastructure by improving logistics and communications so we are ready for the taking back manufacturing journey.

Reduce wasteful regulations that affect our ability to get things done. Regulations slow down the ability to develop new industries. For example, with current regulations, it could take as long as fifteen years for a new extraction mine that would produce the minerals for batteries to start operating, an obvious disincentive for any investor, and particularly damaging for an emerging sector.

We badly need to focus on reducing the bloated and heavily bureaucratic safety, legal, human rights regulatory burdens on business, but, of course, without allowing this rationalization process to harm our safety performance.

Fix the out-of-control housing market with firm action to legislate against external speculation and profiteering. Many experts have defined the solutions to avoid such rent-seeking economics, and these solutions need to be undertaken.

EMPLOYMENT POLICY

Encourage young seniors to work past sixty-five. We can do this through financial incentives that would buy time to support any labor gap before true labor productivity is achieved. This should be optional, not mandatory, and could be incentivized by increasing the amount that seniors can earn if they keep working, without reducing their government benefit payments. Many could be redeployed toward the end of their career as trainers and educators, and encouraged to pass on their knowledge and skills to the next generation in the workforce.

Strive to avoid the need for both parents to work to make ends meet. Yes, it will be a long-term productivity and prosperity goal, but it will mean we will have the option to have our children at home, not in daycares. So, the government daycare-expansion strategy currently being undertaken may be at best a mid-term fix, or a huge expense taking us in the wrong direction.

Avoid and reverse the drift toward a gig economy that badly employs our citizens.... Employment scenarios such as Uber—which forces more cars onto our crowded roads and takes advantage of under-employed labor while increasing pollution and congestion via a cheap communication app—need to be stopped. Government needs to better regulate and force the real solution of improved and effective public transit and support systems, or a regulated private taxi system that is not undercut by such inequitable practices. This is just one example; there are many others.

Develop work-from-home jobs. Parents, particularly mothers, are an option to provide a stretched work force. This could fit with the strategy of reshoring many service-center support jobs currently offshored. This could be encouraged by taxing corporations that use this outsourcing approach. There are tens of thousands of stay-at-home parents and mobility challenged who could fill this role and retrain to re-enter the workforce. This will require we rethink training programs, associated funding, and the recruitment environment. This would also assist gig workers trapped in such low-end jobs and laborers who will need a second, less physically demanding career as they age, and seniors who wish to stay working. Ultimately, it could be a component of a productive economy utilizing untapped talent and capacity we are already in some fashion funding. Better this approach than importing it with more wasteful immigration or funding capacity offshore.

INNOVATION POLICY

Stop giving away our best ideas by better protecting intellectual property within Canada. We must ensure that federal and provincial research funding for innovation from all sources is controlled and retained in Canada so that domestic firms can make use of that technology, rather than see multinational companies benefit and reuse the IP on a global basis. Some of our educational institutions are the biggest leak via international academic funding grants which force IP sharing. This has been the subject of critical review recently.

NATIONAL PROSPERITY GOAL

Generate and communicate a national prosperity goal that everyone can get behind. In 1962, President Kennedy set the goal of "landing a man on the moon by the end of the 1960s," committing to a firm and ambitious goal even though not every part of the plan had been worked out. By contrast, Ottawa has committed to boosting Canada's productivity in only the vaguest terms, verging on wishful thinking, with history showing a half-century of decline. It needs to be an objective-based economic agenda, with a goal of boosting GDP per capita by a certain percent a year. Whatever the goal, it must be well communicated, and a serious focus provided to succeed.

I wish we could redeploy the massive social commitment, effort and energy wasted on the climate emergency agenda toward gaining national prosperity through productivity improvement.

SUMMARY

This will require a strong national-thinking government that can transmit the message that "how we are doing" is much more important than an obsession with "who we are," and make the citizens want to belong to and believe in their nation. The advantage is that public opinion is moving toward the wish for strong leadership that may be more nationalistic and populist than the traditional political institutions. The public is tired of the usual political ineptitude. Most just want it done. Unless such a political transformation is achieved, any economic recovery that demands the mobilization of a nation that will be needed to take back manufacturing will be almost impossible. We live in hope!

And another thing...

As mentioned, a key part of the planning process must be to educate our politicians on manufacturing so they can understand the plans. I have had many bitter experiences trying to explain manufacturing issues to government officials and politicos. Most of them have never been inside a manufacturing facility, and if they have, it's been very superficial and to do with vote-gathering. Many of them have no clue what they are looking at. Also, this lack of manufacturing DNA is prevalent in our media, who never seem able to report the facts of an industrial situation or understand the real issues.

Here is a contrasting scenario. One of my clients running a manufacturing business in Scarborough, Ontario, was building a state-of-the-art paint line and could not get a building permit, which would expand the facility and create jobs. The paint-system technology would emit far less pollution than the local environment standards. In fact, the emissions would be cleaner than the local city air. We convinced the local Member of Provincial Parliament to visit and help our case. He admitted he had never been in a manufacturing plant. He had been a legal advisor before he became a politico, and it was hard to explain the manufacturing technology. We eventually educated him, cut through the red tape, and got the permit, but it was hard work and made us wonder why anyone would want to run a manufacturing business in Ontario. Contrast this with my experience in China, where I worked with a syndicate of manufacturers for five years. I was invited many times to tour the factories with the Chinese government. Almost every time, the senior government party members had a scientific degree or related business experience, and even if they did not, they had toured many manufacturing facilities. They always seemed aware and asked relevant questions. In a few cases, when there were issues they could help with—training funds or facilities or improved government systems—things happened very quickly to rectify the issue.

When given an opportunity, I have made it very clear to our government and media, that our biggest competitor in China is not just their manufacturing capability, but the fact that they have a government, a supporting administration, and a workforce that knows manufacturing, has a maker culture, pays attention to it, and gets things done!.... Just saying...

TBM IMPERATIVE #2:
INTEGRATED INDUSTRIAL LEARNING
SYSTEM FOR SUCCESS

If TBM becomes a reality, we will soon be faced with an economic growth opportunity with significant jobs growth, but a huge gap in capability due to a looming skill gap.

To combat this problem, we will require an Integrated Industrial learning System (IILS) to provide an education, training, and work-experience roadmap for each participant. We need it across all trade, technical, administrative, and professional disciplines to support the manufacturing sectors.

Canada has never developed an IILS because, since the late 1940s, we had imported our skills and knowledge through immigration. This worked in the past, when the quality of imported skills was abundant with immigrants from the UK, Germany, France, Italy, and other industrially mature economies making the move to what at the time was a better life in a wider North American economic market. Most were pre-recruited with a job offer before they applied for entry, or they had a certified and accepted skill that was on the demand list. The past immigration system was set up this way and generated job-ready immigrants who could immediately participate and improve the Canadian economy with their imported skills. Most also had a better grasp of the official language and culture, with many only needing to change their accent to be perceived as Canadian.

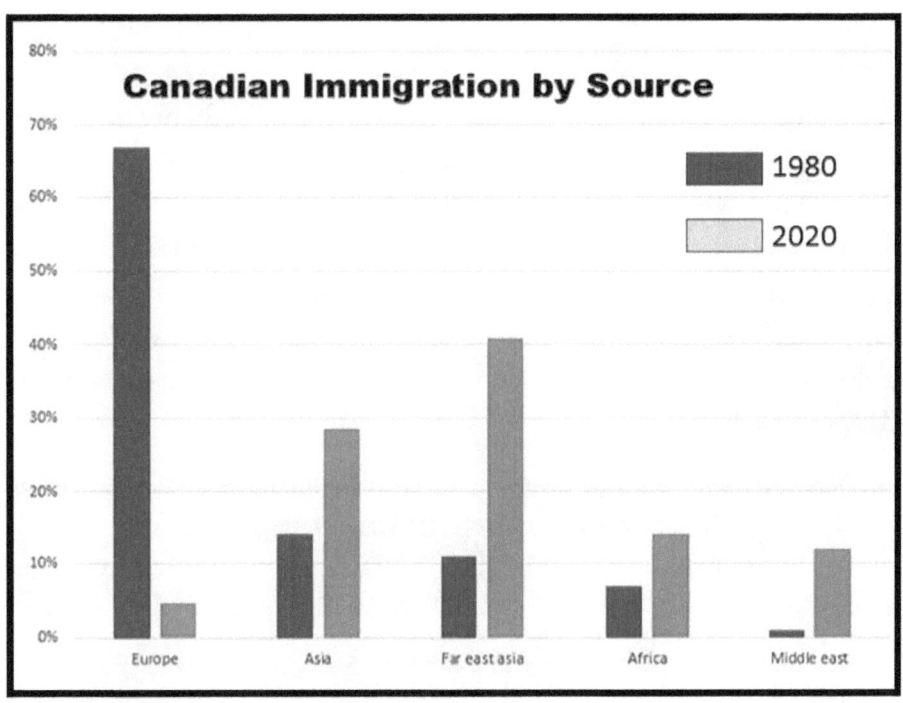

Canadian Immigration by Source

Things have changed drastically, with immigration offering few of these advantages. Most immigrants come with few skills that we need, and they are less equipped to fit into the culture of language and customs. As the graph shows, most now come from third-world economies with less inherent knowledge of how a modern industry functions, or even the cultural experience of how they as citizens should function in a modern society. Many are not screened effectively for the ability to speak the official language, and even lack the basic education to undertake further training. The current immigration rules are apparently not about economic merit, but are focused on a politically charged humanitarian scorecard, including a huge imposition of accepting entrants as refugees, irrespective of their ability to contribute to the economy. Many of us have come to doubt the logic of continuing with this form of immigration, when we have as a minimum 35,000 Canadians experiencing homelessness on any given night, and at least 235,000 Canadians who are homeless in any given year. Of that number, it is estimated that 180,000 are using emergency shelters (including women's shelters), 50,000 are being housed temporarily in other types of non-profit organizations, (such as hospitals or by family or acquaintances), and 5,000 are sleeping outside. But whatever the political views on this topic, the fact is that this current immigration scenario has placed significant pressure on the educational system and the industries that must cope with the capability gap in skills, language, and culture of these new Canadians. Therefore, if this immigration approach is to continue, we will definitely need the IILS approach.

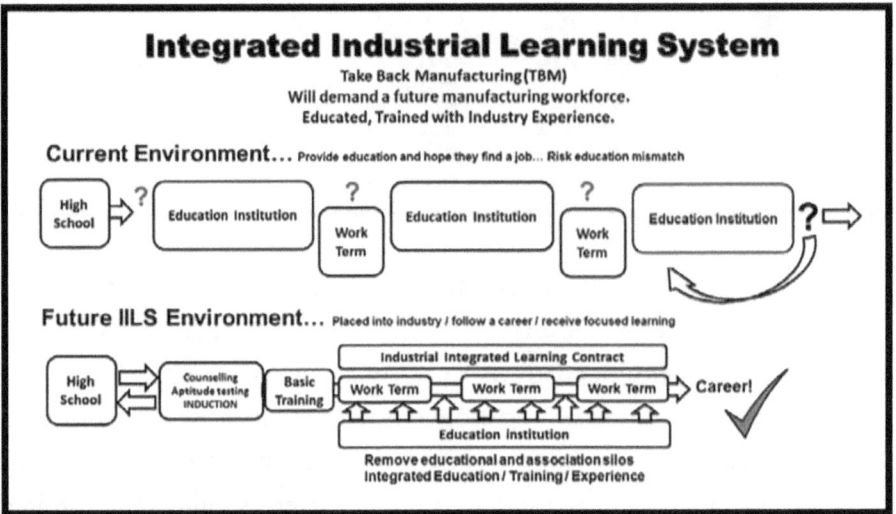

Here is a comparison of the current learning environment and the proposed IILS environment we will need.

Our current learning environment is wasteful, ineffective, and expensive, and although some trade apprenticeship systems and co-op programs exist, they are far from integrated and not implemented at an effective level.

Currently our youth are sent to school and progress through post-secondary education with almost no contact with a potential employer, or, if they are lucky, they may land a final year co-op or poorly paid internship toward the end of their academic journey. Simply put, we spend a fortune educating our youth and hope they find a job, and maybe they get lucky, and it becomes a career.

The current learning system can result in significant misalignment between the needs of the businesses that have a shortage of skills and the massive investment the students are forced to make in the education journey. This can result in little career opportunity at the completion of their education process. The education process can be less motivating for the student who has no pressure to learn without an application in sight. We learn better and faster if we see a need.

Dislocating education from training and experience forces the educational institutions to try to emulate the training and real-life experiences in the classroom or educational labs, and this is more difficult and expensive to do out of the context of an industrial environment.

In the new IILS, youth are briefed and coached early in high school and then recruited into industry at its completion. They would be counseled and recruited to attend at the business. They undertake a planned education and training process and gain experience in industry in an integrated manner, so they quickly become a valuable member of the business environment.

This means there is close coupling of education and practical application, so the process of learning is more effective for the average student and easier for the educational institutions to provide the education.

This would avoid a current issue we see in many of the professions: students attend a university campus for three years to be educated and receive little hands-on industry experience or training, and they end up overeducated and undertrained, unprepared for the real world of their profession.

This IILS solution can be applied to both young and mature entrants, to secure their industry career through on-the-job training and experience, and off-the-job business and technical education.

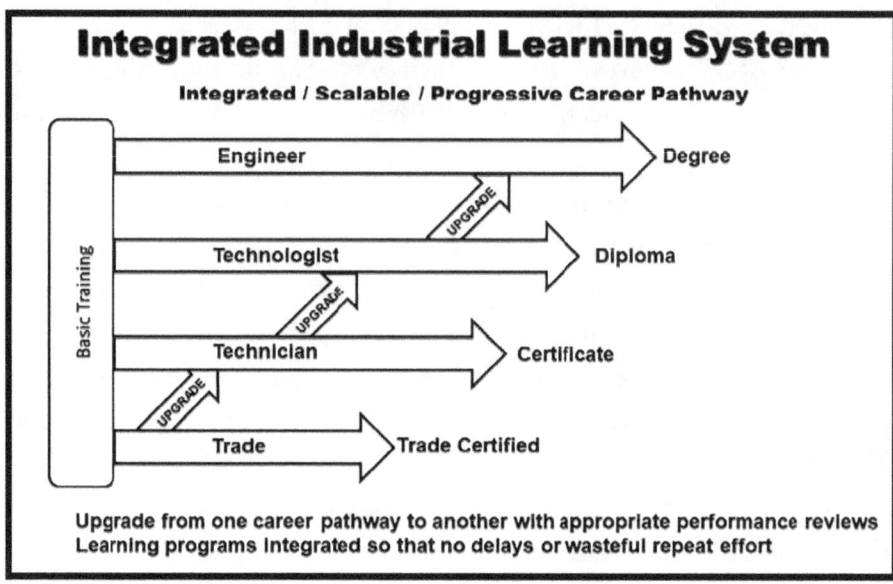

The other attribute of the IILS system would be the ability through entrance criteria for participants to enter at different academic levels in the program, and through progression-grading they can upgrade to a higher career level. This would apply to the mature members of the industry who could engage with the IILS program and further their industrial career, reusing their experience and knowledge gained in industry, and add to this with educational programs offered in convenient downtime from work, such as night school or weekends.

The IILS is a better approach, and a better investment for all concerned. This is like the current German system of industrial training, and the same approach as the British apprenticeship system I undertook from 1966 to 1971.

IT WILL ONLY WORK IF OWNED BY INDUSTRY, COORDINATED BY GOVERNMENT, AND SUPPORTED BY EDUCATION

An IILS approach cannot happen without a strong commitment and realignment from government, the educational institutions, and industry. It will require a governing board for joint industrial learning, which would have the resources to engage students while they are still in school or in the current workforce. Then, assist in placing them into a stable career journey with progressive companies that will propel them through an integrated process to create trade, engineering, and management skills. Government must manage this joint industrial learning board and direct this IILS initiative through effective policy with industry leadership and educational institutional support.

It will require a change in the commitment from the industries to invest in such a learning program for new trainees and their existing workforce. The financial burden should be supported by some form of government assistance in terms of grants or tax reduction. This will enable industry sectors to create, own, and operate a training program that fully trains and qualifies technical and business professionals to fill real industry workforce requirements—now!

It will require a change in operating style by the educational institutions, who must restructure their programs to be seamless and accommodate the off-work hours with industry.

The IILS is a long-term system administering an "earn as you learn" career progression that integrates workplace training and academic education enabled by individual career contracts.

It will offer industry a highly certified and licenced workforce, and a shorter deployment cycle to develop the skilled team members needed. The youth will get integrated learning, a career progression, and higher engagement and career placement experience.

It will require participants signing up to a career contract that will provide reasonable employment continuity and stability and a worthwhile career, as long as they perform and obey the rules of the contract.

We also must take significant actions to attract young people toward such a program. The public image of manufacturing needs work. It's still perceived as dark, dirty, and dangerous. The next generation must see manufacturing as cool, and believe it is something they can build their future upon.

We need to deploy knowledgeable industrialists into our school system to promote, counsel, and recruit. This will include re-educating everyone, including the educators who certainly do not have a good grasp of manufacturing as a career. This is an important culture change. We have had three decades of people thinking manufacturing is bad news, viewed as risky and unstable employment. We have a lot of work to do to change this negative image, and just talking about TBM, telling the real story, and showing what we as manufacturers do for the economy will help. Getting the media to talk it up once they can see the political will and focus will help cement the roadmap as a national imperative.

SUPPORTING MATURE STUDENTS ALREADY IN INDUSTRY

The solution must also focus on industry-friendly learning systems that the workforce can access while still being employed in their busy industry jobs. This must be managed with night classes and weekend programs as needed.

We need to get serious and ensure we maximize the future opportunities for all our citizens and balance education, training, and on-the-job experience into an IILS to ensure we prepare for a balanced economy.

SOME CHALLENGES WITH OUR EDUCATIONAL SYSTEM WILL NEED TO BE OVERCOME

Some educators appear to have lost the real purpose of their role in our society. The pre-secondary educational system at all levels needs to focus far more on STEM education, basic skill training, and personal aptitude discovery to enhance further learning and prepare them for a modern economy.

Currently there is far too much focus on social issues, such as gender, race, and the climate change emergency etc. Many parents remain highly concerned with this form of teaching curriculum. We should be concerned about its impact on young children. We need more education and training, not social conditioning and indoctrination. We also need educators who stay focused on providing a wide range of open viewpoints and positions on subjects, rather than polarized and self-opinionated positions that appear centered on left-leaning woke themes. It is the job of parents to decide on these kinds of topics and not the educational system. This form of teaching curriculum has assisted in breeding the bad cancel culture and woke-driven situations we are now witnessing at our post-secondary institutions, where students have become conditioned to hold extremely polarized views. They must be educated to accept a broad spectrum of viewpoints that clearly promote a spirit of broad learning and discovery that is the essence of a university education.

The other major issue is that we are selling our citizen-funded educational and training resources to the highest global bidder. Higher education has been impacted by financialization. Many of today's universities rely more on paid tuition than state funding to pay for their expenses. This has forced some schools to borrow large amounts of money to pay for luxurious facilities and student housing to attract potential students. The cost of tuition has soared since the advent of such financialization.

Our learning resources, although adequate, are limited and should be predominantly focused on providing for our citizens. This is the only way we can cope with the future load demanded by the IILS. We have far too much of our educational resources, both in the classroom and at the educational admin level, focused on gaining revenue from foreign students. If one citizen is potentially able to have one more hour of class time, more hands-on tuition or more coaching hours spent on them to gain a chance to earn a living and pay more future taxes, then these rare teaching resources should not be deployed to foreign students. Our citizens must come first if we are to have a national image that encourages citizenship as a privilege that, once earned, is of good value.

The fee we charge foreign students is admittedly at a premium from what we would charge our own citizens, but although it more than covers the direct cost of the education, it still does not cover the investment in the overall educational system we as citizens have paid for over our taxation lifetime. So, as taxpayers we are paying to educate the other nations' children.

Further, many foreign students abuse the student system, use it as a back door to work permits, and swell the ranks of the under- and unemployed. Or, just as worse, take jobs that require fewer skills that could have employed existing citizens. Some believe one way to combat this is to eliminate the work-permit portion of the student visa, and this should also disallow co-op work terms.

The sooner we start to see our secondary educational systems as part of our national intellectual property, the better. This will create some debate, as many academics think they live in some kind of global village, and all knowledge is free to be transferred. This open-door attitude to IP transfer needs much more discussion if we expect our businesses to access this environment with their R&D projects.

The real issue is a strong lack of government policy that underfunds our education and training institutions. This not only makes education and training too expensive for our citizens but forces the learning institutions to follow a "sell to the highest global bidder" business model. We need to rethink and re-budget to ensure we service the needs of our citizens of all ages first, and at a far more affordable cost.

Can Industrial employers support time out for education or training?

Due to competitive cost pressure, many businesses tend to hire rather than develop their human resources. This means a stagnation of the learning cycles in most industries and breeds a low learning culture, where the average individual feels unable to plan for career education. The lack of growth in most industries further suppresses the urge to learn and make that next internal career move, as those new openings are scarce. This equates to a non-learning environment in many industries.

WE HAVE ACADEMIC STUDY GROUPS DEVELOPING INEFFECTIVE SPECIFICATIONS

Learning specifications for industry suffer due to the lack of any cogent industrial engagement in the definition of the learning programs. Although many in the educational institutions try their best, more focus is required to ensure education and training requirements are designed and installed through solid representation by industry. This is compounded because we have manufacturing businesses, many of them painfully small, that have been forced through excessive competitive compression to shed much of the infrastructure needed to plan future human-resource development. The overtaxed individual management teams struggle to execute day-to-day decisions, let alone participate in external sessions on the topics mentioned above. These organizations will need much more assistance.

ON A POSITIVE NOTE

The skilled trades program *Skilled trades | Ontario.ca* that is underway by the Ontario government is definitely a strong step in the correct direction, and I hope it can develop into a full IILS approach across all the range of skills we will need.

CANADA HAS AN ESSENTIAL SKILLS PROBLEM THAT MUST GET FIXED

Based on a Canadian government report (Evaluation of Literacy and Essential Skills -Canada.ca) we have a significant percentage of the population suffering with poor essential skills, such as literacy and arithmetic. This will probably prevent them from fully participating in an industrial learning system.

Figure 1: Canada's Scores Compared to Other Countries (2011 to 2012)

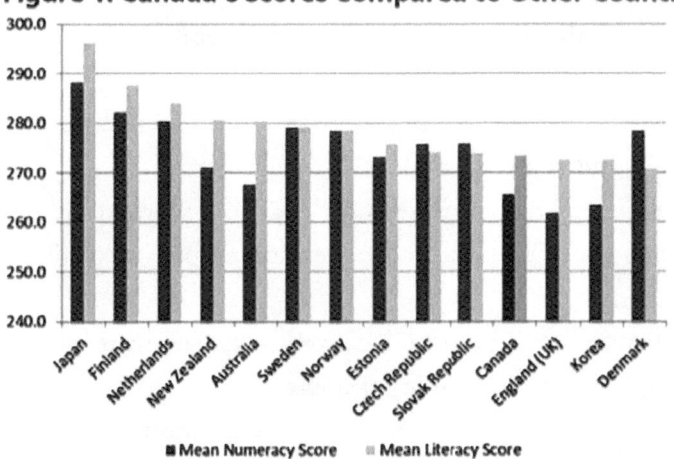

■ Mean Numeracy Score ▪ Mean Literacy Score

Canada gets a C and ranks eighth out of thirteen countries on the percentage of adults scoring low on adult-literacy rate tests. Four out of ten Canadian adults have literacy skills too low to be fully competent in most jobs in our modern economy. Canadian adults with low literacy skills have fewer opportunities than young Canadians to upgrade their skills, because they are outside the mainstream education system. Canada continues to score average amongst OECD nations in literacy, and below average in numeracy, with youth aged 16–24 continuing to underperform relative to other OECD nations. Performance by both immigrant and Aboriginal populations continue to trail their Canadian counterparts.

This essential-skills problem must be factored into the education packages offered by our IILS system.

OUR FUTURE MANAGERS AND TECHNICAL WORKFORCE WILL NEED NEW KNOWLEDGE AND SKILLS

They must have:

- The ability to build an organization with a vision and aptitude for all forms of innovation

- People-leadership skills will also be essential to manage the integration of all this new technology by mobilizing the new technical workforce
- An understanding of the latest trends in industry technology, techniques, and tools
- Strong manufacturing-process knowledge to undertake LEAN implementation and reinstall a mindset for Continuous Improvement
- A capability to rebuild strong localized manufacturing supply chains using balanced sourcing models
- An awareness of the global situation and business trends
- Practical and effective English-language and communication skills
- The ability to be flexible and fill multiple roles within an organization

THE IILS WILL BE ESSENTIAL TO TBM

We need a powerful IILS to support our future industrial objectives to ensure our working citizens and our future youth get an opportunity to fully participate in the prosperity of our balanced economy.

TBM IMPERATIVE #3:
INDUSTRIAL IMPROVEMENTS

Here is a list of industrial improvement strategies that should assist an organization become entitled to be part of the TBM renaissance.

SUPPLY CHAIN OPTIMIZATION

If you are a Canadian business leader, you should start to review the option of a USMCA-based manufacturing plan using a balanced sourcing model, with effective and shorter supply chains rather than overextending your supply base offshore. This means you may as a Canadian corporation end up with a USMCA reach. Many of these kinds of corporations do exist, and they are hardly Canadian anymore, but they can be 100 percent North American.

Of course, many manufacturing-based industries will still exist in Canada and have an opportunity to flourish with a local manufacturing base, but in many cases this may only continue if you have looked at how you can fully compete within USMCA. The real message of the reshoring situation is that the economic landscape is creating a strong need to review and better understand the balanced sourcing factors. This will mean that certain segments of manufacturing will move from globalized manufacturing centered in the next lowest-cost country toward more regionalized manufacturing closer to customers in the best cost-competitive locations within that customer's trade zone or bloc, such as USMCA.

This reshoring and balanced sourcing journey are the early new steps toward waste-free customer-focused manufacturing that is far more sustainable, with shorter supply chains in a world under increasing pressure to meet such goals.

This may force the need to franchise or license manufacturing centers in new markets across the globe, to be closer to customers and avoid wasteful transportation using more portable and transferable manufacturing technologies and better-developed IP and technology-transfer systems via global franchising partnerships.

Manufacturing that will be reshored to the USMCA trade bloc will not be the same products or manufacturing technologies that were off-shored. It will require a well-coordinated and integrated team of experts and organization to do the correct things to succeed.

PRODUCT AND PROCESS PRODUCTIVITY

Product and process productivity-improvement goals using LEAN and Six Sigma, focused capital investments, and technology development may sway the productivity numbers significantly.

An organization with close-coupled product and process design teams and a slick new-product-introduction process should perform these tasks much better than those that do not have such cross-functional business teams operating naturally within the organization. This is because the co-location of product development, manufacturing, and the supply chain, and even better links to the customer, can generate a strong productivity factor and typically reduce risks by improving communication. Also, a product-costing system that can integrate with the new product development team to optimize cost at all levels is a key advantage.

BUSINESS-WIDE LEAN THINKING STRATEGY IS ESSENTIAL

Typically, business-wide LEAN thinking and sustained continuous improvement in all facets of the business tends to be a huge business advantage, and should breed not only strong operating performance, but also a more robust and innovative environment that can be entitled to capital and growth investment.

This requires a stable and visionary management, and this is where strong business leadership can make the difference to the outcome.

There are three LEAN business strategies that should be followed:

1. Use LEAN thinking to eliminate the waste in the non-value-adding parts of the overall business process, and reach a simplified LEAN version of the new business process. This must apply to all parts of the business operation, including developing a supply base organized in a close geographical cluster that will feed local manufacturing and distribution loops. This will require a reconsideration of the business processes and facilities, business systems, and people factors that can be improved and better integrated. Therefore, this overall process of LEAN thinking must be at the top of the business-planning agenda to strip out non-value-added process steps and associated waste.

2. Undertake a formal automation review of what new and emerging business-systems technology and automation science that can be applied to this revised LEANed out business model, using innovation strategies and INDUSTRY 4.0 disruptive technologies. This will also include a review of current and future product and process designs, and how they may better be leveraged by these automation opportunities. Using the latest manufacturing technology, and integrating this effectively with product innovation, is a way to gain an edge.

3. Automate this latest technology into the LEAN value-adding business processes to support the most advanced and integrated business and product set. This approach will possibly make the business the benchmark in the industry. The individuals who can first visualize the outcome and grapple with these three complementary strategies, stay current on the latest technology and scientific trends, relate the output to the latest automation technologies, communicate and implement such strategies, and continuously improve these plans inside an

organization will be the superheroes of the business world, and certainly win the quest to take back manufacturing.

WORKFORCE IMPROVEMENT

The permanent long-term solutions of a formal IILS are still being debated between federal and provincial authorities, and we must all encourage government to facilitate the IILS to correct the skills shortfall as well as solve our significantly high youth unemployment if we are to take back manufacturing.

But in the meantime, each business must realize that to undertake the INDUSTRY 4.0 journey will require the development and training of a skilled workforce, and it is better done through the growth and development of your existing workforce rather than just recruitment.

This will mean doing some IILS-type planning for yourself. Develop a skill matrix for the organization as it is now and into the future, and develop a relationship with local colleges. With their help, define training programs for your existing workforce and set up a pay-for-skills program so that the staff will drive their own development. This also breeds employee commitment and stability.

Plan to take co-op students each year, and select candidates from the disciplines that you want to develop within the organization.

Set up technology-development plans with local academic centers to attract co-op students and jointly undertake R&D projects to access funding and gain talent and new employees that can take the business to the next level.

It does not have to be a lot of work to set up, but the benefits are huge. From my personal experiences, graduating students—if correctly selected and on co-op—are smart and eager to learn and can be your senior team members helping you run the business in only a few years.

FOCUS ON ENTITLEMENT FUNDING TO LEVERAGE ADVANTAGES

A further advantage is to leverage entitlement funding by including SR&ED and other grants, as well as government-sponsored funds for improvements in manufacturing processes and workforce training and recruitment.

THE SMALL-BUSINESS DIMENSIONS

The impact of outsourcing on our small and medium businesses has been huge, with significant decline in this size of venture. The goal of the small business will be to understand where the customers will be, and, if practical, join that localized supply-chain cluster and capitalize on the trend at all levels to be closer to the customer.

This will mean learning how to leverage the broader sectors they occupy in terms of how the customer and supply chain functions, by embracing technology and know-how, and attracting the needed skills. This will be an area of involvement that will generate visibility to be considered a strong player in the more localized and clustered supply base.

Learning how to operate in all three countries within USMCA and how to approach this market will determine success, and this has traditionally been a challenge for a small business. This is an area where assistance should be obtained.

ALWAYS MAINTAIN AN "EVOLUTION PLAN"

Maintaining a continuous improvement culture and measuring results on the progress on all the topics mentioned above with a dynamic "Evolution Plan" is essential to maintaining the ability to enjoy the manufacturing renaissance we all hope will return.

Each business sector needs to learn, develop, and adopt such a plan to achieve an integrated LEAN / INDUSTRY 4.0 business practice and continuous improvement culture.

Unfortunately, most businesses have been poor at making progress on these continuous improvement strategies, and it may need a considerable management focus to make the progress needed to stay competitive. The reasons for this may be too much of a focus in the past on depending on low-cost country suppliers to gain margin, rather than a focus on overall business performance and gaining productivity through recapitalization in more localized manufacturing solutions closer to the customers. Many organizations may need to re-learn the organizational artform of installing and maintaining such a Continuous Improvement culture.

Last word: There never was a magic pill to evolve the business, you just have to get on with it. The productivity message is always the same for every business: you have to improve and manage quality, cost, and delivery continuously through the best improvement techniques, utilizing the best capital and technology that the industry environment can provide, with the support and teamwork of the best people power you can build.

We did not call it "Welcome Back Manufacturing"; it's called Take Back Manufacturing for a reason!

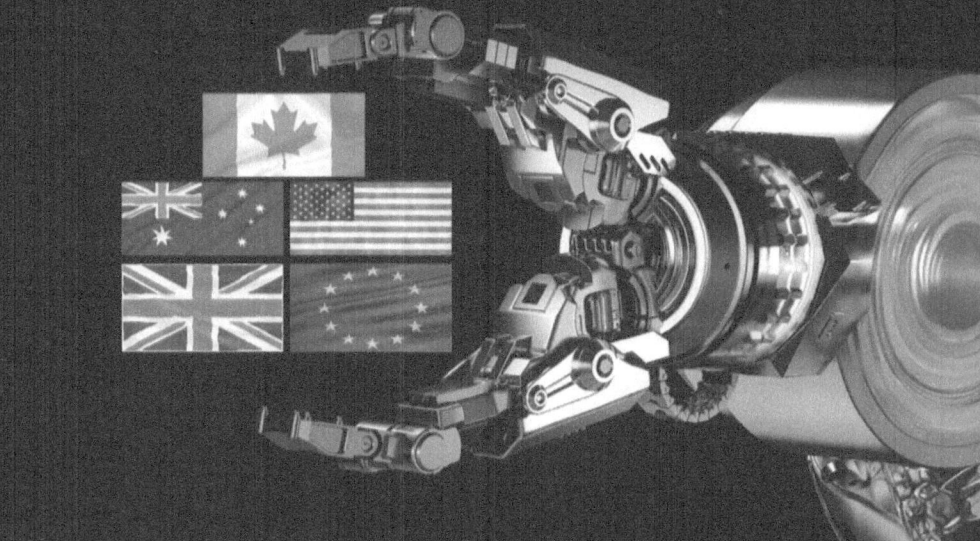

OTHER FACTORS AFFECTING THE OUTCOME

THE IMPACT OF DISRUPTIVE TECHNOLOGIES

AN IMPORTANT AND emerging competitive factor will be to introduce disruptive technologies into your future business using a new imperative called INDUSTRY 4.0, and it's considered to be the next industrial revolution.

The first industrial revolution (INDUSTRY 1.0) was powered by water and steam to mechanize production. The second industrial revolution (INDUSTRY 2.0) used electrical power and introduced mass production. The third industrial revolution (INDUSTRY 3.0) added electronics, computers and information technologies to automate the production process. The fourth industrial revolution (INDUSTRY 4.0) began with the digital age in the last decade, and is characterized by a fusion of technologies such as artificial intelligence, sensors, robotics, the Internet of Things, autonomous vehicles and 3-D printing to generate what is being called cyber physical systems.

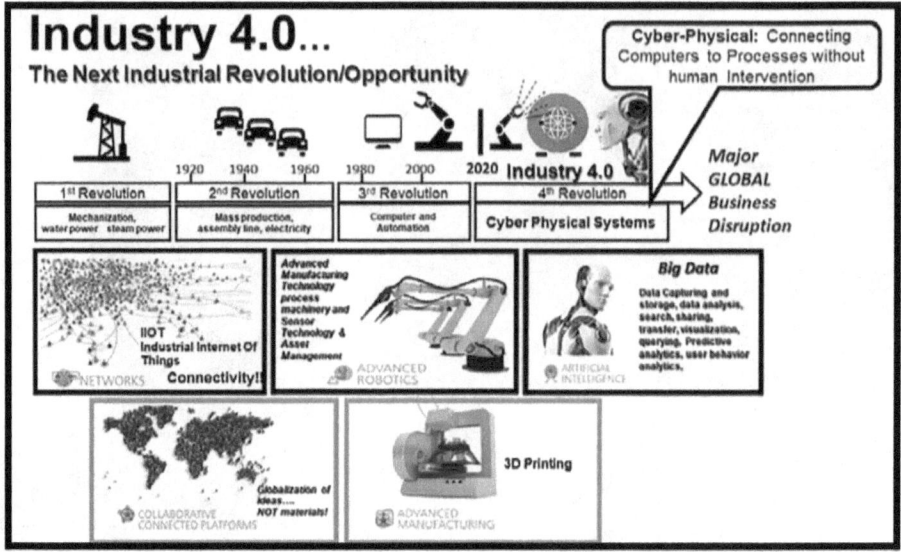

INDUSTRY 4.0 is facilitating what some are calling the age of technological disruption. This is being driven by the emergence of these new advanced technologies that are generating new forms of innovation.

Future products that could return for local manufacturing will not be the products that were offshored. They will have new technology in both the products and the manufacturing process and will demand INDUSTRY 4.0, which will require new facilities, capital, knowledge, skills, and systems, and must be fully integrated with LEAN thinking to implement without automating waste.

Correctly adopting such an imperative will provide an opportunity to change the competitive game and level the global playing field. But much more needs to be done to support the development of these technologies and educate the industries on how they may be applied.

In INDUSTRY 3.0 we added significant computerization to our manufacturing and business processes. But we created many environments in industry where we as humans got trapped in the process and ended up working for the computer, not computers working for the process and benefiting us. This has, in many cases, made us slaves to the computer. An example is how Enterprise Resource Planning systems still struggle with multiple transactions, some of them semi-manual or manual, to keep a firm real-time grip on a dynamic manufacturing process.

CYBER-PHYSICAL SYSTEMS WILL LEAD THE FOURTH INDUSTRIAL REVOLUTION

INDUSTRY 4.0 will employ cyber-physical systems that will eliminate the human interface with sensors and smarter systems, so we will have computers working for us, not us working for the computers. These cyber-physical systems will eliminate the burden of managing computers by humans and allow direct linkage between the computers and the process.

Here are the five key disruptive technologies and how they will impact the future.

ADVANCED ROBOTICS

This means linking traditional computerized machine and automation technology with smart sensor systems, and we are witnessing this technology growth as defined by the upturn in the shipments of industrial robots of all types. These automation systems using smart-sensor solutions are being described as "cyber physical systems" because they place the computer power even more in control of the process without human intervention, which solves most of the major interface issues between computers and process management.

ARTIFICIAL INTELLIGENCE (AI) AND BIG DATA

In the last few years, computer technology has taken a huge leap forward in terms of computing power measured in operations per second. They can operate upon massive and multiple algorithms much faster than human thought, with almost the same level of complex logic and decision capability. This will generate enough information density and complex algorithm management to become a form of artificial intelligence. This improved computing power will enable computing systems to handle what the computer industry calls "Big Data," so that everything we want to know about a subject or event can be stored as a complete body of knowledge and used at will in real time.

THE INDUSTRIAL INTERNET OF THINGS (IIOT).

Although the technical term is "connectivity," the public is embracing the Internet of Things and its industrial version, the Industrial Internet of Things (IIoT). This is suggesting that devices and therefore the knowledge they carry will be connected more than ever before. Again, it is about information and knowledge at the point of use in real time.

MOVE IDEAS, NOT MATERIALS

The other disruptor is the "globalization of ideas" via collaborative and connected platforms that allow remote interaction, and it is breeding a cloud-based mentality and hopefully constructive crowd sharing of resources, skills, knowledge, and funds in an interactive manner. The control of IP may become an issue, but in principle the globalization of ideas is far more sustainable than the globalization of manufacturing and materials.

ADVANCED MANUFACTURING

Besides computerization and automation, there have been many advances in manufacturing techniques over the years. The use of molded plastic materials in products and the associated tooling to support this technology is one, and in electronics the ability to put circuits directly onto a common miniaturized substrate as an integrated circuit chip is another. The chemistry that allows the use of new composite materials used in light structures for aircraft and boats is another.

A recent advanced manufacturing technology that promises to have an impact on the way products are manufactured is 3D printing. The technical term for this is "additive technology," as compared to the "subtractive technology" we have used for many decades, which involves machining away material. in additive technology, we "add" material. The industrial applications for this additive technology are profound in terms of how it can change product designs and provide the ability to rapidly prototype without the overhead of expensive mold or cast tooling. The technology demands a significant adjustment in how products are designed, and, like all new manufacturing technologies, we are in the cycle of defining how the technology will be utilized. It's somewhat like the slow progress made in applying laser technology into products, as the laser was invented in the early 1960s and took a few decades to be incorporated. But today, a significant number of products depend on laser technology to work. We now have this additive-manufacturing technology available in a wide range of plastics and metals, but as mentioned we need a stronger emphasis on designing products for this technology to enable access to the advantages. This must include integrating new design thinking across the whole product life cycle to undertake new and improved 3D-printed rapid prototyping, early production, and adopting 3D-printed high-performance production tooling strategies to revive traditional industries and breed new ones.

Many of us now visualize a strategy to operate a 3D-print electronic warehouse so we can build 3D-printed parts on demand in small quantities at both product early life and end-of-life, eliminate inventory burden, and improve flexibility to customers. New printable materials in composites and food materials, as well as bone and organ building blocks, will take this technology into many sectors that will touch the population more directly and at the point of use than traditional manufacturing. It will aid the thought process of manufacturing being more effective when it is local to the customer.

THE NEXT INDUSTRIAL REVOLUTION IS ON THE WAY

These five technological disruptors have now come together to form the next industrial revolution: INDUSTRY 4.0. This allows the smart-factory concept to be conceived and start us on a journey toward a new factory of the future using these disruptive technologies. These systems use networking technologies, sensors, wireless positioning systems, and connected computing devices with integrated analytics, and they have tremendous possibilities to eliminate transactions and allow factory designers to take the business process to the next level, so they can effectively and cost-efficiently manage a broad scope of physical assets, such as buildings, vehicles, machinery, equipment, and inventory.

Cyber-physical systems using sensor technology, IIOT networks, and advanced wireless position and transaction-system technology will enable not only the advancement of robotics and autonomous guided vehicles, but will allow us to place computers seamlessly into our processes so we can eliminate transactional waste and solve some of the major interface issues between computers and process management. This will allow us to redeploy human skills toward improving our processes and evolve how we do business to better satisfy our customers.

In the future, when manufacturing is re-capitalized with INDUSTRY 4.0, it will be able to service the demand of the local customer in the most sustainable manner, utilizing short supply chains organized into industrial clusters within a certain trade bloc.

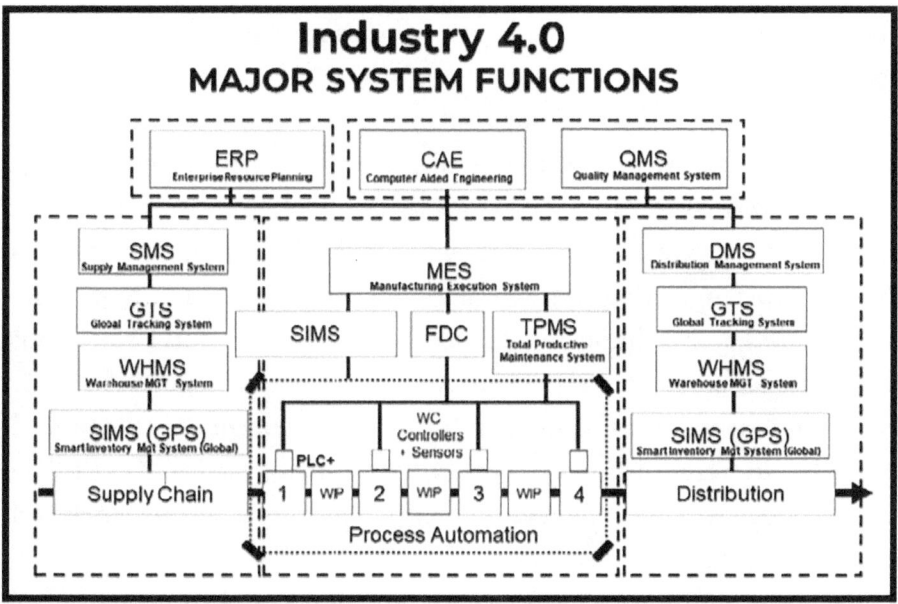

INDUSTRY 4.0 will embrace all major system functions in a business, from the supply chain to the customer distribution, and provide an integrated and computerized business that will integrate Enterprise Resource Planning (ERP), Computer Aided Engineering (CAE) and Quality Management System. (QMS) It will control the whole supply chain and the core manufacturing process, including the management of all the automation processes, and support the customer demand and fulfillment process. We will have the opportunity to completely systematize and manage our business with computers.

ARE WE THERE YET?

For some of us, this has been a long journey from the start of INDUS-TRY 3.0, when we first started to use computers in manufacturing in the late 1960s.

INDUSTRY 4.0 solutions are being developed in each manufacturing sector by the sector-specific manufacturing equipment and automation suppliers and the business-system-solution providers. Much more needs to unfold in this journey but it's well underway, and the goal is to improve operating processes and better harmonize future products and processes to achieve more integrated, waste-free, and sustainable products, processes, and services to meet customer expectations.

A recent industrial study indicates that 70 percent of business leaders in North America are looking at how to embrace the INDUSTRY 4.0 environment, and they are revisiting both continuous improvement and disruptive technologies as strategic differentiators.

The application of INDUSTRY 4.0 and these disruptive technologies have a current global market size specific to the manufacturing industry of about $3.9 trillion and are rapidly growing with investments predicted to exceed $60 trillion during the next fifteen years.

Advanced manufacturing has always been a continuum, but the integration of these new disruptive technologies under the banner of INDUSTRY 4.0 constitutes a near-perfect storm to change the face of business, industry, and manufacturing into the next decade.

INDUSTRY 4.0 provides a window of opportunity to take back the future for our manufacturing sectors and our economy. These technological disruptors are leveling the manufacturing playing field between low-cost labor countries and mature or developed countries, as technology will significantly reduce the labor-cost delta.

When the labor component is removed through INDUSTRY 4.0, any advantage of low-cost labor is far less important. But many are concerned about further job loss due to this next industrial revolution.

Some economists have outlined that automation and related technologies have been and will be the main job killers, rather than globalization in our Western society, but these arguments don't stack up with the facts we have.

First, let's look at white-collar job loss since 2000. We have seen new office practices using computer systems eliminate secretarial, accounting, and administrative jobs. Little real data exists, but it is estimated that about 15 percent of the reduction in the workforce is due to direct computerization. But another 25 percent of these jobs are estimated to have disappeared from our local economy, and they were offshored to low-cost labor call centers and administrative job cells. It was computer systems that allowed these jobs to become mobile and relocated offshore. So, more than half of these jobs were not eliminated, but were relocated by corporations that were allowed to use low-cost offshore services and not pay local tax with limited benefit to our local economy and its citizens.

Now let's look at blue-collar job loss since 2000. This was less effected by automation and systems in the West because we spent far less on automation on our onshore businesses in the last twenty-five years, as our focus was to relocate many of the supply chains offshore, along with most of these local jobs. So, by reviewing labor levels, my estimate is that 20 percent of the 25 percent total blue-collar-labor job loss in manufacturing was relocated offshore due to globalization, and only 5 percent was displaced due to automation.

It is true that INDUSTRY 4.0 will reduce labor content, but it will make any new jobs more viable to become reshored, as such automation will eliminate the cost-differential advantage of low-cost labor. If we take back manufacturing and ensure we have a trained and capable workforce, we will reshore most of the blue-collar jobs, and if we apply this reshoring effort to the white-collar jobs, we are significantly better off even with the INDUSTRY 4.0 journey, as it is always better to have some jobs than none at all.

MANAGING THE CLIMATE EMERGENCY

We have just lived through a huge and destructive globalization period that, as we have explained, has been a disaster for our manufacturing sectors and our prosperity in the Western world, and we are now facing an even more dangerous industrial policy distraction of climate-change mitigation.

Many believe science is being subjugated by over-liberalized political will and woke media hysteria at a level not seen before. Some describe this as the psychological phenomenon of group think at its worst.

I am not a climate-change denier, but I am highly sceptical that it even comes close to being an emergency, and the current climate change appears to be mainly beneficial.

The facts point to some adaptation being needed, but we certainly do not need any mitigation. And even if we did, we could not make a difference to the outcome anyway. The planet and Mother Nature have control of that agenda.

Based on current global events, humankind is far more likely to suffer from the holocaust of nuclear war, not death by climate change.

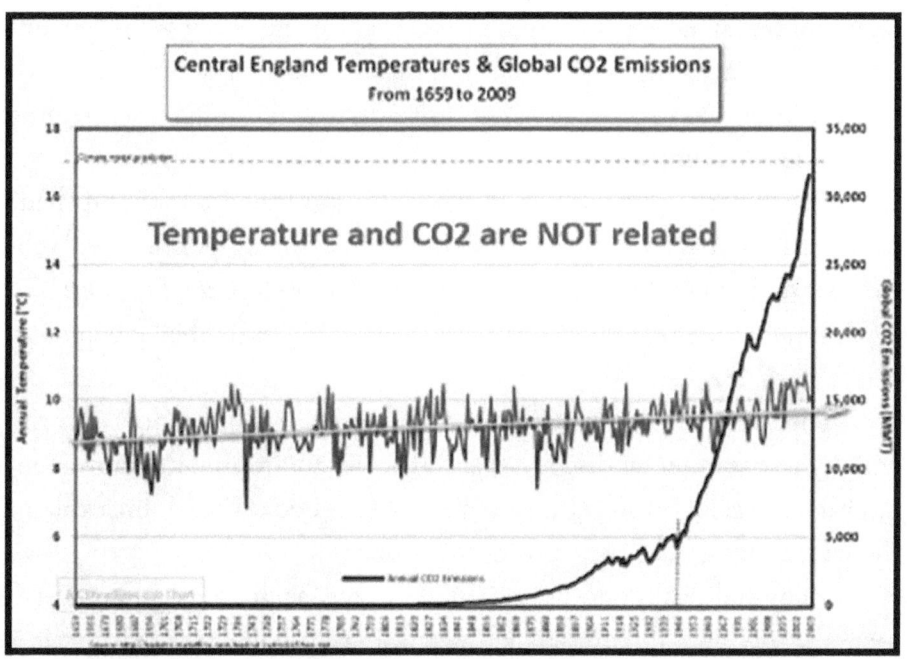

The statement that 97 percent of scientists have reached consensus on a climate emergency is nonsense. There is no such concept of consensus in science. Facts through exhaustive validation and peer review may evolve into a law of science, but with the global climate we are far from that state of agreement. For those of us who have bothered to study the scientific facts on climate change, it's clear that the science is not settled.

The media's hysteria has reached a point that reasonable fact-based debate on the subject is impossible due to almost religious fanaticism from believers that human-made climate change is an armageddon that requires a colossal level of immediate global action. Any denial is treated as evil, and shamed into silence by an increasingly sensitive and polarized society. Scientific experts who disagree with the climate-change consensus are censored with a modern version of old-style religious inquisition that uses social de-platforming to force the suppression of the so-called heresy.

Our governments are being railroaded into renewable-energy management-mitigation policies that will not solve the problem, even if we

179

had one, but which will cripple the recovery of not only what remains of our manufacturing sectors, but the sustainability of our modern civilization in the Western world. It will also destroy the ability of emerging economies to... emerge.

Two experts I have followed who have published books and made presentations that talk the most sense on this highly politicized subject is Dr. Patrick Moore in *Confessions of a Greenpeace Dropout: The Making of a Sensible Environmentalist*, and Michael Shellenberger in *Apocalypse Never*.

They believe that rationalism is in woefully short supply in present-day environmental discourse, and that the environmental movement has been hijacked by political extremists. In his book, Dr. Moore explains the wide range of scientific positions.

Many politically motivated study groups, such as the Intergovernmental Panel on Climate Change, **www.ipcc.ch** have declared that it is extremely likely that human influence, mainly through the rapid increase in Carbon Dioxide (CO_2) in the atmosphere, has been the dominant cause of the observed warming since the mid-twentieth century."

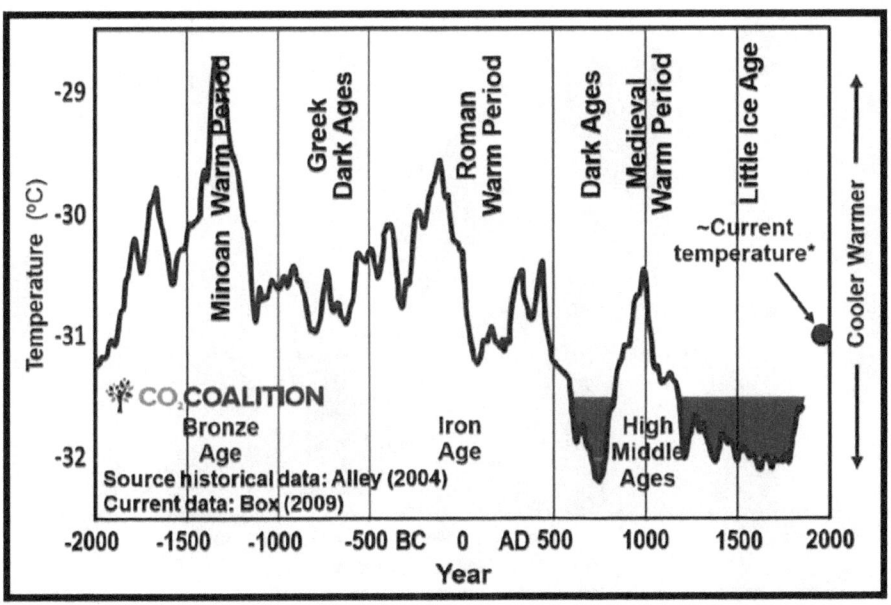

Many other study groups continue to believe, even if scientific facts do not support their predictions, that climate change will cause higher temperatures, lower temperatures, more snow and blizzards, drought, fire and floods, rising sea levels, disappearing glaciers, loss of sea ice at the poles, species extinction including polar bears, more and stronger storms, more storm damage, more volcanic eruptions, dying forests, death of coral reefs and shellfish, the shutting down of the Gulf Stream, fatal heat waves, more heat-related illness and disease, crop failure and food shortages, millions of climate-change refugees, increased cancer, cardiovascular disease, mental illness, and respiratory disease, and some say a devastating effect on the quality of French wines.

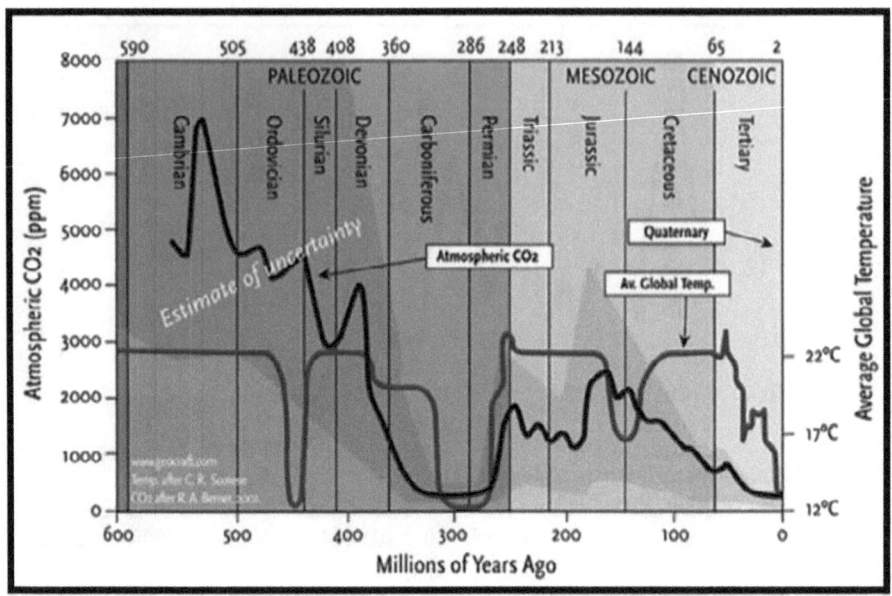

However, 31,000 credible US scientific experts and professionals petitioned are saying "There is no "convincing evidence" that human release of carbon dioxide using fossil fuels such as coal and oil burning, although it has increased, will not in the foreseeable future cause a catastrophic heating of the earth's atmosphere and disruption of the earth's climate.

Many experts make it clear that the science is not settled, as we have a weak correlation between the increase in temperature and carbon dioxide, but this does not mean causation, and many experts see no reason to assume that global temperatures and CO_2 are related. But others have assumed correlation to construct the argument that some people want to hear.

Contrary to this media hype...
Since 1950 the polar bear population
has increased 5 times ...

They are thriving!

Dr. Moore makes a great point that the global climate is always changing over exceptionally long periods, and it is now slightly warming as we are emerging from a cyclic ice age, but it's not significant, not cause for alarm, and may even be beneficial.

This global warming over the last century has been slow. It has stopped increasing and has reduced in the last decade. Also, we have had periods in recorded human history warmer than now, such as the Roman period in 200 AD, and the medieval period in 950 AD. Also, over the long-term history of our planet, CO_2 and global temperatures are now at the lowest average level in 250 million years, which promotes a view by experts that an increase in both global temperature and CO_2 should be welcomed, not vilified.

Although the polarized media will never print this, carbon dioxide concentration has increased for many reasons other than humankind, although we have certainly contributed. But on balance it may be a good thing, as, based on data, we have far less ecological issues such as forest fires, floods, and storms than in recent history. Polar bears are thriving, and the world overall is greening and supports more plant growth, and the food supply has increased across the whole ecological structure of the planet.

We do need to eventually embrace cleaner and more sustainable sources of energy. A modern society needs energy to thrive, and this will exponentially increase in most economies. But our real enemy is pollution in all forms, not climate change. Reducing our dependence on dirty fuels is a worthy goal, but it will be a slow process and must be balanced with the sustainability of our civilizations.

Renewables, such as solar and wind, are non-strategic and impractical, and on balance will use even more carbon energy to produce, install, and maintain, and so will create more CO_2 and pollution than they can save. More importantly, such energy sources will not support an advanced economy that needs energy 24/7 in large and uninterrupted amounts. Hydro power and some other clean-energy solutions may assist, but the most viable and cleanest solution is to switch as fast as practical to nuclear power. We need a nuclear-power strategy now, and this is being accelerated by most nations as they move away from energy alternatives that have a higher pollution footprint.

Politically incorrect climate statements!

The following statements may be considered politically incorrect, but they are technically correct.

We must burn coal to save the trees

In many parts of the world there are no other immediate options, and without coal the population will cut down all the trees.

Stop the focus on wind and solar and biofuels and save our living space

To use these sources and maintain a modern economy, vast areas of our countryside will be consumed, with disastrous results for our ability to feed ourselves. About 25 percent of high-density areas would need to be consumed with wind or solar farms to support that population, and will work only when the wind blows or when the sun shines, and only in the day.

Other forms of so-called green-energy solutions, such as biomass, may be on balance far worse, as in many cases it consumes live trees to keep the new biomass installations busy. Then we have the notion of biofuel that takes away from the food supply with disastrous economic results in some nations.

Geothermal can be applied in only some situations, can only apply to fixed infrastructure, and may cost much more per energy output.

Go nuclear and save billions of lives

The facts show that significantly less harm has been done to humans and the natural world by nuclear power than the other forms of energy production. Nuclear has the lowest pollution footprint and highest energy output of all alternatives. The calculations show that the historical damage to global health, and deaths caused by other forms of energy compared to not adopting nuclear since it became available, can be measured in billions of lives adversely effected.

Avoid nuclear and stay dirty and poor

If we had focused on the latest nuclear technology rather than moved away due to misplaced concerns about the safety of this technology, we would be enjoying the cleanest and lowest cost per energy output. A comparison between France's and Germany's power-generation systems will illustrate this fact, as France is highly nuclearized in comparison with Germany, and enjoys at least 50 percent less cost of energy. As we start to electrify our transportation systems away from oil dependency to reduce pollution, we will need a larger clean-electrical-energy source only offered by nuclear.

Do nothing and save humanity and the planet

It's clear that doing anything to change our energy system until we are fully entitled will be a disaster. An example is Germany, who, although highly industrialized, changed direction from nuclear and switched to renewables, and is now trapped in an energy crisis that will disadvantage it for years to come. Other emerging nations will suffer even worse in growth and poverty if they are not allowed the use of traditional energy sources such as coal until they are entitled to switch to nuclear.

The Paris Agreement

Unfortunately, we still have much political pandering to social pressure groups at the international level on the topic of climate change, and many nations are still focused on a global international agreement called the Climate Accord *Paris Agreement—Wikipedia*.

This UN driven climate accord with its focus on climate change demands targeted reductions on global emissions of CO_2 to control climate change. It forces a carbon and energy austerity program and wealth transfer from mature economies to emerging ones. It is just so much wasted and dangerous political posturing at the international level.

Unfortunately, the bulk of our Western governments, including our Canadian leadership, continue to allow the political-policies cart to be put well in front of the scientific horse. Such policies are not in the best interests of the Western world, and President Trump was correct in not following the herd and looking at the facts rather than listening to the rhetoric, and de-committing the US from such an expensive and economically destructive climate-mitigation agreement. Many other national leaders were upset and horrified at this, but we firmly agree with his position based on how the climate-mitigation agreement was constructed. Trump declared the climate accord a bad deal, as it placed far too many penalties on mature economies. He stated that his focus was the welfare of his own citizens. He has made it clear that he does not believe that mature economies should continue to fund emerging economies. He, like many North American citizens, believe that these emerging economies have gotten enough free rides already in terms of free access to Western consumers through the bad deal of free trade and free IP and technology transfer.

Trump also stated that the future focus should be to gain self-sustainability of energy resources, not continue to be dependent on others outside of the North American trade-bloc borders. He said the focus should be on aggressive pollution control, clean air and water, not the myth of a climate-change emergency. He did not say no to targeted reductions in emissions that cause pollution or that unnecessarily deplete scarce resources, but why should any nation subsidize such a problem outside of its own borders?

So, this was President Trump's response and plan for the US, and, although it was certainly a sudden change in the US's commitment to multilateralism, and extremely nationalistic, it was also more insightful and helpful toward showing strong and true leadership for long-term global sustainability, rather than the climate accord that sets impractical and unnecessary targets.

Trump was undertaking promised policy directions that won him the election, and it was refreshing to see a political leader undertaking the policies he had promised at election time. It's a shame more national leadership cannot understand that putting their citizens first and undertaking what they promised is their main job in a democracy.

Clearly Trump not winning a second term and the reversal of his position by the next administration was a huge disappointment for those of us who understood and believed in his policy directions. But it's clear that something else must move us away from the dangerous and dishonest climate-change-emergency agenda.

CANADA'S CLIMATE MITIGATION PLANS NEED A TOTAL RE-THINK!

Based on recent articles in the Canadian G&M (15 Jun 2022) that the carbon mitigation targets provided by the Canadian government to the UN Climate Accord are not supported with realisable plans. This is now being declared by the stakeholders, such as industry and the local government bodies charged with their measurement. Currently only 50% of the targets can be met without significant reduction in the output needed to support the economy. This suggests such mitigation efforts will be both ineffective and unrealistic, and such a direction needs a total rethink.

It's now clear that the climate mitigation agenda, even if it were necessary, will be a treatment far worse than the disease.

MUCH MORE DISCUSSION IS NEEDED

We must all strive to clear up this climate-change emergency myth and ensure our governments search for the real facts, and not pander to noisy extremism that is spreading unjustified fear. They need to get the policies straight. The adoption of carbon taxes and energy restrictions will make it difficult for prosperity to continue across the globe, with disastrous results for both mature and emerging economies and a destructive penalty toward our civilizations.

We must demand much more open and fact-based dialogue and resolution between all scientists and policymakers to drive an open and fair understanding of the facts. Then this must be better transmitted to the population by a balanced media, so they better educate our population on these topics and stop generating panic over a global climate emergency that does not exist.

We need to allow a much more balanced information exchange, and here are some sources that can balance the discussions.

The Climate Discussion Nexus (https://climatediscussionnexus. com) offers a counterpoint to pro-climate-mitigation thought leaders. They provide some compelling arguments, and they are asking for a serious debate to avoid the dangerous group think on climate mitigation.

The CO2 Coalition https://co2coalition.org was established in 2015 as a non-partisan educational foundation with the purpose of educating thought leaders, policy makers, and the public about the important contribution made by carbon dioxide to our lives and the economy. The Coalition seeks to engage in an informed and dispassionate discussion of climate change, humans' role in the climate system, the limitations of climate models, and the consequences of mandated reductions in CO2 emissions.

The Right Climate Stuff Research Team is a science-based organization in the US composed of a group of NASA scientists, who published a some-what controversial working paper in 2020, with a conclusion based on a pure statistical review of data trends as follows:

> Based on empirical data, the results are clear: The warming of the atmosphere caused by increased amounts of CO_2 are small and insignificant, only about one degree centigrade for this century. Our further studies showed that the claims of climate change causing more frequent and more severe hurricanes, tornadoes, droughts, floods,

sea level rise, forest fires, etc. are false. The actual measured data shows no increase in any of these serious conditions. Our conclusion is simple: Mother Nature is controlling the climate; CO_2 emissions are not. And more CO_2 is beneficial to Mother Nature's work. There is valid proof of significant greening of the earth since the beginning of fossil fuel use. These reports prove CO_2 is good, not harmful.

SOME CLIMATE ADAPTATION MAY BE NEEDED

We may need some focused adaptation projects to improve our resilience to all forms of weather changes. Some local changes in climate may define action, such as improved building codes when we build on flood plains or improve protection on possible sea-level changes, or better manage our housekeeping of forests and grasslands so we better manage forest fires.

THE REAL ENEMY IS POLLUTION

We must all learn that CO_2 is not our enemy, but pollution *is* our problem and can be controlled by national standards. In the main, these standards are being met in most mature economies, and we must migrate to cleaner forms of energy, such as nuclear, as soon as we are entitled.

In the Western world, we desperately need to reshore our manufacturing to enable a balanced economy of resources, manufacturing, and services. The advantage is that reshoring manufacturing closer to the largest consumers will significantly reduce wasteful trade across oceans, which will assist in cleaning up the over-polluted oceans by the reduction of duplicitous trade and the burning of wasteful and dirty bunker fuel used by container ships. Further, by ensuring populations grow, mine, and make locally what they consume, we will reduce pollution created through badly controlled manufacturing in poor countries, and better force manufacturing to clean up rather than pollute close to its own consumers.

SUMMARY

Climate change has become a group-think religion. Many of us who have studied the scientific facts have determined that although global temperatures and CO2 is slightly increasing it may not all be the result of human activity. And even if this were true, its not harmful and may even be greening the planet and improving the food supply. Also, any mitigation efforts will be both ineffective and unrealistic. It will be a huge distraction and a waste of our valuable effort that must be deployed on other issues, such as rebuilding our economies and providing prosperity to all our citizens. Some future adaption may be needed, but we have plenty of time to react, and its certainly NOT an emergency. Let's continue to work on reducing pollution by embracing nuclear power to generate cleaner and abundant electrical energy so we can slowly implement first hybrid, and when battery technology is ready full electrical transportation. We need to be realistic in this journey and prioritize with other important agendas including the need for a strong manufacturing base to achieve balanced economic prosperity.

NEXT STEPS

If we want any recovery of our manufacturing sectors, it's clear that we must come to terms with the climate-change-emergency myth so we can reposition the effort away from a huge, unrealistic global mitigation initiative that will negate an effective energy capability needed to support our industrial renaissance.

My suggestion is that the Paris Agreement should be cancelled and replaced with a re-focus on global sustainability improvement to avoid all forms of pollution and related global waste. But it's going to take considerable political will and leadership to re-engineer the move away from the dangerous climate-change agenda toward global sustainability, even though it would be significantly more productive.

In the next chapter we will talk about how this sustainability agenda should be undertaken.

GLOBAL SUSTAINABILITY: A FAR BETTER GOAL

As we explained in the last chapter, it's going to take considerable political leadership to re-engineer the move away from the dangerous climate-change-emergency agenda and replace it with the more worthy goal of sustainability.

The concept of sustainability provides a better balance for a nation to strive toward. It demands a move toward healthy communities that live in harmony, with great economic vitality now and into the future, yet achieving all this while doing no harm to the future natural environment.

A high percentage of both consumers and business leaders are ready to embrace sustainability, and, if correctly directed by national governments, it should be a productive journey for everyone involved. This will mean inclusive communities that create a waste-free environment, with each nation needing to grow, mine, and make much more of what it consumes.

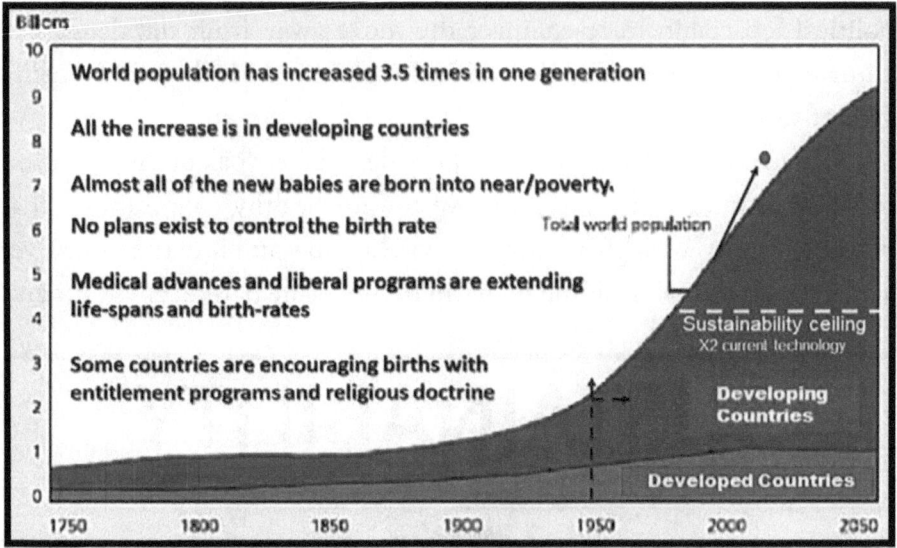

The emerging economies, with their exploding populations that will all want to become modern consumers, are in dire need of being targeted for improvements in sustainability. There are significant issues and challenges with the current rate of global population growth, which, as we display in the diagram, has increased 3.5 times in one lifetime and is predicted to reach a planet-wide population of 10 billion by 2050. It's clear that the developing countries that are responsible for the population growth will need accelerated plans to gain a sustainable economy and move from dirty energy resources to cleaner solutions into the future. However, they must have the right to do this without jeopardizing the trajectory of their economic growth, which the Paris Accord, if implemented, would adversely affect. Most of these economies, such as India and most of the Eastern emerging economies, and most certainly Africa, will have to start with existing carbon-based energy resources such as coal, and then move toward nuclear as fast as practical, but to force them to immediately only use renewables such as wind and solar is irresponsible and unrealistic.

The global sustainability measurements will need to be legislated by some form of controlling body that can load targets and penalties against a lack of sustainability. These measurements must also monitor and reduce the high intrinsic waste of utilizing long global supply chains that employ those dirty container and cargo ships and the other associated waste and pollution of the long supply chains. With this approach we can set specific national targets for each nation to strive toward, and we can together drive toward a sustainable planet.

Implementing a formal program for business sustainability is now a priority of most of the large corporations, and many governments and industrial controlling bodies are adopting the concept. There is a strong push to convince the consumers that good corporate citizens will follow this initiative.

In 2012, the United Nations Conference on Sustainable Development met to discuss and develop a set of sustainability goals for the modern human environment. They defined sustainability as a focus on how organizations strive to meet the three pillars of excellence: economic stability, social well-being, and environmental protection, but without compromising the ability of future generations to meet their own needs.

The ISO (International Standards Organization) has started to develop a set of standards and a scorecard that corporations and nations should follow. This imperative is being embraced by large and mid-sized corporations. This may eventually be driven by national government regulations and reinforced by the growth in consumer awareness and demand for compliance.

We see this business-sustainability initiative as a strong mechanism to force some realignment toward national performance and awareness to eliminate waste in a society.

SUPPLY CHAINS

As globalized manufacturing is reduced and most economies become less globalized, the local manufacturing will be serving mainly the local population, not a globalized consumer. This closer coupling will allow the local consumer population to better drive the reduction of environmental waste in all forms, as the local consumers will balance the costs of production versus environmental discomfort due to the shortfalls of its own manufacturing. The businesses who operate these manufacturing activities will eventually experience significant pressure from their own consumer citizens to improve their overall sustainability performance.

As we have demonstrated throughout this book, physically shipping raw material and product around the world just to take advantage of a quickly diminishing differential of lower labor cost may cut one type of expense, but it will create far more sustainability costs. Many global supply chains have huge amounts of unnecessary intrinsic waste embedded in them, and the short supply chain holds huge appeal and offers a considerably smaller pollution footprint. The key to a sustainable supply chain is keeping it short, as in principle long supply chains attract more waste. We are certain this is a thought process that will be reviewed as part of a formal sustainability scorecard.

From sustainability studies, it's clear that we currently have huge segments of global and national import and export systems handling raw materials and products that could easily be manufactured locally within the consumer country, and they could have been processed and consumed without passing though this wasteful import/export portal. These are foolish and wasteful transactions that add a cost burden to the end user. They are duplicitous and wasteful, and an unnecessary danger to our environment. They will probably be addressed under the scrutiny of sustainability.

So, using these sustainability calculations, we can generate a compelling argument against unnecessary global trade that will utilize long supply chains to support offshore trade, as it attracts significant inventory, transportation, and associated resource waste and has a significant pollution footprint, and must be avoided to meet sustainability goals.

POLLUTION

It's clear that pollution kills all forms of life, and as a post-war British kid I can tell the difference between the polluted 1950s and the clean air we breathe today, and how poorly controlled industrialization is a huge source of health concerns. The emerging economies are trading economic growth through exports against the health of its citizens to feed us the manufacturing products just to save a few cents on the dollar for our corporations. It would be better for us to stop downloading our manufacturing pollution to these ill-equipped emerging economies and take direct responsibility by manufacturing for our own consumers, which would support a responsible and sustainable outlook.

TRAVEL

Travel of any kind adds waste. Public transport so far does not support long commutes due to the size of our cities and the nature of our work activities. This form of transport is not favored or deemed useful by a huge percentage of the inner city and urban population, and results in a large personal transportation footprint that adds to traffic congestion and pollution. To some degree, the COVID pandemic has demonstrated how some work can be performed remotely, but many jobs will still require a commute. Improving and rethinking how we minimize this problem is a huge social science study that must be undertaken.

We will always need an ongoing and balanced discussion about how we utilize transportation technology for maximum sustainability. For example, the immediate reaction for sustainable surface transportation is to insist on the electric vehicle and not the gas engine as the solution.

But currently the battery science shows that for most applications the hybrid solution of gas engine and backup electric traction is currently and for the next decade the best solution. By then enroute recharging stations and battery technology will have become more capable, and we will have learnt how to consume less energy and reduce the pollution in the battery manufacturing process.

(1) The Contradictions of Battery Operated Vehicles | Graham Conway | TEDxSanAntonio—YouTube

RESOURCE ISSUES

Even if we do focus on sustainability and waste elimination in everything we do, we will still struggle with our resources in the future as global population continues to expand, and as those emerging populations move toward modern consumerism.

Economists have authored many books on the future availability of our oil, coal, and gas reserves, as they are not renewable. But even if we move slowly away from these energy sources toward nuclear, we can learn through better technology to extract and use these resources in a more sustainable manner to avoid significant depletions.

The issue of prime concern is fresh and clean water, which may become the most critical, rare, and unsustainable resource on the planet.

Currently, consumerism demands significantly more manufacturing, which is one of the highest users of water, and we have a long way to go to create conservation in this regard.

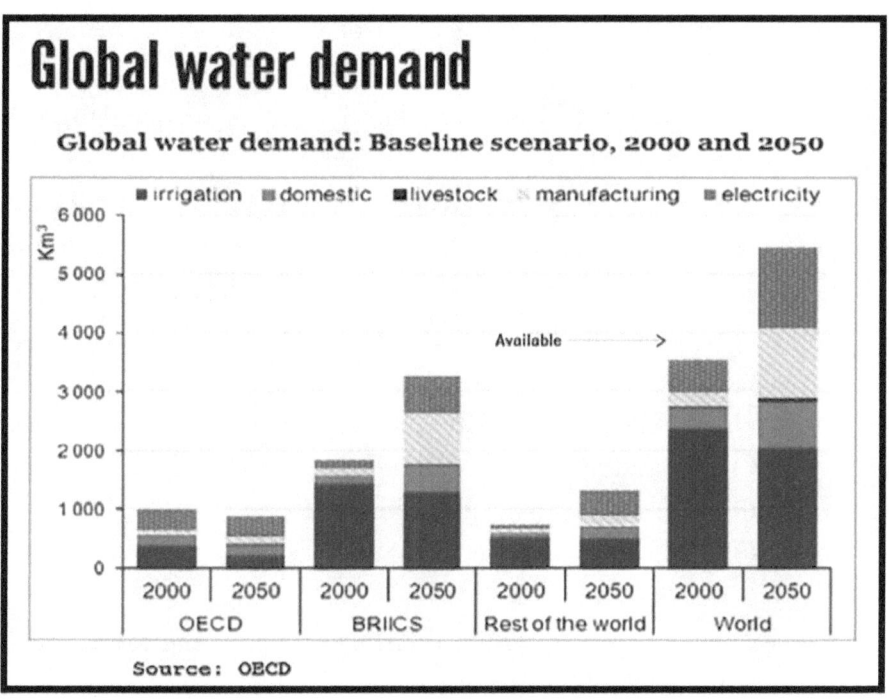

Global water demand

Global water demand: Baseline scenario, 2000 and 2050

Source: OECD

In the future we will have plenty of labor, but we may not have much water. Our social awareness of wasteful practices as far as water is concerned needs to be driven through the art of marketing and consumerism. In many cases, we have been moving in the wrong direction.

A good example is the increasing use of bottled water. It takes 7 liters of water to manufacture the plastic for a disposable 0.5 liter bottle of water. This is crazy when you realize that our private and public faucets have safe drinking water for free. Maybe a tax on bottled water, or even a higher water usage tax is in our future?

But it's just one example of the huge water usage problem:

- A car takes 39,090 gallons of water to make, plus 2,000 gallons for the tires
- A pair of jeans takes around 1,800 gallons of water to grow enough cotton to produce just one pair

- A cotton T-Shirt: 400 gallons of water to grow the cotton required
- A single board of lumber takes 5.4 gallons of water to grow enough wood
- A barrel of beer (32 gallons of booze) takes 1,500 gallons of water
- A to-go latte takes 53 gallons to make: to grow the coffee and sugar, make the plastic lid and sleeve and the cup itself
- One ton of steel: 62,000 gallons of water
- Cement: 1,360 gallons
- One Pound of Wool: 101 gallons of water
- One Pound of Cotton: 101 gallons
- One Pound of Plastic: 24 gallons
- One Pound of Synthetic Rubber: 55 gallons

We North Americans, with a lifestyle the rest of the world wants to copy, use 1.5 Olympic swimming pools of water per year per person, or, put another way: 24,000 pints of beer a week per person, or 13.5 showers a day. Whichever way you look at it, we are the cleanest drunks on the planet!

Future product designs will be key

Water is just part of a bigger problem. We need to look at the overall waste problem as a society. We have developed some unbelievably bad and wasteful habits and systems. Our economies have been designed to need growth to support our corporate profits, and they achieve this through aggressive market-driven consumerism that ensures our wants massively exceed our real needs, so it generates a massive hunger for product. This forces early product replacement and corporations promote planned product obsolescence in ever shorter life cycles.

Further, we have evolved a throwaway product culture. Many products are 100 percent disposable and have significant throwaway packaging to merchandize them. Such packaging waste has further increased due to the need to protect goods over long supply chains and complex delivery cycles. As we extended our supply chains, this produced a wasteful one-way-disposable situation. Our food industry has tried valiantly to minimize packaging, both inside their supply chain and at the consumer level use of bags etc., but with limited success.

We used to do better. As an example, using localized supply chains we used to return milk, soda, and beer bottles to the store, which sent them back to the plant to be washed, sterilized, and refilled, so it could use the same bottles over and over. Glass and plastic bottles and aluminum cans are now used and thrown away. Our recycling efforts are minimal, with most products and associated packaging now going to landfill.

SUSTAINABILITY AS A KEY BUSINESS MEASUREMENT

Many of us believe that soon LEAN practices and the concept of sustainability will combine to move our society in a better direction to achieve a more sustainable way of life. But we badly need the science and measurement of sustainability to stay focused on the removal of waste in everything we do and consume. The products and business waste, the transportation, the waste of time, the throwaway lifestyle—the waste of it all!

THE SUSTAINABILITY-STANDARDS CONFLICT

Unfortunately, there are currently some serious issues with the interpretation, positioning, and ownership of the sustainability agenda and measurements. The United Nations started a serious focus on sustainability in 2006, and has updated it with a position called the United Nations 2030 *Sustainable Development Goals* (SDG). This focused on the management of climate change, inequality, and poverty, mainly for action by the corporate business world. They suggested some measurements called

ESG (environmental, social, governance). Some commitment toward the intent was achieved across the financial community, and planning committees were formed to hash out the ESG-measurement checklist and scorecard that would be used to measure corporate business activities and practice. This was badly standardized before the ESG was rolled out to the financial community, the associated financial consulting houses who perform financial audits, and the rating agencies that advise the investment community. Some recent press reports confirm that the result is a mess of inconsistent performance ratings across different industries, which is creating confusion and lack of clarity to ensure fair investment activities. Another issue is what some are calling the hijacking of the sustainability initiative by the World Economic Forum. The WEF called the initiative the "Great Reset," and this was the theme of the January 2021 50th Annual Meeting held online with global business leaders and national politicos in Davos, Switzerland. According to the WEF, the goal is to "reset and reshape" the world in a way that is more aligned with the ESG measurement, as well as prepare for Industry 4.0 and the future of work.

However, some political leaders have said that the Great Reset's agenda is a set of bad ideas from some of the richest and most powerful people in the world. The concern is that the SDG and the ESG measurements appear to have morphed into a woke wish list of left-wing social constructs than measures of meaningful corporate excellence. The concern is that such measures applied to a business investment process will become a global elitist manipulation of industry, commerce, and society at large. It does include an over-emphasis on climate-change mitigation and carbon suppression. It includes forced international equity, inclusion, and diversity rules, and economic constraints not in the best interests of our nations.

Many of us are concerned about the UN, the WEF, and globalized multilateral organizations setting such agendas for sustainability measurements. We would much rather these sustainability measurements be set at the national and trade bloc level. It's imperative that the national governments ensure such measurements are compatible with national polices.

SUSTAINABILITY CHECKLIST FOR BUSINESS

Business Sustainability Checklist

Product
Product lifecycle extension via smart design
Improved product life cycle through improved maintenance and operator ownership
Improved product disposability
Reduce use of product packaging and ensure recyclable or bio-degradable.
Product material usage
Product material scrap
Product labor productivity
Product Over production
Use of landfill and recycle yards

Resources
water usage
Energy usage

Environment
Pollution (Air)
Pollution (soil)
Pollution (ground water)
Pollution (sewer)
Habitat destruction (local)

Zoning
Land use (production/employment versus other)

Manpower
Income inequalities
Gender inequality

Dislocation of workforce (transient employment practices)
Excessive Under//Unemploymen:
Health and Safety performance
Reduced employee satisfaction
loss of organizational learning

Operational Performance
Poor application of Lean thinking/continuous Improvement.....
Increased operating, admin and capital costs
Reduced revenues and stock value
Innovation loss/reduced new products/market share/new markets opportunities
Increased regulatory intervention
Reduced shareholder satisfaction

Supply Chains
Poor use of supply chains.. Long'complex
Inventory turns (all forms)
Usage of all forms of transportation
Carbon footprint management....
Reduce supply chain packaging and handling materials

Once the correct national measurements for sustainability have been created, business leaders need to think about these measurements as part of the company's overall strategy. Companies embracing sustainability goals will perform better and safer for all stakeholders, investors, employees, customers, and the community.

As shown in the suggested checklist, it will involve measuring all business operational performance, including the products and the resources consumed. It must include how the business impacts the environment, how the workforce is treated, and how the supply chains support the sustainability of the business.

A high percentage of consumers want products and services from businesses that have demonstrated good sustainability in all three aspects of sustainability. They want future product designs and the associated packaging to be as waste-free as possible.

Our business leaders should start now, so the organization starts to build clarity and alignment on how it will address sustainability for all stakeholders. This is a journey, and it's clear that sustainability frameworks and final sustainability measurements are still evolving, and some are certainly subject to change, but it is not a reason to wait any longer. We can begin measuring and reporting on the obvious key business and industry metrics that will direct us toward LEAN and waste-reduction opportunities.

SUSTAINABILITY CHECKLIST FOR GOVERNMENTS

National Government Sustainability checklist

Economic
- High Prosperity
- High equality
- Improved trade balance less dependent on imports and exports
- Shorter less wasteful and more responsive supply chains
- Increasing Productivity % per GDP
- Improved local innovation and IP
- Interest rates at a level to balance lending and investment
- Less non-value-adding transactions across and inside of all economics
- Improved use of local resources
- Improved return on local investment

Environmental
- Less pollution
- Safety and health improved.
- Low-impact on natural habitats by industry and population
- Capable Public infrastructure

Social
- Stronger national governments that can better support democracy
- Improved learning systems to regenerate the utilization of the citizen population.
- Ability to afford government services
- Improved National security of supply chains
- Less dependency on other nations for energy and other essentials
- Improved well-being of our youth with improved and attainable goals
- National sovereignty, individual liberty and economic freedom in all forms

Our national governments need to start operating their own checklists for sustainability. They need to drive improvement in all the economic factors shown in the checklist so that it provides a better platform for business to thrive and the citizens to gain maximum prosperity.

The environmental goals must be realistic so that they are balanced with the economic constraints. It is also an opportunity to revisit the punitive safety and environmental legislations and the bloated government rules and practices in our Western nations. Although they were installed with the best intentions, they have added so much wasteful bureaucracy to how we interact in our society between business, government, our citizens, and our environment. We need to review the concept of LEAN thinking and remove waste in everything we do, including our standards and regulations and how they are enforced, but without reducing the intended goals.

A main goal of government must be to develop tax systems, so that we tax waste in all forms, and reward value-adding and sustainable activities. This is going to take a considerable effort, as currently we reward waste and effectiveness in the way we tax businesses. For example, profit is taxed but most expense is not, which does not encourage waste reduction. It will be a long and worthy journey to recode and rebalance the way we measure and control business and correctly reward its value to our society.

The social measures and actions should be focused on creating a robust society that can self-sustain and promote national sovereignty. This must be communicated as a set of national goals for everyone to follow. Installing and undertaking sustainability will be a long journey, but the results will be worthwhile, and a main initiative in concert with the need to take back manufacturing.

SOCIO-POLITICAL RISKS

We remain hopeful that our modern Western societies will become entitled and capable of rebuilding their industrial bases. But many of us see significant socio-political instability, fragmentation, and divisiveness in most Western democracies, including the US and Canada. It has diminished national unity and significantly distracted governments from developing, implementing, and operating important national policies necessary to take back manufacturing.

POLITICAL AND SOCIAL DISHARMONY

The biggest problem governments face is that the democratic and cultural machine of Western societies has lost its way. We have so many conflicting values, beliefs, views, and political directions, with the democratic process becoming overwhelmed and unable to provide adequate direction on who we are, what we want, how we should behave, and how we should function as a society.

We end up with a polarized electorate that keeps voting for a series of minority governments that don't have any clear mandate and end up inherently inefficient at making any long-term plans or adhering to them.

We have minority pressure or lobby groups that get far too much attention by the media that overwhelms the over-fragmented minority vote.

The balance of power between capital and labor has been lost for many decades due to uncontrolled global trade, with little labor-unionism remaining. The global business elites are controlling increasing amounts of the available wealth, but more importantly they have gained considerable political power that is diminishing the national democratic process, so we have significantly lost the power of the democratic vote.

Based on all this, the government bodies remain in a constant state of disorganized dissent, with no democratic solution that has the best interests of the nation or its citizens in mind.

We see a steep rise in an interest in nationalism, and for many of us this is no big surprise, as there is a growing political and public awareness that most of our current problems have resulted from the past unplanned process of globalization. Unfortunately, nationalism has earned a bad image in political circles, with most democratic systems across the political spectrum resisting this direction, as they have been conditioned to believe that multilateralism within the construct of rule-based global systems, such as the UN, WTO, and NATO and other global alliances, provides the only solution, even though this approach has so often failed to serve the best interest of a nation or its citizens.

We have a wider spectrum of political views and doctrines, from socialism pushing green new deals, to centralist liberal governments that get little done, to a growing right-wing political environment that is promoting a new brand of ultra-nationalism and spawning populist movements. So far it appears that these new right-wing movements better represent the lower- and middle-class citizens than the left wing offering that has become considerably more woke. This left of center doctrine is supported by the elites and the increasingly polarized media. This is creating significant derangement of modern Western society.

One of the best readings on the issue is the book *The Madness of Crowds* by Douglas Murray. He describes the lunacy affecting much of the Western world today, and how just about everything is now a divisive issue with almost everyone wanting to be a victim. He declares that we are living through the great derangement of our time. His summary: Some Western nations are at risk of tearing themselves apart. He investigates the dangers of the woke culture and how it is derived from Marxist foundations. He explains how it has enabled the rise of identity politics, race, class, religion, sexuality, transgender rights, gender reassignment, online cancel culture, symbolic destruction of historical monuments, and the erosion of freedom of speech through the application of political correctness.

This woke doctrine is now spreading through our institutions, starting with university learning centers, and is preaching forced social programming of diversity, equality, and inclusion. It promotes the over-protection of weakness over traditional social strength. It has been instrumental in promoting the identity politics and political correctness that has created a divisive anti-society sentiment and national guilt trips. It generates racial sensitivity and rank acceptance of what some are calling sexual deviation. It is the domain of left-wing politics, and many now see it as the enemy of a robust society and a nation state that believes in itself.

He makes the case that the left has developed an almost fanatical religious belief in its own righteous correctness that has become far more dangerous and totalitarian than the alternative political doctrines. It has started to empower entitlement thinking that will lower productivity and create a breakdown of free enterprise and wealth creation. As said, it certainly creates a victim mentality in minority groups that are being told they are being marginalized, even if some of them disagree.

There is a growing feeling of helplessness by the underprivileged in society that has been accelerated not only by the real social problems of low prosperity, but also by this victim culture.

The outcome of this social derangement is that it will generate political conflict that will only serve to ensure little unity of purpose exists within a nation. It could become a huge distraction for our government at a time when they need to focus on the business of gaining back prosperity.

THE FREEDOM OF THE PRESS

In this book I admit that I have been critical of the media, but I have not singled out anyone specifically. By "media" I mean news outlets of all kinds, professional journalists, social media writers, and the broader information on the internet.

I am not saying that all those in the media are corrupt or dishonest, and many perform their professional best to inform correctly, but some have provided a less than "unbiased freedom of the press" image to the population, and so my comments in general must stand.

As I mention in earlier chapters, the population now has more access to information than ever before, but gets disillusioned and confused with the resolution of the information. We live in a world full of dissention, fake news, conspiracy theories, political correctness, and cancel culture that can suppress free speech. This is now even apparent with so-called trusted mainstream media sources, who often appear subject to dangerous and unbalanced consensus thinking, even on scientific topics, rather than objective, fact-based questioning and reporting. So, we caution the reader to continuously review facts, rather than the current media rhetoric and worldview.

Many official media outlets have been criticized for providing polarized and sensationalized information, probably to gain readership that is dwindling in a fragmented market. Some information networks have openly declared their allegiance to a political or social direction. Many of these media sources are "owned" by powerful entities that may wish to manipulate the message, and this further breeds a level of doubt and contempt. This has bred a distrust and lack of respect for the media at large.

Of course, not all these media sources are biased, but some have adopted a marginal level of reality, where truth and facts get blurred. On some topics it's not *what* to believe, but more *who* to believe, and the difference between fact and opinion has also become hard to decipher.

This distrust of the media may be difficult to fix, and so it will need the general population to become alert and vigilant on what it knows and believes. This situation has made any coherent messaging on any topic much more difficult for all concerned, within a society that badly needs stability and focus to align and get things done.

THE GLOBAL HEALTH PANDEMIC AND SOCIAL UNREST

We have had to cope with the social pressure of the COVID-19 pandemic, with governments, businesses, and households globally shocked and shaken to the core. Public health protocols to slow the spread of the virus were the immediate priority, and this has resulted in unprecedented degrees of business and social shutdowns and economic difficulty in Canada and elsewhere.

This has changed many of the personal freedoms of movement and responsibility that have been stressful for the population. Business disruption has created layoffs and work shortages for a large sector of the working population. At the very least it has changed the dynamics of how business is done, and how employees do their jobs. This includes working remotely, and it has reduced the ease of communication and travel, and the teamwork in some industries. Fortunately, computer technology has eased some of the problems, but several industries have had to modify and reduce their customer-service levels. It has also stressed supply chains, and to some extent forced some thoughts toward the move to localize supply chains and reshoring. That the COVID-19 pandemic is resulting in a global recession and inflation is sadly a given, and we will have debt, mountains of it.

Although the facts from health records clearly show that the COVID vaccines reduce the risk of serious illness by at least seven-fold, many in the population have refused to be vaccinated, and so we still run the risk of this overwhelming our health system, and it has prevented the undertaking of normal medical procedures. This has developed social unrest, with many organized demonstrations demanding the elimination of pandemic health controls. Some of these demonstrations, which are more like occupations in some city centers, have escalated to significant civil disobedience and loss of governmental control and polarization of support across the population and the political environment. This breeds social unrest that will create a huge distraction for government activities.

One by-product of all this social unrest is the need for a clearer definition of "freedom." It's clear that Western governments will need to bring in new legislation so that, although it will always ensure that the ability to assemble and demonstrate will be a citizen right, it will have stricter time limits, so that these disruptions do not turn into destructive blockades.

SUPPLY-CHAIN SECURITY

Governments have mandated "national critical supply capacity" in products such as vaccines, face masks, medical devices, and certain technologies. This has forced some selective reshoring due to the firm need to improve national security of the supply of these essential items to fight the virus. The lesson is that globalization can lower national security and sustainability.

Another national security risk that is now being resolved, and which underpins the need to move back to local products and manufacturing, is the restriction on Chinese telecom products for 5G networks, the next generation of internet technology. We can expect many other technologies that may need similar localization as the impact of globalized security issues surface.

Trump had correctly targeted steel and oil and other energy products as those that should be secured within the control of the North American trade bloc, and he was well on the way to having full energy independence from the global supply. This included his approval of the Canadian oil sands pipelines, but this approval was immediately reversed by the next administration, driven by the climate-change agenda, and probably vindictiveness to anything Trumpian. This resulted in oil being purchased from Russia. Well, that decision proved to be a huge mistake, as we now have the Russian / Ukrainian conflict forcing a move away from trading with Russia—yet another example of why Trump was correct to develop a local trade-bloc economy, with plans to move away from the problematic global-trade environment. The message to any future national administration: Any global trade should be an option of last resort.

The pandemic may have accelerated current changes in global trade and investment that were already set in motion by more "buy local" trade tariffs and reshoring initiatives already underway in the United States. Canada and Canadian business will have to decide how to position themselves for this global decoupling.

Global people movement was also affected and is now recovering fast. Some countries at the time of writing are still restrictive on travel visas. University student bodies will be less internationalized, and leisure travel outside of national borders may decline as people self-select to limit travel. International business travel may be reduced as part of pandemic-related corporate risk management and move toward the option of internet meetings.

UNDER-EMPLOYMENT AND SKILL MISMATCH

More than 9.5 million Americans were unemployed at the end of 2021, and many will still be looking for work, according to the latest Bureau of Labor Statistics data. At the same time, job openings in the country hit 9.2 million, a new record high. Statistically, there is an open job for every person looking for one. But even as employers signal that they are ready and willing to hire, they are having trouble finding workers ready and able to fill the jobs. This is a trend shared by the Canadian labor market.

This apparent labor shortage is blamed on a range of issues. Some employers believe job seekers don't want to work because they are making too much money on extended unemployment benefits due to the pandemic, although these benefits are expiring. Economists are split on whether this is the driving reason businesses can't find enough workers, and by one estimate only four in ten workers make more in jobless benefits than from a paycheck.

There are other factors at work, including continuing health concerns around COVID-19 and the lack of affordable childcare, with the impact of children staying home from schools forcing one of the adult members to stay home.

Yet another factor is the acceleration of the mismatch between the skills workers have and those that employers want. And this is going to be the same story in Canada.

Of course, this problem can be fixed, as we have explained in earlier chapters, but it's a real problem at this time.

THE SOLUTION.... A NEW SOCIAL CONTRACT

I have already mentioned many times in this book that it will take significant political will and leadership to recover our prosperity. Some experts now believe that the poor state of the western democratic systems will mean that most democratic governments must rewrite a ***New Social Contract.*** This contract will need everyone in the nation to sign up to focus on a plan and a set of policies to recover our prosperity that can benefit all citizens. Although government must lead this journey, it will need all the stakeholders to understand and undertake their role and responsibilities. The stakeholders are Government, our industries, our educational institutions, our banking system and our investors, and of course our citizens.

Selling a new social contract is a huge undertaking, and will need very strong leadership, but will be essential, as many citizens have lost confidence in their democratic system, and believe it has been eroded and lost its way. Many believe democracy is no longer the mechanism by which the needs of the majority are met. Many believe the democratic process has developed the disease of trying to please everyone on every issue to maximize votes. Also, it has lost the ability, with a scattered and wide political agenda, to focus and make meaningful policy plans, take action, and achieve progress for the democratic majority. This is clearly demonstrated by the low voter turnout in most elections.

The socio-political issues mentioned above have made our North American populations almost impossible to govern, let alone be able to mobilize them to undertake another industrial revolution to take back manufacturing and gain back prosperity.

So, here is a process to follow to reset and mobilize the population with a new social contract.

1. Appoint a strong democratic but focused leadership that is aligned with the solution
2. Form a coalition from all political representative across the political spectrum who have the best ability to assist with the solutions. It's clear that the fragmented party-political system just won't get us the focus we need.
3. Resolve to focus primarily on a national prosperity agenda
4. The focus will place citizens and national interest first
5. It will avoid any discussion on all the social discord and dissent issues, and defer and force the use of existing laws to manage any of these social issues
6. The democratic processes would be focused only on majority needs rather than over-liberalized minority pandering
7. The outcome would be a **New Social Contract** for the nation to follow…

It would clearly be a government focused on "how we are doing" not "who we are." I should mention that this type of government approach is a knockoff of the British Government War Measures that were successfully adopted in the British coalition government of Winston Churchill in May 1940 to fight World War II. I guess this is a war, on prosperity, so all we need to do is find another Churchill?

I hope our currently distracted, and somewhat dysfunctional western governments can focus on undertaking such a process to develop a new social contract, and mobilize the common will of the citizens. I hope they can move forward by keeping the government agenda simple and focused on prosperity and national sustainability. It will take a strong focus to not be distracted by the other less important agendas so that we may have a chance to take action to Take Back Manufacturing and gain back our prosperity.

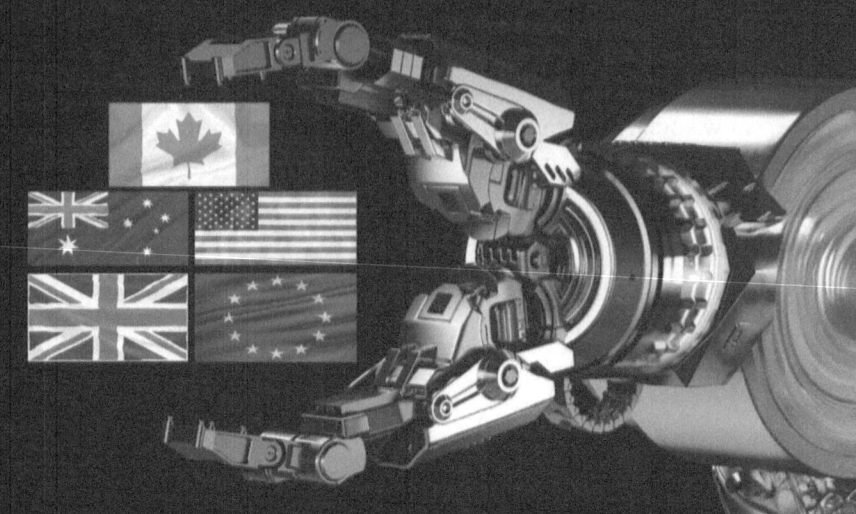

WHAT'S NEXT?

THE RECAP

I WROTE THIS book to explain how much manufacturing has been forgotten and allowed to be destroyed in our Western societies. Yet it remains an essential part of our economies, and a strong mechanism to recover our prosperity for all our citizens.

WHERE ARE WE?

As I will report in this chapter, the US now appears to be experiencing some solid reshoring activity, with predictions of more to come, which is good news for them.

I am going to be frank. Contrary to what our Canadian government and some economists may say, we in Canada are still losing significant ground on prosperity. Yes, we still have an opportunity to change the future, but there is no magic pill. It's going to take considerable effort from all involved to protect our future.

Here are the significant things we need to consider. In one lifetime, we have gone from pencil and slide rule to powerful handheld computers that have revolutionized our lives in mostly a positive manner, yet, in parallel, we have lost the plot as far as national democracy, citizenship, and prosperity is concerned.

Global trade has increased eight times since 1980, but global GDP has only increased three times. So global trade has been an inefficient generator of real wealth, but it's been excellent at transferring wealth from mature economies to emerging economies and the global elites. It creates unplanned economic migration and harmful population dislocation.

If global trade is to continue at all, it must be far better controlled within each nation, and this will mean a firm move away from a blind application of globalized manufacturing driven by free trade. Global free trade has been a major and uncontrolled destructive force against national sustainability for Western nations. It facilitates unfair transfer and dilution of wealth and sovereignty loss, and is the largest contributor to the growth of inequality within an economy. In the emerging economies, it generates the most pollution and unsafe living conditions, and enables the destruction of the planets eco-structure.

Without question, if we in the Western economies remain trapped in the current global free-market ideology still being preached by some global-centric economists, then our manufacturing sectors will continue to lose ground on all fronts and our prosperity will continue to trend worse. The warning signs are now apparent to most of us.

The good news is that globalization is reversible. It has been and gone before. It is not an irresistible force.

National sustainability, not economic growth, must be the real driver of economic prosperity. If we cut down on global waste, we can maintain and improve economic prosperity with a far lower growth rate.

North America has the inherent ability to become self-sustaining. We have extraordinarily strong and essential consumerism. We have people with skills, knowledge, and educational ability. We have technology, capital, and most natural resources, along with, on a good day, a rule of law. Hopefully, we can cut through the great social derangement we have mentioned and muster enough political will and leadership to move toward sustainable solutions and avoid the blunders of the past.

THE MISTAKES MADE

History shows that all modern democracies have made blunders over the last few centuries, with some resulting in wars or economic disasters, but over the last two decades most Western governments have created a perfect storm of mass blunders. They appear to have significantly lost the plot on prosperity.

The first blunder is recent government that has allowed social issues to become a larger agenda focus than the economic issues. We have accepted a democratic environment that thinks its mandate is to be more concerned about "who we are" than "how we are doing." Even the social scientists are concerned we have an overextended and over-heated agenda on social topics that we must all come to realize just don't pay the rent.

Let's not dissipate or distract any more governmental energy on social and human rights, and the other minority interest topics. These should be managed by existing laws and regulations, and we have plenty of those already.

This is the downside of an over-liberalized democracy, and a media body that typically gets more excited about human rights and associated social fringe issues than the wealth of the nation and its citizens. Who knows, maybe some of them will refuse to read this book because they would find it politically incorrect.

In the future, we must have a government that can create a sustainable focus on the real economic priorities that concern most of the population, rather than the noisy fringe elements. It's clear that we need to guard against ending up prim and proper but poor. This wrong agenda is beginning to create social unrest, and although we can agree that this has been compounded by the virus epidemic lockdowns, it's now a real issue the population is focused upon, and they are beginning to demand strong government action.

The other blunder in which all Western governments have been fully complicit is following the herd on free-market ideology, while not paying attention to our economic stability and the well-being of our manufacturing base and most of its citizens.

A further blunder is not insisting on energy independence as a trade bloc. We have a resource-based economy, with some available resource sectors within the trade bloc without pipelines and effective distribution systems. Yet we still import from less stable global actors. Governments need to stop listening to high principles on social and environmental issues from the same people who will expect free handouts from the economy they have been blocking.

Another blunder is having no plans to add more value-adding content to these local resources, with the outcome that we continue to ship raw resources to other economies with limited value to our economy.

A major blunder was signing up to support the climate change emergency without due process of balanced scientific review. This means we will be forced to meet stringent mitigation targets that are proving to be both unrealistic and unachievable. This will significantly disadvantage our resource-based economy, and our energy dependent manufacturing base, and will further jeopardize our future prosperity.

THE ISSUES

Our Canadian politicos must look in the mirror and start to realize how they look to business leaders. They will continue to struggle to invest in a country that is not a cost-competitive destination, has a questionable political will to set a consistent national industrial policy, a comparatively small consumer base with flat growth, a traditionally unpredictable resource-driven exchange rate, high overall energy costs, non-competitive transportation and border transactions, high labor ownership expenses, and punitive safety and environmental legislations. Our advantages of a slightly lower corporate tax rate and a strong yet fast-eroding skilled workforce no longer offsets the longer list of disadvantages.

We need to reverse the drift we have seen toward the gig economy that badly employs our citizens, which is a symptom of an unstable and inequitable economy that creates a significant under-employment situation.

Another issue is that most of our manufacturing and STEM learning centers are full of foreign students. The real point is that our education resources must be primarily a service that improves the prosperity of our own citizens, not a product sold to the highest bidder.

The past uncontrolled global trade has also allowed inequitable transfer of intellectual property that was developed and funded by the Western nations. This knowledge theft also exists within our gullible academia, who have also been complicit in allowing the hijacking of our nation's educational system. Steps must be taken to redress this issue.

Recent geo-political events such as the Chinese saber-rattling toward Taiwan, and certainly the Russian invasion of Ukraine, provide a strong lesson we must consider for future national policies. As these geo-political issues and conflicts unfold, we will see significant effects on our own supply chains and commercial activities, which proves that the globalized supply system is far too interconnected and subject to instability. It will mean forming more stable, localized, and inclusive trade blocs to avoid the need to trade with distant nations that may lack socio-political stability.

THE OPPORTUNITIES

We need to start to believe that we have an opportunity to take back manufacturing, so we need our economists to stop preaching about a post-industrialized Western world and admit that the concept of a global free market is at best a nice dream that has become our worst nightmare.

So, for Canadian manufacturing and our resource sectors to recover, we will need a significant government focus and a bold political will to reverse the current going-out-of-business plan. Saying hopeful and willing words won't change the situation. Most industrialists are saying "fix it quick or forget it."

We need industrial policy to target and focus on industries and sectors we want to see thrive that have the intrinsic advantage and opportunity to succeed, such as an ability to add value to our resource sectors. Then we need focused assistance for education, consulting, and evolution planning and associated development support. We need to ensure a total industrial approach organized by targeted sectors, not isolated centers of excellence.

Our best leverage will be a focus on products that add value to our natural resources that we already mine, gather, and grow using new technologies in innovative ways. This will apply to many food products that can be enhanced, and supply chains that can be localized and better integrated. Some metal-working products may be supported when linked with local raw materials. Furniture and semi-finished wood products can leverage local resources, and may be a value-adding export opportunity rather than the export of fully raw-wood materials. Oil products in all forms leave our borders with little refined value-adding activity. There are many options here to add value in products leveraging our natural resources that we can sell within and outside our borders.

A more difficult candidate to retain in Canada is our automotive industry, with our OEM plant recapitalization share being only 15 percent of our entitlement from past decades. Mexico and the Southern US are now getting the lion's share. Experts predict another 20 percent minimum overall decline in our auto-manufacturing footprint in the next decade, unless something significant is done to reverse this trend.

There is ongoing talk by the Canadian government about a focus on high-tech as a growth area. But this may not have any significant leverage. We may have some of the intellectual capital in our universities to perform the R&D, and we are putting significant funding effort into academia for R&D and innovation that may create a lead, but we currently lack a strong manufacturing and supply base to act as the industrial commercialization incubator. This means a foreign competitor, who already has the industrial commercialization leverage, will quickly adopt the IP, and catch up fast to close any advantage gap. Also, high-tech will never employee a lot of people. So, we need to refocus our plans on the target industries that have natural leverage to succeed.

Each business sector needs to quickly learn, develop, and adopt an Evolution Plan to achieve an integrated LEAN / INDUSTRY 4.0 business practice and a Continuous Improvement culture, and strive to meet sustainability targets that we are sure will soon be government legislated.

The whole INDUSTRY 4.0 culture of automation and systemization is being adopted very slowly into our manufacturing base, due to the uncertainty of reshoring into Canada. Getting corporations to spend large capital without a competitive need is a contradiction in terms. It will demand a coordinated industrial policy that funds long-range plans for each specific industry sector.

We need to focus on improving our success at attracting employees to the targeted manufacturing industries. We have a whole generation of young people not significantly engaged in STEM, who are not suitable for the future manufacturing workforce. Instead, we have the educators offering what some are calling "hobby subjects," rather than professional career-building disciplines. We need to fix this, or we will have a skill gap that will grow as the baby boomers retire.

As we undertake an INDUSTRY 4.0 implementation to become productive, we will need to re-train our own citizens and adopt an IILS so that education/training and on-the-job knowledge is fully integrated in a career-development journey within an industry sector.

We should become far less reliant on immigration and scale this back considerably. The reason is that, although the current industrial baby boomers were mainly immigrants, they came from mature economies and came job ready, and quickly built the current skill base. The current-day immigrants are entering under-educated and under-trained from mainly third world countries. It's clear they are not at the same skill set or education quality as the baby boomers when they joined our society. In some cases, we even need to teach these recent immigrants our language and culture so they can hope to be productive. It will be far better to focus on the retraining and recertification for existing citizens within the workforce, and for those that want to re-enter the workforce. Also, adding more to the population does not help with productivity, as well as adding to the drain on infrastructure and housing. INDUSTRY 4.0 will require far less labor but a higher-trained workforce, and even with the retirement of the baby boomers we will certainly have enough people. We just need to focus on improving their utilization to gain productivity and prosperity.

It will also mean a refocusing of the financial and corporate sectors to better serve the national good rather than their globalized agenda. This will require much more government control on how corporations operate and pay their way within a nation or a trade bloc such as USMCA.

We will need to take a hard look at resetting interest rates, exchange rates, and import/export tariffs to better position the nation's financials for the new economic journey.

Remember, the only way to get prosperity is to get more productivity, which means doing more with less for the same level of growth. This will demand a balanced economy of well-utilized resources and an integrated manufacturing base that adds solid value to these resources, an aligned and supportive service sector, a streamlined and well-trained workforce, with a government that listens to its citizens and maintains a long-range plan to achieve prosperity.

DE-GLOBALIZATION IS NOW HAPPENING

My ongoing position, now shared by many I have talked with, is that in the past we have over-reached on all forms of trade globalization, and it needs to reverse in some organized manner using the local trade-bloc logic that I have outlined in this book.

Of course, not everyone agrees with the reversal, and it's been reported that the economists who presented at the recent World Economic Forum 2022 in Davos have coined the negative-sounding term "fragmentation" to describe this reversal of globalization, or what I would prefer to call "de-globalization," or reshoring. but however much these reluctant global economists may wriggle and squirm, it's got to happen.

The expert view from the WEF economists is that the choices of both business and government are expected to lead to greater fragmentation in the global economy, and unprecedented shifts in supply chains. These choices are expected to create further difficult trade-offs and choices for policymakers, and the whole process will need significant coordination. You can read more about fragmentation at "This is globalization in reverse"—CNN Politics.

It is true that de-globalization is a journey that must be undertaken carefully over time, with the correct national policies to allow supply chains to adjust and reshore capacity to be built. It took more than thirty years to get our Western nations into this mess, and it needs to be reversed in an organized manner to avoid a reverse repeat of the herd behaviour we experienced when we started the uncontrolled globalization journey decades ago.

Of course, besides the powerful seeds of change sown by Trump, we have experienced the COVID pandemic, the Russian-Ukraine conflict, and the threatening attitude of China, which have all contributed to the need for a journey away from long and unsustainable supply chains and fragile internationalism.

There are many signals that fragile internationalism is now unraveling the global business relationships that will reverse the global trade ideology:

- China's ride-hailing giant Didi is scaling back its once-grand global ambitions, and officially delisted its shares from the NYSE

- Starbucks pulled out of Russia after McDonald's, continuing the mass corporate exodus over the war in Ukraine.
- Airbnb said it would pull all of its listings in China, citing "costly and complex" operation constraints tied to the COVID-19 lockdowns
- Malaysia moved to restrict exports of chicken to its neighbors, saying, "The government's priority is our own people"
- Huawei, the Chinese telecom giant, has been excluded from Western business due to a lack of trust in security issues
- Microsoft is slowly scaling back its China practice

Western nations will probably have to move away from the many multilateral free-trade agreements in which they have become entangled. This will be necessary as they rationalize and consolidate within localized trade blocs. This may take time but will be an important reset for most of the western economies.

From a Canadian perspective, the major trade deals outside of the USMCA that must be reviewed is the Comprehensive and Progressive Trans-Pacific Partnership (CPTPP) trade agreement and the EU-Canada Comprehensive Economic and Trade Agreement (CETA).

Some parts of these existing agreements may not need much change if they are just simplifying the transactions on trade that is not disadvantaging either economy. But each commodity trade activity must be reviewed on its own merits for wasteful duplicity or a high level of hostile mercantilism. This is when a nation practices a process of maximizing its own exports while limiting imports from others via selective tariffs. It's probable that most of the CPTPP deal will need to be either rewritten or withdrawn, and that is why Trump withdrew from this deal, as most of the transactions would support hostile labor arbitrage using low-cost Asian labor. The CETA deal may need less adjustment, but here are some examples of what could stay and what may need to change. The export of timber and wood products from Canada to the EU is a necessary transaction to support the EU economy, as sufficient and sustainable local materials do not exist in that region and need to be supplemented. However, CETA allows Germany to ship completed autos and parts from the EU with limited or zero tariffs. If a realistic tariff were applied, it would encourage the automaker to locate local production to Canada. The point is that the trade rules must be set to encourage localized added value as much as is practical yet support the sustainability of both economies.

Please note that we are not suggesting trade cannot exist outside of a local trade bloc, but that it needs to be far better controlled and must follow rules that are in the best interest of both trading partners, and will never be free, and should be discouraged if it distracts from the success of a localized trade bloc. Also, let's be clear about the new rules. We do not owe other nations balanced trade, and it certainly should not be a bartering or trade swap system to achieve balance. In fact, we need to start to understand that trade outside the trade bloc should be considered an option of last resort. We don't owe others outside of a trade bloc any trade at all.

Recently, there has been discussion about a US pact with Asia called the Indo-Pacific Economic Framework for Prosperity. This may be more of a discussion group about security and climate change, but every time such talks start, the business lobbyists are lured to them like moths to a light as they get scared they will miss some business opportunity. This and other "lures" will require firm resistance by national governments to not deviate from the local trade-bloc concept.

SIGNIFICANT RESHORING IS NOW HAPPENING IN THE US

Although international trade pacts may still be discussed, it's clear that the localized trade-bloc approach and the import trade tariffs set up by President Trump on some key industries and materials are now paying off and yielding significant reshoring activity.

According to a recent Thomas report, the interest in reshoring has increased more than 50 percent since 2020. <u>Free Report: State of North American Manufacturing 2021 Annual Report (thomasnet.com)</u>

The report declares that 83 percent of manufacturers indicate they are "likely" to "extremely likely" to reshore.

Probably the best example that reshoring is well underway in the US and will positively reshape the US industrial future is the recent announcements from the semiconductor industry. For cost, supply lead times, and national security reasons, the semiconductor manufacturers Samsung, Intel, and Texas Instruments recently announced reshoring plans for new fabrication factories in the Southern United States. <u>(55) What Samsung's Return to U.S. Chip Manufacturing Means for the Economy | WSJ—YouTube</u> This is an extremely good start for an electronics industry that was completely decimated by offshoring. The industry has a long way to go to be fully reshored and will require significant support and capital to fully return, but it's a key industry that needs to reshore to support many other industries.

RESHORING SITUATION IN CANADA

We are not sure yet. Historically, when the US economy sneezes, Canada gets a cold. But when the US economy parties, we get invited. But so far, it's just not happening this time around as far as reshoring is concerned. Even though the US is moving forward significantly on reshoring, it's not yet clear how much Canada will participate. In this book I have painted a very pessimistic picture for Canada being an ideal destination for significant reshoring without significant action, and I hope I am proved wrong. It's true we have had some increases in manufacturing business levels, but we still have not seen much concrete reshoring activity.

WE ALL BETTER KEEP ON ADVOCATING.

I remain hopeful, but so far, we do not have the correct level of political will and focus to generate the new social contract to position Canada to undertake the Take Back Manufacturing initiative, or benefit from significant reshoring. So, it's clear we all need to continue our focus as advocacy groups, and through the many channels of communication, ensure we assist in generating the correct level of political will.

One Canadian advocacy group to follow is the Reshoring Canada team that was formed in early 2021 by Tony Clement and Sandra Pupatello, who are past Canadian Members of Parliament. They have partnered with other groups, such as CME, the Automotive Parts Manufacturers' Association, and the Ontario Mining Association to look at how Canada can not only participate in reshoring, but how it should improve its supply chains. It's not yet clear what direction their initiative will take, and how much they can help.

Another Canadian advocacy group to follow is the Coalition of Concerned Manufacturers & Businesses of Canada (ccmbc.ca). The CCMBC was formed in 2016 with a mandate to advocate for proactive and innovative policies that are conducive to manufacturing and business retention and safeguarding job growth in Canada.

As well as our own TBM forum (www.sme-tbm.org) there are many other like-minded groups, societies, and associations that may want to assist, and we will need all the help we can get.

I hope this book will promote discussion and focus to enable us to get on with the important journey to…. Take Back Manufacturing.

CONCLUSION

How should I conclude this book?

All I can do is offer the two possible destinations to the journey I have taken you on.

THE BAD-NEWS DESTINATION

We all do nothing, or very little, and continue down the current globalized free-trade road of trade imbalance, poor productivity, ongoing high-debt loads, rank inflation, and terrible prosperity.

The manufacturing facilities that remain in Canada look more like small hobby shops when compared to the USMCA manufacturing facilities and the global manufacturing competition.

None of this gets noticed by a continuously distracted Canadian government and media that continues to be consumed with worrying more about "who we are" rather than "how we are doing," and dissipates energy pacifying the minority-interest groups, who continue to tear apart our social fabric. They all continue to follow political and economic agendas that don't "pay the rent."

The climate-change agenda continues to force alarmism and significant mitigation efforts, rather than a mild need for some future adaptation. The expensive and distracting goal of reducing CO_2 continues, even though CO_2 and global temperatures are at the lowest average level in 250 million years. All this mitigation happens even though it's established that increasing CO_2 is a net benefit by greening the planet and improving the much-needed food supply. This bad journey in the wrong direction blindsides our ability to focus on the real prosperity issues, such as TBM, and so our prosperity sinks lower.

We become a poor and irrelevant nation, which is an OK place to live, if you can afford it.

THE GOOD-NEWS DESTINATION

We get extremely lucky: we all vote for governments on both sides of the border that work together and form a working coalition to create a national social contract with a focus on a no-nonsense productivity and prosperity agenda.

All governments finally agree that the notion of building an economy around just services while also supporting significant levels of imports, even if you have resources to trade with, is not the way to get prosperity. All agree we will need strong manufacturing, resources and services blended in a balanced economy. This way, we minimize the need for imports and can reduce the need for exporting resources to pay for them.

The unified North American governments make the USMCA a true trade bloc that enforces the suppression of past wasteful international agreements. This reduces unnecessary offshore imports to localize trade and leverage the advantage of local natural resources. This starts a significant and much needed reshoring gradient that better manages the trade balance.

Firm focus and action to support this journey is undertaken by government, the educational institutions, and industry-support organizations to respond to the challenge to take back manufacturing.

An IILS is launched, and it becomes a strong thrust for the citizen population to re-life itself and get back to solid and meaningful employment. The whole learning syllabus of our elementary and secondary schools are revisited and better focused around providing a solid education in STEM subjects to better position our youth for a solid career. Also, the image of manufacturing is improved with solid PR by a supportive media, and youth starts to see industry as cool, and a new maker culture emerges.

INDUSTRY 4.0 is the main investment focus across North America, and the financial institutions assist our governments in an investment plan for the long-term restoration of manufacturing using these strategies.

Due to this INDUSTRY 4.0 approach, we will need far less new labor to drive productivity and growth. Therefore, less immigration will be needed, and future immigrants must come with employment offers, and ready and aligned to join our society and contribute.

A long-range energy plan to support industry is undertaken, with nuclear power as the main thrust to support industry and the electrification of our modern society, so we can reduce unnecessary pollution. Also, overall energy strategies, including oil and gas, are developed, including transnational pipelines to ensure overall continental energy self-sufficiency through the short to long term.

The issues of climate change are revisited and debated in a mature manner, and a more realistic perspective is achieved, so that we avoid the blunder of climate-mitigation projects. Some adaption projects are included in new infrastructure projects that are undertaken to support the re-industrialization journey.

We significantly reduce the energy and investment at all levels on wasteful social-political agendas. We make the economy and prosperity the main agenda. In other words, less about "who we are" and much more about "how we are doing"

We eliminate government and public sector waste and bureaucracy in all forms. We develop a plan for sustainable and economic development. The whole nation starts to develop a "get it done" attitude.

As part of the new social contract we stop the housing market financial casino, and other areas of over financialization of our economy. We agree to add stricter controls on the movement of capital into our banking, investment, and business sectors with appropriate policies.

With assistance from our powerful media, we communicate the social contract and the prosperity plans and progress. We re-install hope for future prosperity back into the minds of our citizens, and especially all our youth. Also, we ensure that everyone has a clear view of their own roles and responsibilities to undertake this prosperity journey.

We reinstall the image of a nation with citizens who have rights, but also civic responsibilities, and we learn the common ground between the differences between ourselves, so we can live in harmony. Our youth becomes our greatest generation ever, and they fuel the new industrial environment so that it is productive, prosperous, and highly sustainable, and together we take back manufacturing!

These are our destination choices. You choose!

FINAL COMMENTS

The notion that I am advocating as a hard-right nationalist is inaccurate. But I believe that the unrestrained globalization and the uncontrolled financialization practiced in its present form in our western economies, is the wrong direction.

It's now a clear fact that globalization has weakened our national sovereignty, security, and increased our sensitivity to swings in our economic demand.

It has made our economies and prosperity far less sustainable. It has also made us dependent for a range of essential products and services on global actors that may not always have our best interests in mind.

For these reasons we should reshore most products and services and gain as much resource and energy independence as possible.

We need to especially secure local capability to provide for such products as pharmaceuticals and medical devices, as well as key modern society foundation technologies, such as electronic devices.

I don't believe the world is ready for a new world order or being dependent on the concept of the global village, or any other form of internationalism, cosmopolitanism or globalism.

Such concepts are now fast evaporating as realistic national policies.

So, as global trade, security and safety declines due to conflicting power struggles between nations e.g. Russia and China versus the US and the rest of the west, its clear that long supply chains supporting a globalized economy will be much more difficult and unsustainable.

This will further encourage deglobalization or regionalization of supply chains. It will demand the need to take back manufacturing within localized trade blocs to create far more balanced and stable national economies operating inside regional trade blocs that are highly sustainable.

The nation-state organized into these localized trade blocs must be the economic operating unit for some time to come.

This will ensure a nation can have a prosperous, healthy, equitable, and secure society. In this manner it can provide a meaningful cultural environment and an optimum level of opportunity to flourish for all its citizens.

Dani Rodrik, a leading economist, now suggests in a recent article called The New Productivism Paradigm that there are obvious signs of a major reorientation toward an economic-policy framework that is rooted in production, work, and localism instead of finance, consumerism, and globalism.

This is exactly the solution I have described in this book.

It remains to be seen if this "Productivism" solution will develop into a new policy model that gets real traction.... I most certainly hope so!

As a Canadian, I have mainly focused on the Canadian situation or the North American environment in my examples, and as an entitled Canadian citizen I have been extremely critical of my own political environment.

However, its very clear that a significant amount of the issues and solutions are common across western nations.

Currently, an increasing portion of citizens in most western nations are disgruntled with declining prosperity, free trade globalization that has killed local industries and productive jobs, climate change mitigation that is affecting basic cost of living, affordability, uncontrolled immigration, and a movement away from the security of nationalism. They are awakening to the need for change and increasingly are taking to the streets and voting in national elections to move away from the past centralist governments that had embraced these destructive ideologies or allowed them to impinge on the well being of these citizens. It will be interesting to witness how this unfolds.

The many suggestions I have stated in this book are no longer a fringe opinion, and are fast moving mainstream, and I hope these thoughts can support the discussions and actions needed for our western nations to Take Back Manufacturing.

ACKNOWLEDGEMENTS

I would like to thank many people who directly or indirectly contributed to the writing of this book.

To Sheila, who has always supported me on any journey I have taken.

To the whole TBM team for their support throughout this journey. Thanks to Marie Laird, who worked with me early to form the genesis that became TBM. And especially Ron Kurtz, who has been with me from the start and has helped me through all the thought ware needed to write this book.

Thanks to Dr. Patrick Moore, who has assisted me on the comments on climate change and allowed me to quote from his excellent books on the subject.

Thanks to Ian Fletcher, who assisted me with some of the free-trade theory and allowed me to quote from his books.

Thanks to Harry Moser of the Reshoring Group in the US, who has been my prime kindred spirit in the USA.

Thanks to Jeff Rubin, who authored the book *Why Your World Is about to Get a Whole Lot Smaller: Oil and the End of Globalization*. He allowed us to quote from his book in our presentations in the early days of the TBM advocacy.

Thanks to Jim Stanford, who, as a progressive economist, has been very supportive and provided insight into the conflicting economic theories we face in the modern world. And, for allowing me to mention his report and conclusions on the lack of focus on automation and effective business process improvements in Canada.

To the many technical societies and associations that were supportive of the TBM journey and have encouraged me to continue to write on this topic.

To the various writers and editors at the Toronto *Globe & Mail* who inspired me with their many special reports and opinion pieces over the years, some I violently disagreed with, but which still forced the thinking process, and provided some of the excellent research material necessary to write this book.

To the many industry trade magazine editors who asked me to write articles over the years on this topic, which in some manner generated the inspiration and material to put it all together into a book.

To the Project Syndicate article and blog site that allowed me to expound my theories, some of which enabled some spirited discussions.

To the many writers of trade and economic books and articles, many are mentioned in the appendix, who have assisted me to position my thinking about the subject of manufacturing and its future.

To my many manufacturing clients and industry contacts who showed interest in the writing of this book.

APPENDIX

BOOKS

Free Trade Doesn't Work .. .. .Ian Fletcher

Confessions of a Greenpeace Dropout. .. .. .Dr Patrick Moore

The Madness of Crowds. .. .. .Douglas Murray

Woke .. .. .Titania McGrath

Ship of Fools .. .. .Carsen tucker

The Conservative Case Against Free Trade. .. .. .Shearer & Fletcher

The Great Reset . .. . .Glen Beck

Globalization and its Discontents.. .. .. .Joe Stiglitz

The Case for Trump. .. .. .Victor Davis Hansen

The Case for Nationalism.. .. .. .Rich Lowry

Green Fraud. .. .. .Marc Morano

Global Inequity.. .. .. .Branko Milanovic

Freefall .. .. .Joseph Stiglitz

American Alone.. .. .. .Mark Steyn

The China Price. .. .. .Alexandra Harney

Boomerang .. .. .Michael Lewis

Economics. .. .. .The Economist

The wealth of Nations. .. .. .Adam Smith

The End of Normal.. .. .. .James K Galbraith

Why Your World is about to Get a Whole
     Lot Smaller .. .. .Jeff Rubin

That Used to Be Us.. .. .. .Thomas Friedman

The Price of Inequity .. .. .Joseph Stiglitz

The End of Growth.. .. .. .Richard Heinberg

The Affluent Society .. .. .Galbraith

Keynes/Hayek.. .. .. .Nicholas Wapshott

The Map and the Territory .. .. .Alan Greenspan

The Shock Doctrine.. .. .. .Naomi Klein

The End of Poverty.. .. .. .Jeffery D Sachs

Naked Economics .. .. .Charles Wheelan

Free to Choose .. .. .Milton Friedman

The Rise and Fall of American Growth Here
     and Now. .. .. .Stephen Harper

An Extraordinary Time .. .. .Mark Levinson

The End of the Free Market. .. .. .Ian Bremmer

The Age of Over Supply. .. .. .Daniel Alpert

Post Capitalism .. .. .Paul Mason

The Maligned Hand of the Market .. .. .John Staddon

The next American economy .. .. .William Holstein

The Age of Stagnation. .. .. .Salyajit Das

Reinventing Prosperity .. .. .Maxton/Handers

Currency Wars .. .. .James D Rickards

The Great Degeneration. .. .. .Naill Feguson

Power Inc.. .. .. .David Rothkopf

No Ordinary Disruption .. ..Richard Dobbs,

23 Things They Don't Tell You About Capitalism . .. .Ha-joon Chang

End This Depression Now .. .. .Paul Krugman

The Expendables: How the Middle Class Got
     Screwed by Globalization .. .. .Jeff Rubin

Cycle Time Management: Time-Based
     Productivity Improvement. .. .. .Northey & Southway

The Contradictions of Battery Operated Vehicles | Graham Conway | TEDxSanAntonio—YouTube

Websites

TBM Website . .. . .www.sm

Authors Business Website .. .. .www.nig

Articles & Internet

Premarket stocks: Globalization is coming undone, and th
    flag—CNN

POLITICS, POLICY & PROSPERITY by Patrick Brethou
    AND MAIL | SATURDAY, FEBRUARY 26, 2022

BIS-15-604-english-apprenticeships-our-2020-vision.pdf   (pt
    gov.uk)

[2018 Issue Briefing: Youth Employment—City of Toronto]

Big polluters: One massive container ship equals 50 million car

Total Cost of Ownership Estimator | Reshoring Initiative (resh

Skilled trades | Ontario.ca

Evaluation of Literacy and Essential Skills—Canada.ca

The Climate Discussion Nexus at https://climatediscussionn

The Right Climate Stuff Research Team (https://therightclin

The CO2 Coalition https://co2coalition.org

This is globalization in reverse—CNNPolitics

Free Report: State of North American Manufacturing 2021
    (thomasnet.com)

(56) 83% of manufacturers want to reshore—YouTube

(55) What Samsung's Return to U.S. Chip Manufacturing Me
    omy | WSJ—YouTube

Energy sector presses Ottawa to clarify how climate targets v
    G&M 15 Jun 2022

The Puzzle of Low Interest Rates—The New York Times (n

Canadian Workers Need More Technology, Not Less—Centre
    (https://centreforfuturework.ca/2022/04/25/where-are-t

www.ingramcontent.com/pod-product-compliance
Lightning Source LLC
Chambersburg PA
CBHW021618120626

46545CB00001B/291

Websites

TBM Website . . .. <u>www.sme-tbm.org</u>

Authors Business Website .. .. <u>www.nigelsouthway.com</u>

Articles & Internet

<u>Premarket stocks: Globalization is coming undone, and that's a huge red flag—CNN</u>

POLITICS, POLICY & PROSPERITY by Patrick Brethour THE GLOBE AND MAIL | SATURDAY, FEBRUARY 26, 2022

<u>BIS-15-604-english-apprenticeships-our-2020-vision.pdf</u> (publishing.service. gov.uk)

[2018 Issue Briefing: Youth Employment—City of Toronto]

<u>Big polluters: One massive container ship equals 50 million cars (newatlas.com)</u>

<u>Total Cost of Ownership Estimator | Reshoring Initiative (reshorenow.org)</u>

<u>Skilled trades | Ontario.ca</u>

<u>Evaluation of Literacy and Essential Skills—Canada.ca</u>

The Climate Discussion Nexus at <u>https://climatediscussionnexus.com</u>

The Right Climate Stuff Research Team (<u>https://therightclimatestuff.com</u>)

The CO2 Coalition <u>https://co2coalition.org</u>

<u>This is globalization in reverse—CNNPolitics</u>

<u>Free Report: State of North American Manufacturing 2021 Annual Report (thomasnet.com)</u>

<u>(56) 83% of manufacturers want to reshore—YouTube</u>

<u>(55) What Samsung's Return to U.S. Chip Manufacturing Means for the Economy | WSJ—YouTube</u>

Energy sector presses Ottawa to clarify how climate targets will be reached... G&M 15 Jun 2022

<u>The Puzzle of Low Interest Rates—The New York Times (nytimes.com)</u>

Canadian Workers Need More Technology, Not Less—Centre for Future Work (<u>https://centreforfuturework.ca/2022/04/25/where-are-the-robots/</u>)

(1)   *The Contradictions of Battery Operated Vehicles | Graham Conway | TEDxSanAntonio—YouTube*